A Constitution in Full

American Political Thought

Wilson Carey McWilliams and Lance Banning
Founding Editors

A Constitution in Full

Recovering the Unwritten Foundation of American Liberty

Peter Augustine Lawler
and
Richard M. Reinsch II

 University Press of Kansas

© 2019 by the University Press of Kansas
All rights reserved

Published by the University Press of Kansas (Lawrence, Kansas 66045), which was organized by the Kansas Board of Regents and is operated and funded by Emporia State University, Fort Hays State University, Kansas State University, Pittsburg State University, the University of Kansas, and Wichita State University

Library of Congress Cataloging-in-Publication Data

Names: Lawler, Peter Augustine, author. | Reinsch, Richard M., II, author.
Title: A Constitution in full : recovering the unwritten foundation of American liberty / Peter Augustine Lawler, Richard M. Reinsch II.
Description: Kansas : University Press of Kansas, 2019. | Includes bibliographical references and index. | Series: American political thought
Identifiers: LCCN 2018058252
  ISBN 9780700627813 (hardback)
  ISBN 9780700627820 (ebook)
Subjects: LCSH: Constitutional history—United States. | United States. Declaration of Independence. | Constitutional history—Political aspects—United States. | Liberty—United States—History. | Individualism—Political aspects—United States—History. | Universalism. | BISAC: POLITICAL SCIENCE / Constitutions. | LAW / Constitutional. | POLITICAL SCIENCE / Political Ideologies / Conservatism & Liberalism.
Classification: LCC KF4541 .L387 2019 | DDC 342.7302/9—dc23
LC record available at https://lccn.loc.gov/2018058252.

British Library Cataloguing-in-Publication Data is available.

Printed in the United States of America

10 9 8 7 6 5 4 3 2 1

The paper used in this publication is recycled and contains 30 percent postconsumer waste. It is acid free and meets the minimum requirements of the American National Standard for Permanence of Paper for Printed Library Materials Z39.48-1992.

Peter Augustine Lawler, *In Memoriam*

This book began in the respect and admiration that Peter Lawler (1951–2017) and I had for the great American nineteenth-century political and social thinker Orestes Brownson. Unfortunately, this book comes to its readers with lamentation for my esteemed coauthor, Peter Lawler, who died in his sleep on May 23, 2017. In the aftermath of Peter's death and the realization of how much he had shaped my own thoughts and research, my thoughts turned to this book. Peter had delivered to me his contributions, and most of what remained was making revisions and edits. But it seemed too much. After some thought, encouragement from mutual friends and Peter's widow, Rita, and the University Press of Kansas's continued belief in this project, I resolved to bring the book to completion. I am so very glad to have had the opportunity to do so.

Lawler's memory and unique argumentative style have been the largest presence in my mind throughout the process of writing and completing this book.

Contents

Acknowledgments

Every book is also about the people in a writer's life who make possible the time and energy needed to write. For me, that person is always my wife, Evelyn. She is the rock, the strength, and the indomitable spirit of our family. Augustine, Clare, Noah, Lillian, John Paul, and Dad are always looking her way to know what we should do. True, I add some energy to her decisions. But I rise each morning and work each day secure in the thought that my wife is a blessing and a source of love and great joy. And for that I am grateful.

This book is sent with gratitude to Peter's widow, Rita, and to his daughter, Catherine. I hope that it will be one more of the many great memories you have of Peter's mind and wit.

Special thanks to Paul Seaton, Ralph Hancock, Brian Smith, and Daniel Mahoney for your excellent comments and thoughts on the manuscript. The great Lockean and editor Lauren Weiner provided important questions to ponder on the manuscript, and I am sure our conversation on these matters will go on.

Liberty Fund is a tremendous place to work and to pursue a vocation in study, reflection, and writing. For its generosity that made this project possible in so many ways, I am very thankful.

Thank you to the University Press of Kansas for encouraging me to go forward with this book after Peter passed away. Your support was invaluable.

I am thankful to the University of Notre Dame Press and its wonderful editor Stephen Wrinn for permission to use Peter's chapter "Locke, the Puritans, and America: Reflections on the Christian Dimension of Our Personal Identities," which appeared in *Natural Right and Political Philosophy: Essays in Honor of Catherine Zuckert and Michael Zuckert*. Special thanks to the Intercollegiate Studies Institute for permission to use our jointly authored essay "The Unwritten Constitution," which appeared in *Modern Age*, summer 2016. Thank you to *National Affairs* for letting us use portions of the jointly authored essay "Freedom and the Human

Person," fall 2014 issue, Peter's essay "Our Country Split Apart," winter 2017 issue, and my essay "Envisioning a Constitutional Restoration," summer 2017 issue. Finally, thank you to *Anamnesis* for allowing us to use the essay "A Constitution in Full," which appeared online in 2013.

A Constitution in Full

A Brownsonian Prologue

Some of our most familiar political and intellectual categories, originally adapted to suit twentieth-century debates, now cause us to fall into a contest between progressivism and a simpleminded individualism that seems increasingly ill-suited for the economic, political, and cultural trends sweeping us along in this century. Regaining our balance will require us to open our eyes to the simultaneously disturbing and encouraging trends before us. But even more than that, we are required to reflect anew on who we are as free and relational persons. We can and must think more deeply about the contents of a fully human life, as knowing who we are is an indispensable prelude to figuring out what to do to sustain the future of personal and political liberty. Too many conservatives persist in the tired distinction between individual freedom and collectivism. They fail to understand that the reality confronting the United States isn't the unending growth of progressivism, but its attenuation. And their view of the individual person is often inadequate.

The good news is that the road to serfdom Friedrich Hayek feared in the mid-twentieth century probably never gets to its destination. The current demographic situation—too many old people and not enough young and productive people—will only get worse, thus undermining our entitlement system. Other aspects of our safety net—such as pensions and unions—are likely to succumb to the dynamic realities of global markets. We can also note on a more political level that progressivism can no longer put together legislative coalitions that endure session after session. Today's progressives can only dream of the congressional power once exercised under President Franklin D. Roosevelt and President Lyndon B. Johnson.

But if progressivism is receding, what is the alternative? The most commonly voiced alternative to big-government progressivism is a Lockean natural rights constitutionalism, a doctrine that many of our Founders deployed in their own battle to secure American liberties. However, we have to ask whether a purely individualistic understanding of who each of us is by nature is really stable enough to sustain limited and representative (or generally democratic) government. That question, of course, has been a perennial conservative concern in our country.

That bifurcation helped discredit the communist or fascist reduction of the particular person to nothing but an expendable cog in a machine, plugging away in pursuit of some glorious paradise to come at the end of History. But today that distinction too often ends up placing in the same repulsive category any understanding of the person as a relational part of a larger whole—of a country, family, church, or even nature. It thus causes conservatives to dismiss what students of humanity from Aristotle to today's evolutionary psychologists know to be true: that we social animals are "hardwired" to find meaning in serving personal causes greater than ourselves, and that reconciling freedom with personal significance is possible only in a relational context that is less about rights than about duties.

The same simpleminded individualism leaves us unsure about how to approach the difficulties of the modern American economy. Given the complicated challenges posed by globalization, the fading away of the middle class, the breakdown of the family among the poor, the growing economic distance separating our "cognitive elite" from the decreasingly "marginally productive" ordinary American, and the indisputable need to trim our entitlements in order to save them (for a while), our current ways of speaking about responsibility, work, mobility, and opportunity are increasingly out of touch.

Most know that success in the marketplace requires skills and habits that are usually acquired through good schools, strong families, and even solicitous and judgmental churches and religious institutions. Those relational institutions, however, are threatened, albeit in different ways, by the unmediated effects of both the market and big, impersonal government. We also know that most people find that worthy lives are shaped by love and work, and that the flourishing of love and work are interdependent. We even know that love and work are limits on government, even as we know that middle-class Americans who have good jobs, strong families, and "church homes" are also our best citizens.

What we really know should point our political life in rather definite directions. Does our familiar political vocabulary provide us what we need to articulate those directions? Or does it confuse us more in this already confusing time? We have every reason to wonder whether we still have access to a plausible account of the reality of our personhood, an account that could serve as the foundation of a public philosophy that would properly inform and direct a sustainable political life for free persons. What we lack is an authentically empirical theory adequate to the complexities of American life in our time.

The natural inclination is to seek out such a theory in our deep and diverse tradition of liberty, rather than invent one out of whole cloth. And if our search is guided by a sense of how our changing circumstances require us to reflect on the relational character of the human person, our tradition will not disappoint. But we also need to look beyond the most familiar fixtures of that tradition to some neglected American theorists of liberty who have highlighted the shortcomings of an overly individualistic understanding of American life. Complacently excessive individualism is the opiate of the American "public intellectuals" of our time.

America is becoming more "Lockean," not less. As evidenced by Justice Kennedy's evolutionary understanding of the Constitution's view of liberty in *Lawrence v. Texas* and *Obergefell v. Hodges*, America is now more attuned than ever to the individualistic philosophical principles that guided some of the leading Founders. And by reconfiguring, even against the intention of Locke himself, every feature of human life, our individualism is pushing us in the direction of a postpolitical, postfamilial, and postreligious fantasy that would make our free republic unsustainable.

ORESTES BROWNSON (1803-1876)

The common sense of our country for most of our history has been to take the view defended most ably by our great (and unjustly neglected) nineteenth-century political thinker Orestes Brownson. This New Englander's insights into our constitutional republic are an important aspect of this book's diagnosis, analysis, and prescription for how we might be a better constitutional people. His biography itself situated him to engage the unique opportunities and challenges of American constitutionalism and citizenship.

Brownson emerged from the poverty and obscurity of backcountry Vermont where he was born in 1803. He excelled as a writer of English prose. Although lacking in formal education, he taught himself Latin, French, Italian, and German. An autodidact, he had incredible command of subjects and languages that enabled him to critique the latest trends in politics, philosophy, and theology with a gravity few American contemporaries could match. Lord Acton declared Brownson the most intellectually formidable figure he encountered during his visit to the United States.

Between the 1820s and 1840s the young Brownson underwent a series of intellectual and spiritual conversions: from Congregationalism to Unitarianism and atheism. He also aligned himself philosophically with the New England transcendentalists. In terms a liberation theologian would understand, Brownson pragmatically enlisted Christological imagery for social and political reform, channeling his formidable energies into radical movements that called into question the distinction between labor and capital. But he didn't remain a man of the left for long.

Brownson campaigned steadfastly for Democratic president Martin Van Buren's doomed attempt for reelection in 1840. That same year he published "The Laboring Classes" in the *Boston Quarterly Review,* where he predicted a future class struggle between laborers and capitalists. This fight, he claimed, would be won by the workers and would pave the way to a revolutionary new social order that would erase inheritance, special privileges, and the wage system.

Brownson's explosive essay made him, in the words of Arthur Schlesinger Jr., a "Marxist before Marx." His socialist-sounding ideas stirred a hostile reception and provided Brownson with a realist education in politics. The Whigs highlighted Brownson's radicalism because of his influential status as a Democratic Party court philosopher. President Van Buren's loss to the Whig candidate, William Henry Harrison, left Brownson permanently disillusioned with partisan politics.

As we might say, Brownson was "mugged by reality," and he soured on the overblown promises of democracy and the sovereign people as the voice of God. The people were easily deceived by the Whig's populist appeals that had no real substance, he thought. Brownson became more conservative, we might say, appreciating more sober insights about politics and religion. He labeled socialism "social despotism." He fostered a newfound appreciation for the idea of limited government.

Interestingly, however, Brownson did not rush headlong into the radical individualism that was powerfully expressed by the sundry radical liberals of his day. Brownson looked to an intellectual tradition that justified liberty under law in civil society. He studied the great Western thinkers, particularly Aristotle and the Christian philosophy of Augustine and Aquinas, and he found deep resources in the classical tradition of natural law that he would unfold in later works.

Brownson's intellectual and also religious conversions were largely complete by 1844, the year he entered the Roman Catholic Church. He ended his contributions to the *Democratic Review,* an influential journal of what was then "liberal" opinion, and he founded *Brownson's Quarterly Review.* He wrote as an uncompromising Catholic apologist, a stance that, at a time of intense anti-Catholic sentiment, weakened his popularity and damaged him professionally.

Brownson, inspired by Catholicism, embraced French philosopher Pierre Leroux's (1798–1871) principle that all persons live in communion with God, humans, and nature. He transformed this "life by communion" philosophy into a foundational justification for constitutional government. Brownson argued that every human is, by nature, a relational person who exists with others to work, to love, and to pray. These higher ends of humans provide the principles that limit government precisely because these relational ends cannot be defined by law; they are above the state. Humans' need to provide for themselves and those they love means that government cannot subjugate economic freedom. A person's need to love and serve others, most notably in family life, means that the family cannot be undermined by government, and humans' need for meaning and purpose, their desire to know the truth about themselves with others, equates to religious freedom. The term "relational personhood" that we use in this book stems from Brownson's understanding here.

Brownson sobered as to the real possibilities of government. He thought a humane political order must be reflective of a people's history, as well as their deeper cultural, philosophical, and theological assumptions about humans, society, and God. This unwritten constitution of a people must anchor their extant constitutional settlement. Brownsonian political theory provides a clear and coherent set of principles that we will develop in this book because of their richness and applicability to our own set of constitutional struggles. He believed in applying the genius of the federal Constitution to revitalize America's political life, restoring republican self-government while holding together state authority and individual liberty under the anthropological understanding of a human's relational personhood, as revealed in multidimensional social, familial, religious, and economic life.

THE UNWRITTEN CONSTITUTION

We Americans have embraced the self-evident truths of our Declaration, which proclaims that each of us has been created equal with inalienable natural rights, but we have also ignored Locke's nominalist method of establishing those truths. Instead of the written Constitution being grounded merely by abstract natural rights and autonomous individuals, we have looked to a prior, unwritten, "providential" constitution. Providential here, to be clear, does not refer to some intervention of divine Providence into history. It has to do with the fact that no written constitution could emerge from nothing, but is necessarily dependent on various "givens" that limit and direct what is possible for statesmen at any particular time. The "givens" from this view aren't oppressive constraints but civilizational accomplishments that make the written Constitution and constitutional order possible. "Providential," in this sense, means to be guided by what one is given by custom, tradition, and prior political experience, and even from philosophy and theology.

This unwritten constitution is found in a people's political culture, mores, customs, disposition, and peculiar talents. The constitution of the government is built on this assemblage of order and is deeply connected to it. Thus, the authoritative law of a particular country can't be viewed apart from the context of the unwritten constitution. No government built to stand the test of time can be a merely willful construction that defies the historical, spiritual, and cultural materials that have shaped or formed a people.

Notice that the constitution that emerges from Lockean contract theory is consented to by self-interested individuals, and it exists to secure their universal natural rights. Governments are monolithic in their origin, form, and purpose, because individuals are monolithic in their origin, form, and purposes when uprooted from particular inheritances and even biological differentiation. This constitution devised solely in the interest of the rights of individuals is based on the unrealistic abstraction of unrelated autonomous individuals, beings divorced from the privileges and responsibilities of being parents, creatures, and even citizens. Lockean thought, thus, isn't political enough to be the foundation of government, and it isn't relational enough to properly articulate the limits of governments with the family or organized religion in mind.

It is true that Locke's social-contract teaching was for many Founders the way they justified their independence from Great Britain and the formation of the American union. It is a fact, however, tempered by the statesmanlike compromises they made to secure political unity. The content of those compromises, from Brownson's view, made what they built better than what they knew through their theory, insofar as they took into account the political, religious, familial, and other relational dimensions of the human person that were slighted by Locke's individualism. The process of political deliberation gave our country's foundation particular or providential content that fleshed out Locke's otherwise abstract theory.

Brownson affirms the equality of human persons as a fact, but one that entered the world through Christian revelation and was later affirmed as self-evident by philosophers. Equality, as Lincoln says, is our proposition that inspires our devotion. It was brought to America, as Tocqueville says, by our Christian Puritans. That self-evidence, Brownson contends, is undermined by the pure Lockean dimension of the Declaration, where individual sovereignty becomes the foundation of government. Every man, as Locke says, has property in his own person, and for Brownson that assertion of absolute self-ownership is, in effect, "political atheism." But, with the providential constitution in mind, the Declaration really does become about the equality of all humans by nature under God:

> under the law of nature, all men are equal, or have equal rights as men, one man has and can have in himself no right to govern another; and as man is never absolutely his own, but always and everywhere belongs to his Creator, it is clear that no government originating in humanity alone can be a legitimate government. Every such government is founded on the assumption that man is God, which is a great mistake—is, in fact, the fundamental sophism which underlies every error and sin.[1]

Brownson's rejection of the implicit atheism of the Lockean effort to transform all of human life in terms of contract and consent is based on his observation that such misguided liberationism or individualistic "secession" inevitably led to the interlocking vices of modern political life: anarchism and consolidation. Social contract thought lacks an external standard higher than a human's will that could limit, shape, and condition it. The highest being is the human, who would self-create government by consent to provide a protection against violent death and to secure property rights.

Brownson contends that the transformational project of self-sovereignty or political atheism as laid out by Thomas Hobbes, John Locke, and Jean-Jacques Rousseau aims, with its misguided conception of human liberty, to displace the complex relationship between the nature of the human person and political order with a world full of self-consciously autonomous individuals. The goal is the enlightened deconstruction of the free and relational human person in order to reconstruct political order as consciously utilitarian, or representing the truth about free and contracting individuals to themselves.

The individual armed with a bevy of rights before the state is likely to be swallowed, Brownson observes, by a collectivism made possible by the elimination of various types and scales of communities that stand between the individual and that state. There would, it follows, be no context and content for being a truthfully free and relational person. Only if the person is understood to be more than a consenting individual can the limits to government be more than "negative" or empty. To be sustainable, they must correspond to the fuller truth about who we are. Brownson, for this reason, wrote of humanitarian liberals as "abolitionists" about the business of abolishing the real human distinctions that make up the world of particular persons in favor of the leveling of humanity.

The unwritten or providential constitution thus replaces the social contract and grounds the actual Constitution, limiting the range of potentialities it can develop. These limits also provide reasons for affirmation of an architecture of devotion to a country's actual constitution, its way of life. This particular or political way of thinking recaptures something of the Greek polis, but with the Christian addition that each of us is more than a citizen through our relational devotion as creatures to the church. The American republic is also to be distinguished from the tribe, by its devotion to a common good that's much more than collective selfishness. The American idea of the providential constitution places our particular country under the universal yet still personal God.

Thus, America's written Constitution of 1787 has to be understood by the unwritten order. That order encompasses America's common law heritage, the colonists' practice of self-government, the positive good of religious devotion and pluralism, the colonies as separate and then unified political actors in war, largely democratic emigration patterns, and colonial resistance to an empire that had abused historic common law rights and its own tradition of limited government. Our Framers built as statesmen, and as such they drew from all the sources that history, philosophy, political precedent, religion, and the rest of our civilized tradition had given them.

In the United States, the citizen is a member of both the state and the nation. This dual status reflected, in part, the preexisting political settlement of the colonies. Brownson believes that two facts are salient: the colonies had instinctually united in their push for independence from the British Empire, and as subjects of the Crown they had voiced their political grievances through their colonial political bodies. The colonies themselves, Brownson notes, had united as a protest against abuses of their English liberties and then to declare independence. Once independence was achieved, America eventually jettisoned the Articles of Confederation, its wartime constitution. This rejection, Brownson argues, was an affirmation of experience in favor of a political articulation more suited to the actual unity of the colonies during their war for independence.

The constitutional framework of 1787 thus expressed the dialectical form of national and state political organization in America. In their ideal relationship, Brownson urges, the national (general) and state (particular) governments are not inevitable competitors and are called to realize in their work humans' natural requirements that move from the local community outward to larger spheres of interaction: "The simple fact is that the political or sovereign people of the United States exists as United States, and only as United States. The Union and the states are coeval, born together, and can exist only together. . . . The Union is in each of the states, and each of the states is in the Union."[2]

Brownson reconciles the particularity of the states with national unity in a way that makes federalism compatible with republican loyalty. Sovereignty inheres in the American people only as they exercise power in their membership in the States United, Brownson argues, and not in the singular states as is demanded by the compact theory of John Calhoun, whereby the Union was created by the separate states, with the consent of the states replacing the consent of the people as the principal of the Union. The individual states in their particularity are completed, Brownson urges, through union with their opposite, the United States. This dialectic of order helps us understand the difficult relationship of dual sovereignty, and also justifies Brownson's opposition to Southern secession.

Of course the idea of the States United entails the legitimate identity of the states within the republic and fully affords them their rightful authority under the Constitution. For this to occur, however, the states must acknowledge that their legitimacy is in their union. These United States authorize the political existence both of each state and of the national government. Brownson corrects both the secessionists who deny the reality of the nation and the abolitionists who do away with the states in favor of a consolidated union. He argues that "if the principle of unity" is removed, then "the state is dissolved." But "take away the principle of plurality, and the Union would be a simple, centralized despotism." Therefore, "The true American statesman . . . will guard with equal vigilance against consolidation and against disintegration."[3]

TERRITORIAL DEMOCRACY

Complementing the unwritten constitution is the notion of territorial democracy that Brownson recommends as the correction to the modern political temptations of hypercentralization or excessive individualism. Territorial democracy is Brownson's way of expressing the irreducibly republican dimension of every free political order. Political loyalty pertains to the way of life shared by a particular people occupying a particular part of the world. The idea of natural rights, as so many contemporary libertarians contend, makes the very idea of legal borders seem unjust. Free individuals should be directly open to each other in an unmediated marketplace freed up from the "rent-seeking" of political force and fraud. The truth, however, is that we embodied beings necessarily find ourselves at home in particular places, and even natural rights, to become effective, have to be secured by a particular order. Political order, Brownson adds, is about justice understood as a good shared in common, as opposed to the selfish loyalties demanded by tribes, tyrants, and dislocated individuals. But it is still limited in important ways.

For Brownson, a good polity will connect and reconcile the free and relational person with self-government and law and thereby engender devotion to the common good. Citizens occupying a particular part of the world, joined together by borders, law, and defined accountability of rulers to ruled—this is what makes republican government possible. Brownson's territorial democracy, as a political order, is not open to ongoing redefinition by majorities, nor is it created purely by contractual consent. Principles of popular sovereignty, equality, and majority rule operate within the context of territorial democracy.

Brownson dismisses from republican government abstractions like the sovereignty of society or of individuals creating government from a putative state of nature, making government an artificial rather than a natural institution that flows from humans' sociability. Power, Brownson responds, is a public trust, not a form of obedience either to majoritarian suppression of particular liberties or to the endless rights claims lodged by autonomous individuals against society. Instead, it is ordered to the demands of a shared political enterprise that emerges from humans' social nature.

Brownson's project does not entail constructing a new philosophical basis for American government so much as putting the Founders' philosophic views in the larger context of the magnificent accomplishments of their deliberative statesmanship. Our country's self-understanding finds the mean between "humanitarian" political centralism and "secessionist" atomism in the limited but real political unity of citizens who are both more than and less than citizens. The American republic isn't to be confused with the comprehensive republicanism of the polis, although it is richly deserving of civic loyalty. American citizens are also free economic actors responsible for taking care of their material needs. They also flourish as spiritual beings who find their home in a corporate religious body.

BROWNSON TODAY

It goes without saying that the whole that is a particular human person living in light of the universal truth about the equality of all persons under God is not free of tensions. Brownson, for example, says that the Catholic Church has the freedom it needs in America to fulfill its mission of evangelization. But it still remains the case that "the free exercise of religion" can clash, at times, with the imperatives of political loyalty and even those of the globalized competitive marketplace. Brownson would not be surprised to see that in the proudly particularistic American South, some of our most ferociously devoted citizens have been our most observant Christians, but that's not to say that proud particularism still doesn't stand in tension with being dedicated to the universal political proposition that all persons are created equal.

Brownson doesn't provide any fail-safe recipe for resolving the conflict today between our devotion to "nondiscrimination" and, say, his Catholic Church's defense of the sacramental understanding of marriage between a man and a woman. Libertarians and others, following the lead of Justice Kennedy, say the American idea of liberty has evolved, in accord with the intention of the Founders, toward an ever more expansive individualism; but conservatives emphasize the violence that a progressively more abstract or abstracted understanding of liberty does to our relational lives. The natural tendency of providential constitutionalism is to look for truth on both sides of such conflicts, but that's not to say that the result can be some doctrine that authoritatively resolves partisan conflict on the level of high principle.

The providential emphasis is resolution through civic deliberation that often produces compromises that capture the whole truth about each of us better than either of the parties to the compromise. We've seen how that was true with the Declaration of Independence. It was equally true with the religion clauses of the First Amendment. As Steven Smith notes in his important book, *The Rise and Decline of American Religious Freedom*, there was no magical or grand philosophical solution produced in the First Congress by the members that debated and drafted the religion clauses. They merely affirmed the consensus that the federal government wouldn't establish a national church, but that states would be free to regulate morals with legislation that was informed by a religious argumentation and belief. It was a legislative compromise crafted by Congressman James Madison that produces a result better than the anti-ecclesiasticism that deformed even his "Memorial and Remonstrance."

And today it's natural for Brownsonians to be in favor of a kind of judicial restraint that curbs enthusiastic natural-rights nationalism based on the presumption of liberty and leaves as much space as possible for civic deliberation on issues as diverse as abortion and the future of our entitlements. It's especially important in defending the dialectic between universality and particularity that is the genius, Brownson explains, of American federalism to create a larger "safe space" for always-tentative legislative resolutions of issues that should be illuminated by the whole of our providential constitutionalism—and not by efforts at definitive resolution by judges spinning high principles from the single word "liberty" in the Due Process Clause of the Fourteenth Amendment

For Brownson, to think clearly both about our Constitution and about particular human beings means avoiding the excesses of thinking too universally (or abstractly) or too particularly (or selfishly). It requires finding a mean between the two extremes of American political thought. On one side, Americans properly appropriate the truthful dogma of human equality, and remembering that all persons equally possess rights is what directs us away from the excessive concern for particularity that characterized aristocratic Southerners in Brownson's time, with all their secessionist, racist, and even pagan impulses. But at the opposite extreme, humanitarians and their abstract egalitarianism have divorced the theory of equality from its properly personal theological context. What remains is an empty universalism that overstates the possibilities for human redemption in political reform and denies the truth about personal being, and therefore about personal rights. As the Yankee Brownson acknowledged, despite their many faults, the Southerners were right to defend the particularity of relational individuality; they claimed to know and love real persons and so to have no need for any interest in abstract "humanitarianism."

The American constitutional mean between abstract universalism and tribal secessionism, according to Brownson, is a limited political unity of citizens who know they are more than and less than citizens. All of us equally are shaped by natural, personal imperatives having to do with flourishing as material, political, and spiritual beings. When we forget any of the three, we get into deep trouble. The material being is concerned with the personal subsistence of self and family. The political being is concerned with the common good shared by citizens in a "territorial democracy" in a particular part of the world. And the spiritual being is concerned with discovering his or her relational duties to a loving personal Creator and sharing that personal news with fellow creatures through a religious institution.

Fully human beings attend to all three parts of who they are. They don't regard themselves as less than they really are by thinking of themselves as only producers and consumers or only citizens, and they don't think of themselves as more than they are by confusing their limited and dutiful freedom with the unlimited freedom of God.

The American Constitution, Brownson explains, reconciles "liberty with law, and law with liberty" through the devoted affirmation of mediating constitutional principles such as self-government, federalism, the separation of powers, and religious freedom. Rightly understood, we can see in Brownson's idea of law and liberty a theoretical justification for an enduring practice of American liberty that affirms a constitutional order that "secures at once the authority of the public and the freedom of the individual—the sovereignty of the people without social despotism, and individual freedom without anarchy. In other words, its mission is to bring out in its life the dialectic union of authority and liberty, of the natural rights of man and those of society."[4]

In the way we have suggested, Brownson can help today's Americans think seriously about the complex interplay between political and economic liberties and the relational life of creatures and citizens. It is that kind of thinking that the friends of liberty require if they are to overcome the confusion that marks our time and the increasing inadequate character of twentieth-century categories.

1 · What Distinguishes America?

What distinguishes America? From one view, of course, ours is a middle-class country full of prosaic, bourgeois men and women who all understand themselves to be free beings who work. Orestes Brownson's view, however, is that America is the dialectical reconciliation—someone else might say prudent compromise—between two idealistic extremes. One extreme is the egalitarian idealism of Puritan New England. The other is the love of liberty of the Southern aristocrats. As Alexis de Tocqueville reminds us, each extreme had its founding as European civilization planted itself on our soil in both New England and Virginia. Our two founding regions, Brownson explains, are characterized by "opposite" political tendencies.

The antebellum South, for Brownson, was characterized by personal democracy, that is, government built on the principle of pure individualism. The North—through the dominant influence of New England—was characterized by humanitarian democracy, that is, government built on the principle of egalitarianism. Each of these extremes, by itself, is equally "hostile to civilization" and "capable of sustaining governments only on the principles common to all despotisms."[1] What the South "loses" is "the race," or the truth that all human beings are created both free and equal. It tribally suppresses the truth that rights are universal or "catholic" or encompass us all. In that respect, it dismissed the truth, embodied in Puritan New England (even in its post-Christian manifestations), about the "unity" of the whole human race. What New England loses—as it makes the transcendentalist move from Christianity properly speaking to a kind of pantheism—is "the individual" or the irreducible liberty of each particular person. When Brownson calls the humanitarianism of New England "abolitionism," he means that its theoretical tendency is to obliterate all the distinctions that constitute the truth about who each of us is, made in the image of a personal and relational—or Trinitarian—God.[2]

Abolitionism serves justice insofar as it aims to negate the barbaric oppression of race-based slavery and the patriarchal chauvinism that excludes women from equal

13

citizenship. But it moves on to deny what we can see with our eyes about the natural differences between men and women, as well as the distinction between citizen and noncitizen, which is an indispensable feature of political life, which, in turn, is necessarily territorial or shared by people occupying a particular part of the world. Brownson goes as far as to say the abolitionist movement cannot end until "all individualities" disappear. Humans are to become apolitical and indistinguishable members of a species, and our species will then be no different than all the others. Abolitionism so understood, of course, reminds us of C. S. Lewis's "abolition of man," as it does Nietzsche's "last man" and "the end of history." It also reminds us of the Southern saying that Northerners love humanity, but Southerners love particular men and women they really know. For Brownson, abolitionism so understood replaces charity with philanthropy, as "philanthropy, unlike charity, does not begin at home and is powerless unless it operates at a distance."[3] Charity is the virtue that flows from our love of those persons made in the image of the loving, personal God, but the philanthropist isn't concerned about this or that person in particular.

Brownson echoes St. Augustine when he reminds us that true religion is "catholic," but it was never meant to abolish the diversity of a world separated into nations with their own "providential constitutions" or destinies rooted in their traditions, customs, and complex array of circumstances. The despotic civil religions of the Greeks and Romans denied the truth that each of us is more than a loyal citizen, but the modern efforts to reduce the political community to merely a contract that autonomous individuals without a history and an inheritance consent to denies that we are citizens, and that political belonging is a real and admirable feature of who we are. The mean between the extreme positions of the unreserved or supreme devotion demanded by the ancient polis and the selfish liberation—or what Brownson calls political atheism—of modern or Lockean liberalism is civic loyalty under a personal God (in whose image all creatures are made and who is no mere creature of any particular city). What G. K. Chesterton called "the American romance of the citizen" is that each of us is equally more than a citizen, but an equal citizen too. It's on the truthfully Christian foundation of the Roman Augustine that the United States escapes the aristocratic error of living in denial of "the unity of the human race" and the democratic, or humanitarian, error of obliterating the territorial distinctions that separate persons into particular political communities. Nations have separate political destinies, but it's also true that "all Christian nations belong to one and the same family, have the same Christian idea, and are (each in its way) developing and laboring to perfect one and the same order of civilization."[4] No nation or state should be explicitly Christian politically, but they can be united by a shared Christian culture or civilization, which ranks higher than their diversity of political forms.

BROWNSON ON FOUNDING STATESMANSHIP

Brownson's capacity to incorporate what's best about both the South and New England into American constitutionalism properly understood depends on understanding the Framers not as theorists, but as statesmen. They were, on the level of theorists, innovating Lockeans who aimed at the revolutionary reconstruction not only of government but of all life with the individualistic spirit of contract and consent. But they didn't build as theorists, but as statesmen, whose enduring accomplishment was to take into account all they were given in framing our political institutions. That means our written Constitution wasn't meant to obliterate the inheritances Americans received from their first foundings in New England and in Virginia, although it was meant to avoid the extremism of each of them taken alone. They certainly didn't mean to somehow create a civilization out of nothing, displaying the opposite of gratitude to everything our people and our nation have received. As statesmen, they did not understand themselves simply to be implementing the theory of the Declaration of Independence, which is all about sovereign individuals instituting government to serve their personal, apolitical, asocial, and areligious needs. The theory of the Declaration, taken as a self-sufficient foundation of government, is, Brownson observes, "political atheism," insofar as it recognizes no authority above the individual's sovereign rule. It's also "state suicide," insofar as a sustainable political order depends on more than consent that can be withdrawn at will. The theory of the Declaration, as Jefferson saw, lays the foundation for permanent revolution, with no place for the territorial character of political attachment, the social consensus for political loyalty over generations, or any effectual restraint on the "secessionism" that is the tendency of uprooted, assertive individuals.

That doesn't mean that Brownson is particularly uncritical of the content of our written constitution, even as he places it in a providential context. He goes as far as to ground federalism, which, for our Framers, was more a compromise than anything else, in the truth about human nature. Moreover, he affirms social but not political aristocracy. Democracy of some sort is what Americans have been given as a possibility, and there is no way we could or should choose against it. But democracy is not without its defects, and that's why Brownson, in American fashion, calls our country more a republic than a pure or Rousseauian democracy. And democracy is not necessarily a universal political possibility that's destined to be actualized everywhere. But Brownson is, overall, a loyal American democratic republican. Democracy is more sustainable and more elevated by social aristocracy—or some place for a beneficial deference to the natural aristocracy of talented and virtuous leaders—and the antebellum south, which was democratic in political form, displayed this to a certain degree.

In the same way, Brownson highlights the singular American separation of church and state as not only prudent or customary or inherited but deeply truthful. He says that his Catholic Church in America has all the freedom it needs—the freedom to evangelize—and he suggests that it's always wrong for the church to push for "more" politically.[5] That separation, in fact, is grounded in the Christian truth about the transpolitical character of the church and of each of us as persons open to the whole truth about who we are. True religion is nonsectarian, and so it rises above (and is not about) serving the diverse needs of territorial political forms. Because true religion is catholic—and because American political power is limited by that fact—Brownson could say without irony that America, in form, is a Catholic country.

That, however, means that religious liberty can't be sustained by mere religious tolerance, much less religious indifference.[6] Religious freedom is not, in truth, the negative freedom of the individual's isolated sovereign conscience to choose spiritual preferences. It is positive freedom, or freedom for being a member of a church (or an organized body of thought and action).[7] Religious freedom can't be sustained by "political atheism," because it has no effectual limit on individual or political will. That means the Constitution's silence on God is a rejection of sectarian civil theology—or the chaining of religion and citizens wholly to the sovereign nation. Thus it's an affirmation of the understanding of God found only among the Christians. In that crucial respect if in no other, ours is a Christian nation. Even if many of our Founders regarded themselves as atheistic enlightened rationalists in the theoretical mode of John Locke, it turns out that they and even Locke himself were more Christian than they knew. It's from the Christians that we learned the truth about our dignity as more than merely natural or political beings chained in some civic "cave." Locke and our founding theorists slighted, of course, the fact that our freedom depends on being relational beings as well, but that accusation works better against the theory than the statesmanlike practice of our Founders, who created, or better, preserved safe spaces for the relational flourishing of local political communities, families, and churches.

Brownson's understanding of the place of Christianity and even aristocracy in our providential Constitution seems, at first, too quirky to be of much use.[8] And it's true enough that it has had no influence worth speaking of in our political tradition so far. But it might still be more relevant than ever. One argument against the idiosyncratic character of Brownson's providential constitution, after all, is that it is strikingly similar in many ways to the description of America found in the best book ever written about America and the best book ever written about democracy, Alexis de Tocqueville's *Democracy in America*.

TOCQUEVILLE'S AMERICA

Brownson, like Tocqueville, understands America to have two foundings—one in New England and the other in Virginia—with opposite tendencies. Moreover, he goes even further in understanding the American Constitution as not simply the implementation of the theory of the Declaration of Independence. Rights, for Tocqueville, are a point of honor—a proud assertion detached from merely material need. Tocqueville, in fact, notoriously doesn't mention the Declaration at all, showing that the Constitution and the minds and hearts of democratic Americans can be accounted for without its theory about individuals in the state of nature. He does observe that America was transformed by its revolutionary generation, but his emphasis is mostly that that democratic transformation of our country was deliberately incomplete. Unlike the far more comprehensive and radically centralizing French effort, the American revolution left intact "free local institutions," an inheritance from aristocratic England, that Americans do not regard as aristocratic, freedom of religion combined with a more or less universal acceptance of Christian moral precepts, and the family.

Christianity, Tocqueville instructs legislators, should be regarded as America's most precious inheritance from aristocratic ages. Christianity is as democratic as any religion can be that preserves the inegalitarian distinction between God and humans, teaches that we have souls and irreducible social duties to be discovered and performed in common, and preaches that each creature made in God's image has a high and singular destiny as more than a merely biological being. And the Catholic Tocqueville, like the Catholic Brownson, thought that American freedom was quite compatible with a secure future for the church, for a church that would likely grow as an authoritative countercultural antidote to the aimless and apathetic permissiveness of individualism. But Tocqueville, also like Brownson, thought that pantheism—a kind of indiscriminate humanitarianism that ends up even abolishing the distinctions that separate God, humans, and material nature—was the democratic threat to individuality that most needs to be opposed by the true friends of human liberty.[9] Tocqueville, it's true, displays no awareness that the Puritanism of the New England founding had morphed into transcendentalist pantheism, and so he doesn't join Brownson in describing pantheism as a particularly American form of post-Christian heresy. He and Brownson do agree that the movement forward to pantheism is a far greater danger to the future of human liberty than some relapse to aristocracy, although he also warned of the possibility of an industrial aristocracy that would have many of the privileges of the European political aristocracies without any corresponding sense of paternalistic responsibility. An industrial aristocracy that would think of itself as a meritocracy based on productivity and as deserving what it has, and think of others as beings to be controlled or scripted by their mental labor.

One antidote he presents is an aristocratic education—reading the Greek and Roman authors in their original languages.[10] Another is the American belief in the equality of all personal creatures with souls, and that includes some attention to the limited truth in the Puritan spirit of egalitarian political reform. The Americans, because they are Christians, don't believe that political reform can remedy every human ill or produce perfect equality. But because they are Christians, they are truthful critics of the aristocratic assumption that slavery will in some sense always be with us, including the alienated drudgery of this or that point in the progress of the division of labor. One part of the enduring American legacy of the Christian Puritans is the belief that universal education isn't just the techno-vocationalism of free beings who work, but the genuinely higher education that allows every creature to read the Bible and other great and good books for himself or herself. Both work and leisure are possibilities given to us all. That's why Tocqueville defends the Puritans' Sunday—a day of preaching and personal reflection about each of our high and singular immortal destinies as beings with souls—against the encroaching spirits of materialism and commerce. In that respect, religion is our most precious aristocratic inheritance, a source of both chastened humility and proper pride, something Socrates himself would praise as indispensable for personal elevation against the democratic grain.[11] Organized religion, in that respect, is both highly egalitarian and a form of social aristocracy. So Tocqueville shows us that America at its best is some combination of middle-class, aristocratic, and Christian (meaning, first of all, Puritan) self-understandings.

In describing the "social state of the Anglo-Americans," he observes that all Americans understand themselves alike, as free beings who work. The good news, we can say, is that they are free, like aristocrats. The bad news, we can add, is that they have to work, like slaves. There is, in America, no leisure class that understands itself to deserve to depend on the work of others to pursue higher or nobler and intrinsically beautiful pursuits. American justice is that each of us was made to work, and so each of us has every right and even duty to love money. One reason we love money is that we have every reason to expect that our efforts will be rewarded with more of it. The equality of opportunity to be rewarded for our real productivity is justice. And, in justice, there is no genuine meritocracy but the one based on productivity. There's no denying that the rich deserve what they have—money—and other claims for status are lazy and unjust vanity. In America, the rich have to work hard to make it clear that they're only quantitatively and not qualitatively better than most people. So they have to hide any unjust contempt they've picked up for the vulgarity of the many, and even when their ostentation becomes conspicuous it remains vulgar, because they either pretend or, more typically, really have no way of knowing better.

That means, Tocqueville adds, that the imperative to be middle class "to a certain point . . . extends to intelligence itself." There is, in fact, no place where there are "so few ignorant and fewer learned men than are found in America." Middle-class intelligence is somewhere in between being ignorant and being learned. A certain level of learning is shared by most everyone, whereas in the aristocracy ignorance is pervasive and higher learning is prized as one purpose of the leisure the few deserve to enjoy. As Tocqueville observes, "In America a certain middling level of human knowledge is established. All minds have approached it; some by rising, others by falling."[12] America, we can say, has a common educational core, which, from an intellectual view, makes some people better and other people worse.

Now this combination of elevating and leveling characteristic of the middle-class social state works only to "a certain point" in achieving intellectual equality. That's because, Tocqueville explains, "Intellectual inequality comes directly from God, and man cannot prevent it from always reappearing."[13] In a middle-class democracy the main way that inequality is displayed is through amounts of money, and there's no denying that one's intellect and one's money are one's own to use pretty much as one pleases.

Still, it's undeniable that middle-class democracy is a form of indirect social engineering to recast everyone in the same mold. Or you could say that modern or middle-class liberal democracy is not only a form of government but a way of life. It's that comprehensive intention that's only partly consciously chosen that Tocqueville attempts to capture with the somewhat ambiguous phrase "social state." In Brownsonian terms, the social state is partly the result of a written and partly the result of a more providential constitution.

The result in America is that "primary education is available to every one; higher education is hardly available to anyone."[14] There is an equality of opportunity and lack of opportunity. In America, just about everyone is "comfortable" enough to find the time to "readily procure for themselves the first elements of human knowledge." And working for oneself does depend on basic literacy when it comes to reading, writing, and computation. Most Americans have no real alternative but to choose a profession, and so most education beyond "the general cultivation of intelligence" is basically an apprenticeship. That means, from an aristocratic view, real American education "concludes when ours begins."[15] It also means that more advanced American education is specialized with money in mind. Science itself becomes a kind of "trade" with only its immediate utility in some "applied" setting in mind.

In this connection, Tocqueville calls attention to and criticizes an American dream. Get rich while you're young, and then turn to serious study or higher education somewhere down the road. The problem is, of course, that it's young people who have "the taste for study."[16] The mind and the longing for learning function better and are more readily and deeply aroused early in life—as the example of Pascal shows. He was so deeply animated by his pursuit of truth—including the quest for God—hidden from view that he, in Tocqueville's telling, pretty much thought himself to death before he was forty. It is also between very hard and impossible to switch off the love of money and switch on the love of truth for its own sake. Minds formed in a middle-class social state are formed by monetary and professional concerns—by being a free individual who works and nothing more. It's between hard and impossible to choose, at a certain point, to be more or different than you've been for most of your life. That's why the key democratic distinction is not between work and leisure, but work and recreation, and why, as Tocqueville observes, even literature becomes an industry. Certainly it's not middle class to buy into the aristocratic claim that leisure is the basis of culture. Culture becomes an amenity you're free to choose (or not) in your free time.

One piece of good news is that middle-class America is an "ever-growing crowd of readers," but that means almost all authors become "vendors of ideas" for people who only know how to read for information and entertainment. Readers and writers profit from books that can be quickly read and don't require much learning to be understood. Nuances elude them, because they have neither the taste nor time for them. Democratic readers, to be sure, have moments in which they "taste the pleasures of the mind furtively." They do not—they believe they cannot—"make those pleasures the principal charm of their existence," but they consider them "as a passing and necessary relaxation in the midst of the serious business of life."[17] The aristocrat holds that work is for leisure, the middle-class democrat says some relaxation is indispensable for sustaining the "serious business" demanded of those free and equal workers.

Tocqueville, of course, thinks that the middle-class view—like the aristocratic view—of who we are is partly true and partly not. The official doctrine of the aristocrats was "sublime" because it was detached from mere utility, and so it functioned to sustain the higher, proud, immaterial qualities that distinguish members of our species from all the others: those that cause us to have thoughts and perform deeds that stand the test of time, that keep us from being merely pointless momentary specks in a universe indifferent to the greatness of particular persons. The tendency of democracy, by contrast, is to empty individuals of particular relational content that keeps them from being absorbed into some impersonal system. Tocqueville's key criticism of the middle-class understanding of freedom is that it's unsustainable, mainly because it distorts and denies—without being able to extinguish—the needs of the soul.[18] One result is the decent materialism of democracy is deformed (thank God!) by outbursts of spiritual madness, the diversion of incessant restlessness that has no material cause, a kind of insane ardor that drives the frenzied pursuit of happiness through material acquisition. Despite or because the middle-class democrat brags that he can reduce everything to self-interested calculation, madness, Tocqueville reports, is common in America.

Tocqueville adds, however, that while aristocrats constantly spoke of the beauty of virtue, in secret they studied the ways in which their doctrine was useful in sustaining their power. Middle-class democrats are less hypocritical by being loud and proud about the utility of science, virtue, and everything else useful for being rich and productive. Their view of freedom, in obvious ways, is more real and less imaginary than the aristocratic one. It is also more just, insofar as it doesn't subordinate the many—who are publicly regarded as beings with interests to be recognized—to the interests of the few. The middle-class democrat candidly admits that no one should be regarded as more or less than a being with interests, and that's why the love of money is (and should be) universal. That universal conclusion, Tocqueville ventures, is in accord with the mind of God, who has given each creature an equal right to liberty. Jesus coming down to earth, Tocqueville explains, revealed a truth about us all that we can confirm with reason as justice. In that respect, part of our providential Constitution is the New Testament, insofar as it's what we've been given that can't be forgotten, but only distorted or deformed. Tocqueville himself understands that when he attempts to enter into "the mind of God," he finds that he must prefer the justice of equality to the greatness of the few.

But like Brownson, Tocqueville understands that the choice for equality—in the absence of any concern for the greatness of particular examples of individuality—morphs in the direction of an abstract humanitarianism and finally pantheism. And it's pantheism, Tocqueville asserts, that most of all needs to be resisted by the true friends of human individuality. The tendency of aristocrats is to think too particularly, and so not even notice what they share in common with human beings not of their class. But the tendency of democrats is to think too generally, with generalizations that become plausible only through abstracting from the distinctions that constitute the truth about human nature. God, Tocqueville says, has no need of general ideas—a need that flows from the weakness of the human mind and not really from the nature of things. God sees each of us just as he or she is, similar to in some ways and different from in others. The egalitarian impulse toward "unity" that produces humanitarianism and then pantheism is really, in large part, anxious and ultimately failed attempts at self-forgetfulness. However, purely democratic poetry—poetry free from all imagined illusions—gets beyond both aristocratic focus on gods and heroes and the democratic focus on abstract humanity and impersonal nature.

It's all about the strange and wonderful being who exists for a moment between two abysses. At the end of the day, the truth is that each of us is put in a predicament not of his or her own making and has a singular destiny.

That means that the democratic tendency to reduce science to technology is, from one perspective, a candid and considerate effort to use what we can know to make lives better. But from another, it's a diversion from what we can know about the invincible limits of such efforts, as well as about their degrading materialistic obsessiveness. In democracy, metaphysics and theology lose ground, as all of language is transformed in a technological direction. When aristocrats think about human perfectibility, they focus on the progress toward wisdom and virtue that occurs over particular lives, and they assume technological development and political change don't really transform who each of us is. The aristocrat's view of perfectibility is definite and particular, but it unrealistically underplays what science can do to improve the human condition. Democrats, by contrast, have a very indefinite view of perfectibility; the individual gains significance as part of a long process heading away from nature toward who knows what. Technological progress is therefore given broader significance as evidence of moral and political progress, as if technology couldn't be deployed by those tyrants and didn't inevitably have a cost in the relational lives of individuals.

Aleksandr Solzhenitsyn says that the fundamental fact of the modern world is that it's "a world split apart" into unrealistic extremes: There's the displaced person who proudly understands himself or herself as an abstracted role player living by the code of "human rights" detached from the security and loyalty of any particular community. Our cognitive elite is made up of humanitarians who say "we are the world," while not sharing the real egalitarian devotion of our original people. There's also the person detached from the stability of family and church and secure employment and sometimes full of xenophobic resentment (and other stuff in Hillary Clinton's "basket of deplorables") but in other ways mainly decent and often touchingly nostalgic for the relational dignity that comes from being a responsible citizen, parent, and friend.

BROWNSON'S RECONCILIATION OF AMERICAN LIBERTIES

On this point, Brownson would agree with Solzhenitsyn that technological progress gains significance for us, but this occurs through a particularly intricate trial of free will. It is a gift flowing from both our natural capabilities and our tradition that has facilitated the progress of science. But it's not to be confused with the "one true progress" that is the self-disciplined and relational movement toward wisdom and virtue that occurs over each particular life. Brownson sometimes tended to think that technological progress is almost inevitably at the expense of self-knowledge and relational life, but at other times he was more confident that America was the place where scientific progress could be reconciled with the truth about political and religious life.

In Brownson's eyes, what's distinctive about our country is its reconciling of apparent opposites—universal and particular, cosmopolitan and tribal, South and North, the church and the polis, mind and body, and so forth—while it's the providential constitution that does justice to the whole truth about who each of us is, by incorporating what's true and rejecting what's not in the key moments of self-understanding—from Greek philosophy and republicanism to modern liberalism and humanitarianism—that make up the constitutional context in which our written Constitution was constructed by the Founders, who built far better than they claimed to know through their Lockean theory.[19]

Brownson would note, to begin with, the disappearance of mediating categories of church membership and citizenship, places where all Americans used to meet in common despite sometimes vast disparities in talents, wealth, and status. Our cosmopolitan elite lacks political loyalty and civic responsibility, sometimes thinking, as did the aristocrats of old, that people not of their class are to be viewed with condescension and contempt. Actually, of course, they're colder and more detached than those discredited aristocrats, because the latter often were able to connect their unearned privileges with the personal responsibility they must fulfill to particular human beings not of their kind.

To be a member of a meritocracy based on productivity is to be given to believe that you deserve what you have, and even that you serve society best by "relating" to others in the modes of manipulation and control. That means you're basically unbothered by progress in the division of labor that strips the workplace of personal qualities such as loyalty and security and that freedom really means the unfettered ability to think of others as basically producers and consumers. That also means thinking of churches not as authoritative and truthful places where we learn who we are as more than merely economic and political beings, but as sources of arbitrary discrimination that resist progress and hobble the global marketplace. From Brownson's view, it also means a false thinking about citizenship itself as simply an arbitrary form of rent-seeking that also impedes the free movement of peoples and so rigs the competitive marketplace. And again (and finally) from Brownson's view, it means disrespecting the patriotic warrior spirit of the most loyal Americans, those most willing to give their lives to protect American freedom and security. It means, in other words, reducing all Americans who are not part of our meritocratic cognitive elite or not compliantly willingly to be scripted by said elite to brutes.

Here, Brownson would look to the proud spirit of the genuine meritocracy of virtue of our democratized South, of what we see portrayed, for example, in *Friday Night Lights* and *American Sniper*.

Brownson would claim that it's the absence of shared religious understanding about who each of us is—a sharing that flourishes best under religious freedom or the proper separation of church and state—and the demotion of the privileges and responsibilities of citizenship that are the main symptoms that our country has been split into an intellectual elite that aims to script those they have reduced, in their own minds, to bodies to be controlled. If he were among us now, we might see the stirrings of the young socialist all about justice for the working class. But the more mature, less abstractly humanitarian Brownson saw the remedy to be the recovery of the whole truth about who each of us is: more than a mind or a body, but a real, relational, loving person open to the truth about all things, including the personal Creator in whose image each of us was created.[20]

Brownson's paradoxical conclusion is that if America were merely a middle-class nation, a people understanding themselves as nothing more than free beings who work, we wouldn't be able to sustain a middle-class life that reconciles inevitable social aristocracy with civic and religious equality. That's why we can say that the techno-vocational or utilitarian standard is more omnipresent among our experts and leaders, but the actual middle class seems to be withering away. In our world split apart, it seems that Americans have fewer common experiences than ever, even as their thought and art languishes in the kind of vague mediocrity that flows from a world unable to find the words to articulate the content of human lives.

Brownson would even say that our time has become way too Lockean, too much about individual liberty. The resulting individualism empties each of us, depriving us of the spirit of resistance to the homogenizing forces—the global marketplace and centralized administration—that surround us. The two alternatives aren't really individualism and collectivism, because radical individualism produces indistinguishable beings readily absorbed into this or that scripted collectivity. It can produce the dependency of socialism, but also the dependency that comes through being scripted by the cognitive elite and its "corporate values" of compliant competency and sensitivity to diversity.

The real way to make America great again is to honor and facilitate the relational dignity of the lives of whole human persons open to the universal truth through their deep participation in particular personal institutions. That means that even we conservatives have to see some good in what remains of our Puritan devotion to political egalitarianism, expressed, as Brownson himself did, through a renewed devotion to the Catholic principles of solidarity and subsidiarity.

A DIALECTIC OF LIBERTY

All creatures are open to the truth they can share in common as particular beings dependent on, and so indebted to, the social life embedded or embodied in particular institutions, principally the family, the nation, and the church. True cosmopolitanism we experience through philosophy and especially religion, but those truthful experiences not only do not negate but actually depend on experiencing ourselves as particular beings with privileges and responsibilities as loving members of families and loyal citizens. And even economic freedom—which Brownson also unreservedly embraces as a limit to the scope of political power—is understood as what we've been given to provide for ourselves and our own; it's not the freedom of people who are sovereign producers and consumers and nothing more.[21]

Brownson opposed the emptiness of cosmopolitanism insofar as it undermines the social attachments, moral virtues, and real friendships that made particular lives worthwhile. As Christopher Lasch pointed out, Brownson's "Christian radicalism" states that "man grasps the universal only through the particular" and that personal truth can be affirmed without the aid of biblical revelation.[22] Or, as the philosopher-pope Benedict XVI observes, logos, we can see for ourselves, is personal; it is a feature not of abstracted minds or materially determined bodies but of the third reality each human person is.[23] That means, if you think about it, that if all of truthful reality can be shared joyfully by persons, in some sense being itself is both universal and particular all the way down. The world is the home not of the mind, but of the person, and personal existence is necessarily both universal and particular. The emptiness of humanitarian cosmopolitanism is reflected in the theoretical construction of the unrealistically abstracted or content-free person—the orbiting, ghostly tourist—detached from any place and any people in particular. The cosmopolite is really a homeless person who readily surrenders his anxious experience of particularity to the "we are the world" that is pantheistic humanitarianism.

For Brownson, the cosmopolitan truth about the limits or partiality of every particular human community is discovered through participation in the universal City of God. There, personal reality comes into its own in the communion that is the church, where every creature retains his or her personal and relational identity in love with the personal God. It's true, at first, that pantheism—which is a poetic form of materialism—seems more reasonable or unified than Christianity, just as, at first, the idea that God is a person seems to be an oxymoronic offense against reason. For the ancient philosophers as much as the contemporary physicists, philosophy (or science) is "learning how to die" or getting over all illusions about your personal significance. God, meaning "the Laws of Nature and Nature's God," neither knows nor loves particular persons, and all our personal pretensions dissolve in the light of God's cosmic indifference. But pantheism, in truth, can't account for the personal being who can live in the truth, including, of course, the personal God and those made in God's relational image. The Cosmopolis, in truth, is not a union of knowing minds, but a community of loving persons. And, of course, the City of God can't be confused with cities or nations in the properly political sense. Political cosmopolitanism—or dedication to a nation with no geographical or proper human borders—is an oxymoron.

From this view, Brownson criticizes the New England of his time as basically post-Christian and the South as basically pre-Christian.[24] And the dialectical interplay between the two excesses, in his mind, returns us to the Christian truth of our providential constitution. In the wake of the South's defeat, humanitarian abolitionism becomes the greater threat to America's truthful self-understanding. That's partly because egalitarian leveling is such a potent and often a seemingly irreversible feature of the modern world. But it's also because Americans might understand the defeat of the South on the battlefield as a repudiation of the partial truth it embodies at its best.

That's why Brownson worked so hard to keep the war from being understood, as it often was in the North, as "between the Northern democracy and the South aristocracy." He wanted it to be a war "to abolish slavery so far as it can be done without appealing to humanitarian or revolutionary principles."[25] He wanted to contain the spirit of abolitionism to the barbaric injustice. Against the spirit of revolution, in fact, he mostly wanted the war to be understood as fundamentally conservative, as a "vindication of national integrity, and in defense of American constitutionalism." And he didn't think that vindication gave the North the right—nor did he have the "wish"—to "revolutionize southern society."

He noted that the South is "socially" but not "politically" aristocratic and so is in no need of political revolution. And its social aristocracy, with its defense of a kind of "natural aristocracy" based on talents and virtues, was an advantage during the war. Its "society has proved relatively stronger and more energetic than Northern society," because its leaders were both "intrinsically superior to the mass" and "felt to be so." In the South, democracy "is less socially defused" than in the Northern states, and the result is that it "has always, as a rule, elevated abler men," and their "ascendancy in the Union . . . has provoked Northern jealousy." When democracy becomes too social, in addition to political, it's not the "best men" who are elevated to office, but "the most available men," who are typically mediocre at best and demagogic at worse.[26]

It's possible to "let all be equal before the law" and still favor "a social aristocracy; families elevated above the commonality by their estates, their education, culture, manners, tastes, and refinement." The truth is no "community can long subsist where such an aristocracy is wanting, to furnish models and leaders for the people."[27] The correspondence between the convention of the social aristocracy and the natural aristocracy of talents and virtues is, of course, imperfect. But it embodies the common sense that those with the qualities of leaders are always few, and it resists the democratic tendency to raise people "to places of honor, profit, and trust" who would be rightly regarded as unworthy under any other social forms— a tendency fueled by the democratic excesses of "substitut[ing] public opinion" for "trust, justice, reason, . . . and the criterion even of moral judgment."[28]

The South's orientation around the greatness of leaders came from the slaveholders who "studied the classics" and "admired Greeks and Rome." They imagined that they were returning to the classical virtue of republican civilization, which did, in fact, depend on slavery. And it's true that the South's honorable devotion to the military spirit, and the honorable profession of the military officer, "supply an element needed in all society, to sustain it in the chivalric and heroic spirit." Insofar as America is a republic, as opposed to a democracy animated by some combination of individualistic indifference, irresponsible deference to public opinion and demagoguery, and commercial selfishness, it owes much to the Greeks and Romans, and their spirit is most alive in the South. Not only that, insofar as America aspires, as Brownson holds to be our destiny, to "be a great military and naval power . . . the old hostility to a standing army and the only attempt to bring the military into disrepute must be abandoned."[29] As subsequent experience has shown, America will depend more than ever on the virtues of the comparatively honorable and violent South. And some military spirit—the willingness to risk and to wage war, our experience suggests—is required for members of our natural aristocracy to desire and take on positions of political leadership.

The contributions of the South to our self-understanding aren't limited to political leadership and martial virtue. The New Englander, Brownson claims, "need[s] the slower, the more deliberate, and the more patient and enduring man of the South to serve as his counterpoise."[30] Like all aristocrats, the Southern man prefers leisure to restless activity, thoughtful deliberation to incessant calculation, and the permanent things over the ephemeral success of disruptive techno-innovation. He has a high opinion of the human mind and his singular greatness, and he's less in a hurry because he's less obsessed with time, less haunted by his mortality, and less anxious about his status. His is, as Brownson puts it, "the marked individuality" of "the nobility of thought and purpose, and the high sense of honor, so common in the medieval world, and the better parts of antiquity."[31]

In Brownson's mind, one high purpose of America's providential constitution— the mission our country in particular has been given—is to sustain and complete what's best politically and intellectually of "Greco-Roman civilization": art, science, philosophy, and political life. This requires overcoming our chauvinistic misperception that their accomplishments have simply been supplanted. The Civil War had the magnificent accomplishment of purging from our nation the "grand error" of slavery, but that can't or shouldn't be at the price of forgetting the ways in which the Greeks and Romans knew better than we do. The American destiny is to rival or surpass the Greeks and Romans in science or philosophy, but that could only happen by being attentive to their great accomplishments and texts.

Surpassing can't be grounded in forgetting, and that's an advantage of the leading Southerners' conviction that classical philosophy was of perennial relevance as an articulation of truthful thought and noble action. Even Mr. Jefferson, we can say, taught the superiority of the middle-class doctrine of rights in public, but he lived the classical doctrine of friendship with great men and free thinkers like himself in private. It's after Jefferson—and outside the South—that Americans became increasingly convinced that the free person is a being with rights and nothing more. And that dogma, of course, has the tendency to empty out the content by which the free individual can display genuine individuality—or moral and intellectual virtue. Brownson himself became increasingly convinced that middle-class American life came at the price of the decline in thought. It is true, he observed, that "education has been more generally diffused," and that is, to a point, genuine progress. Still, "it is doubtful that the number of thinkers has been increased, or real mental culture extended." The truth is that profound thought and high culture have always come from a natural aristocracy, and they have never had a merely middle-class audience. In science, there's been progress in the invention of comfortable conveniences and weapons, and in knowledge understood as information—all of undeniable benefit to free beings who work. But there hasn't been corresponding progress in "really scientific classification and explanation," in theoretical science prized for its own sake. Even in political science, the vain vulgarities of "all the democratic theories and tendencies of modern liberals" find "unanswerable refutations" that can be discovered by "anyone who has read Aristotle's Politics."[32] The refutations are, of course, indispensable for anyone who thinks that liberal and democratic theories can explain everything about who we are as moral and political beings.

Brownson's balanced judgment is that the world has been progressing physically in ways that have raised up ordinary people and produced less gratuitous violence and cruelty. It's good—and undeniably Christian—in many ways that "manners, habits, and sentiments have been softened, and become more humane."[33] But it's also true that "characters have become enfeebled and debased." Brownson's undeniably aristocratic overall judgment is that "in the moral and intellectual orders, America has been losing rather than gaining." That aristocratic tilt privileges, it would seem, the perspective of the natural aristocrat, of great leaders and thinkers, over the peace and prosperity that benefit us all. But it's also a "medieval" or distinctively Christian judgment. It's true that middle-class Americans are more tolerant than their predecessors, but they're also more "indifferent" when it comes to truthful answers about the fundamental questions about God and the good—the questions that present themselves to persons who are born to know, love, and die and who clearly, in their freedom and responsibility, have more than a merely biological destiny. The "Ages of Faith" can be condemned for their "barbarism," "violence," and "terrible crimes." But in one respect their freedom was greater; they had much greater confidence in higher purposes of "individual reason and conscience."[34] All in all, Brownson's view of the highest truth about American liberty depends on the Southern counterweight to both middle-class restless materialism and post-Christian abolitionist humanitarianism, just as it depends on New England's Christian and post-Christian modern antidotes to the selfish tribalism of aristocratic assertiveness.

So, in Brownson's view, "Southern society must be respected," even in defeat.[35] And the natural leaders must remain natural leaders if Southerners are going to be free and equal citizens of the nation again. That means that southern society shouldn't be revolutionized in the commercial direction of the North, and even that the freed blacks shouldn't be totally integrated into political life, for now. Brownson, questionably, was willing for a good amount of injustice to be perpetuated so that the South could continue as a counterweight to New England. His opposition to "negro suffrage," however, was merely prudential, and he had full confidence that it would come soon in a civilized, republican, and Christian nation.

Still, Brownson is emphatic that what the leading Southerners slighted is that Greece and Rome were great despite their slavery. And it was the truthful "infusion of Christian dogma" into "the lives, laws, and the jurisprudence of all nations" that doomed slavery everywhere. Southern democracy was, from that view, less territorial than personal. Authority wasn't held by those devoted to the common good of all persons living in a particular part of the world. It was, instead, held by those who contended that "as only the white race has been able to assert and maintain its personal freedom, only members of that race have the right to be free."[36] Freedom depends on personal assertion, and not the subordination of one's own will to the truth and the rights shared in common.

In its honorable but selfish assertion of class-based liberty, the "slaveholding class" was "the American imitation of the feudal nobility of medieval Europe." It actually, of course, was less chastened by Christianity than was the feudal nobility. Not only was "the tendency of the South[ern] democrat . . . to deny the unity of the [human] race, he tended to deny all the obligations of society to help the weak and helpless."[37] The Southerners might have often displayed magnanimity and generosity toward their inferiors, but that's different from recognizing society's duty to care for the unfortunate—a duty recognized so clearly by New England's Puritans in the public provision for the poor. The duty of charity, of course, has its Christian and post-Christian modes. It is, in both cases, a specifically Christian contribution to republican government.

Brownson's criticism of New England's humanitarian impulse for unbridled reform, for that reason, was tempered by his acknowledgment that such progressivism reflects Christian truth. Even socialism, which he presents as an extreme form of an egalitarian denial of particular individuals and countries (not to mention the basically transpolitical mission of the church) is inspired, in some sense, by Christian love. Brownson is not so polemical as to fail to observe that "much at least of what is most living, least groveling, least servile, most manly, and most elevated, outside the church, is found today" in the ranks of the socialists and other philanthropists, despite their meddlesome moralism. That's because socialism, like so much of "modern civilization," is a mistaken and defective result of "serious and earnest efforts to realize the Word made flesh—or the Christian idea—in their social life."[38]

Not only that, Brownson understood the humanitarianism or this-worldly reformism of New England as an understandable "reaction against the exaggerated supernaturalism of the [theological, Calvinist] reformers and their descendants," against all those, in fact, who privilege the truth of revelation over human reason and human science, who see no real connection, as a result, between Word and flesh.[39] Following Brownson's own tendency as a young man, they aimed to reform this world with charity and universal truth in mind. And even the mature or chastened Brownson didn't deny the proper, beneficial influence Christianity had had on reforming political life everywhere in the civilization of the West. The error of the humanitarian political reformer is a mirror image of that of theological reformers, and the socialist and otherworldly extremes each contain part of the truth.

Brownson thought the Southerners shouldn't be treated as criminals—as traitors—because their erroneous interpretation of the Constitution was sincere and far from implausible. The Southern defense of liberty understood as assertive individuality was clearly a cause for real men, even if it favored a particular class of men more than the good we share in common, just as it favored the proud particularity of the states over the general welfare provide by the national government. The Southern impulse needed not to be extinguished, but to be moderated by the truth found in its dialectical opposite. From this view, the cure of the spirit of secession—a spirit, after all, fueled by the Lockean theory of our Founders that viewed government as a contract to be nullified at personal convenience—is the correct view of America's providential constitutionalism, one that puts individual particularity and national unity in their proper places, just as it—with the correct view of federalism—puts the nation and the states in their proper places. That correct view reconciles a country split apart, just as a correct view of the whole human person corrects the division of modern philosophy into the pure universality of the mind or spirit and the pure particularity of the body, just as the correct view of the nation and its providential constitution reconciles the modern split between cosmopolitan humanitarianism and racist or tribalist xenophobia.

Political life must be in accord with the truth about who we are, and we can't live freely or effectually protect universal rights without states and borders. And so Brownson's aim was not at all to extinguish what we now call progressive, egalitarian reform in our country, but to contain it within realistic boundaries. The Southerners, remember, unrealistically slighted (and typically still slight) what government might do to improve the lives of the unfortunate, and that was an error even our original, or genuinely Christian, Puritans did not make. "The demand for the amelioration of the condition of the poor and more numerous classes, or the effort to put the poor in the way of helping themselves," Brownson even observes, "is only a catholic exposition of the precept to give alms."[40] And, as Tocqueville explains, our original Puritans, out of charity, gave government the duty to provide for the poor, a duty that our Southern states slight even today.

Brownson was rightly and genuinely concerned with the intersection of the spirit of humanitarian philanthropy with that of centralization. In both unifying tendencies, it's the distinctive reality of the particular person that gets lost. But Brownson finds in New England our most effective antidote to the spirit of centralization. That "New England system" is the town that has control over local matters; it's the system of the original Puritans. There, public provision for the unfortunate was often less philanthropic—or impersonal and abstract—and more genuinely charitable and animated by the public spiritedness of active citizens. Brownson even predicts that that localism will spread through the country in the wake of slavery's abolition.[41] And localism is the best beginning for containing, but not extinguishing, the spirit of humanitarian reform in New England and awakening it in the postslavery South. True solidarity depends, therefore, upon subsidiarity, upon political reform occurring at the most intimate and personal possible level. Government involvement inevitably compromises to some degree the voluntary spirit that must animate the personal virtue of charity, but that's less so when the government agency in question is run by citizens you might actually know and even love.

The modern tendency, Tocqueville reports, is to "treat poverty as a crime, and hold honest labor should be endured by none who can endure it." And "one of the greatest services Christianity has rendered to the world has been its consecration of poverty, and its elevation of labor to the dignity of a moral duty."[42] The antebellum South, by contrast, was indifferent to the poverty of the many and driven by the view that the best people are, in fact, too good to labor. Christianity is the deep source of the genuinely middle-class view of the dignity of work, which has nothing to do with the love of money as such. That dignity, in fact, flows mostly from the fact that nobody, even Socrates, is exempt from practicing the virtue of charity. And the dignity of poverty, illuminated by both Socrates and Jesus, is the fact that who we are is not defined by our productivity or material success. The affirmation of the dignity of labor is one place among many where modern liberalism shouldn't be opposed, because they "are borrowed from the Gospel, are taken from Christian civilization, and are, in themselves, true, noble, just, and holy."[43] It's more true to say that modern liberalism "misapplies" them by separating them from their Christian justification.

When it comes to the practice of virtue, the nation, in some respects, is still superior to the Greek polis, which tended to claim comprehensive control over whole human persons, at the expense of the truth about each creature's religious destiny. The nation, as Brownson says, is marked by diversity, replacing the loyalty to small tribes and ethnic solidarity with the less personal and more territorial loyalty of citizens. The nation, in many respects, is the political form that corresponds to the truth about our limited but real capabilities for knowing and loving. It is larger than the polis, it's true, and it's far more diverse, but those qualities awaken our capacity to trust and respect the strangers that are our fellow citizens. The ancient polis and the Puritan township were too meddlesome and intrusive at the expense of freedom of conscience or religious freedom, and so the political pretensions of the nation are chastened by the proper separation of church and state. The church, after all, aims to be meddlesome and intrusive in its care for souls and in its practice of charity, but it does not proceed with the political coercion aiming at an artificial uniformity.

That means that the nation doesn't correspond to our limited powers of knowing and loving in every respect, which is why Brownson understands our civic loyalty to the United States to include devotion to the states as particular bodies as well. It's also why he says that government's concern with the well-being of the poor, the disabled, and others deserving of charitable attention should be properly local. Even the category of citizen is too abstract or general to do justice to personal relationships and especially to those unable to flourish freely without special assistance.

2 · The Privileges and Responsibilities of American Constitutionalism

Responding to Anti-Federalists' demands for a set of amendments in the form of rights to be added to the proposed Constitution, Publius states in *Federalist* No. 84 that the Constitution is a bill of rights. Hence, any attempt to make individual rights an additional pillar of the Constitution was at best superfluous and at worst an invitation to open-ended power grabs. The logic of the Constitution, Publius observes, is a national government of delegated, enumerated, and limited powers. To further list rights that the federal government could not encroach upon, where it was already not given such power, was to suggest that rights not listed might be fair game for the new government to abolish or limit. Whispering into the federal ear that its powers may not be those that are explicitly delegated, but are capable of expansion provided that it does not violate the provisions in the first eight amendments, was to invite the undoing of the constitutional handiwork of defined powers. Hamilton's reply on this score did not carry the day, while the hypothetical point of his argument was met with the Ninth and Tenth Amendments, which ensured that unlisted rights of individuals and states were not constitutionally forsaken.

Yet we are forgiven for wondering if his essential point about constitutional structure and rights might deepen our understanding about the way we do constitutionalism now more than stale debates focusing on originalism versus living constitutionalism. This chapter will consider the manner and the extent to which the privileges and responsibilities of American constitutionalism and citizenship have been redefined by the court, to be a set of expansive rights, thin on duties, meant to liberate individuals from public and private constraints in order to fulfill the demands of autonomous persons. This view necessarily makes the autonomous individual an end in itself and therefore struggles to make sense of mediated communities of family, religion, local government, and associational life as equal complements to ordered liberty that must be constitutionally affirmed. The argument in this chapter is that the human person's relational capacities are the needed complement to autonomy and should be accorded equal weight in constitutional law.

THE CONSTITUTION AS A BILL OF RIGHTS

Publius's argument regarding a federal bill of rights is almost incomprehensible to the contemporary American. Given the power currently claimed by the Supreme Court, we should consider anew Publius's reply in *Federalist* No. 84 to the Anti-Federalist appeal for a bill of rights. "The truth is, after all declamation we have heard, that the Constitution is itself, in every rational sense, and to every useful purpose, A BILL OF RIGHTS."[1] The Anti-Federalists looked precisely to rights and immunities from government power because of their plausible concerns regarding the new powers the federal government would hold under the proposed Constitution. They thought its powers were immense and vague, a dangerous combination. They fretted over representation in a large republic that would elevate an elite governing class to rule the larger body of citizens whose sentiments and opinions would be disregarded. They feared the executive branch would dominate the federal government, entrusted as it was with general grants of power.

The Anti-Federalist Brutus had argued that judicial review was a kind of stealth weapon embedded between the lines as an undeniable implication of our written Constitution. The Constitution would have control of the legislature, and that would mean, in practice, that the Congress couldn't correct judicial interpretations of the Constitution's meaning.[2] Meanwhile, the Constitution includes no rules for its judicial interpretation, leaving the court free to mold it in new directions according to its view of its "reason and spirit." And the molding would characteristically be in the service of the transfer of power to the national government. The court, after all, is in effect an allegedly impartial referee that actually plays on the national government's team, and its own power and privileges expand with a more national or intrusive Constitution. For Brutus, the key threat to American federalism—and American democracy—is the absence of any effectual checks on the completely independent or wholly unaccountable court. This is the death knell of popular sovereignty.

Publius agreed that popular sovereignty must be protected. In the context of this debate, Publius recalls to his audience the fundamental difference between the British Constitution and the American Constitution. Bills of rights, he says, are appropriate for governments whose origins are in their "stipulations between kings and their subjects, abridgments of prerogative in favour of privilege, reservations of rights not surrendered to the prince. Such was Magna Charta, obtained by the Barons, sword in hand, from King John." Now here's the contrast, Publius says, that is provided by the American Constitution: "According to their primitive signification, they have no application to constitutions professedly founded upon the power of the people, and executed by their immediate representatives and servants. Here, in strictness, the people surrender nothing; and as they retain everything they have no need of particular reservations."[3] The British Constitution had been a contest between the Crown, Parliament, and the nobles for sovereignty over the realm, for power that is complete and full. Bills of rights make sense in that context because of the need to carve out liberties, rights for individuals in a situation where the Crown, and by the eighteenth century the Parliament, claimed sovereignty over the empire.

In the American Constitution, Publius states, the people surrender nothing and they retain everything. Sovereignty in the American political order resides not in the president, the Congress, or the Supreme Court, but in the people, and the people do not surrender their sovereignty to the government. What the sovereign does is delegate certain powers to the government through the Constitution. Moreover, the Constitution is only "intended to regulate the general political interests of the nation" and not "every species of personal and private concerns."[4] Powers that have not been assigned to the federal government are retained by the states and by individuals.

The Bill of Rights will only serve to confuse things. For example, if you say that the Congress shall not impair the freedom of the press, but nowhere was such a power given to the federal government in the first place, have you not implicitly suggested that the enumerated powers are not really enumerated. Here's Publius:

> Bills of Rights, in the sense and to the extent they are contended for, are not only unnecessary in the proposed constitution, but would even be dangerous. They would contain various exceptions to powers not granted; and on this very account, would afford a colorable pretext to claim more than were granted. For why declare that things shall not be done, which there is no power to do? Why, for instance, should it be said, that the liberty of the press shall not be restrained, when no power is given by which restrictions may be imposed?[5]

In this way, Publius says to critics, you have inverted the constitutional design. Notice what Publius points to as the guarantor of liberty of the press: public opinion. Its protection "must altogether depend on public opinion, and on the general spirit of the people and of the government. And here, after all, as intimated upon another occasion, must we seek for the only solid basis of all of our rights."[6] Today, we are told and we accept that the basis of constitutional rights is a federal government dominated by a judiciary enforcing unenumerated rights, with its legitimacy guaranteed by a supposed higher morality that it exercises, lifting its verdicts above the discomfiting prospects of deliberation, compromise, and imperfect agreement.

Publius does recognize protections in the Constitution for rights, but they are the rights tied explicitly to a republican form of popular government: the Impeachment Clause, habeas corpus, a prohibition on a bill of attainder, and the Ex Post Facto Clause. Along with this, the Constitution disallows granting titles of nobility. The jury trial must be accorded to those accused of federal crimes, and the crime of treason is defined with detail. The point of these rights is that they serve the ends of republican government.

What does Publius point to as the essence of our constitutional order? He cites the Preamble to the Constitution: "We the People of the United States; to secure the blessings of liberty to ourselves and our posterity, do ordain and establish this constitution for the United States of America." And he adds, "This is a better recognition of popular rights, than volumes of those aphorisms, which make the principal figure in several of our state bills of rights, and which would sound much better in a treatise of ethics, than in a constitution of government."[7] His focus is on rights not in some kind of detailed list, but rather in the body of the document, which structures the ways that we the people will conduct our politics in the three branches of government. Rather than government by judiciary, our constitutional order is premised on federalism and separation of powers and self-government in view of the fivefold ends of government: security, justice, peace, liberty, and the common good.

The rise of the Bill of Rights and the Fourteenth Amendment, and the claimed supremacy of the federal judiciary in the binding articulation of these provisions, is thus a symptom of the fundamental reworking of Madisonian constitutionalism. A government of few and defined powers, however, confronts the problem of power not as a moral issue, but as a basic question: does the branch or constitutional agency have the power? Moreover, the concept of enumerated powers would take off the table a range of topics and issues that were appropriately left to the states. As Russell Hittinger has argued, "Rather than listing all the moral norms that ought to guide the use of legislative, executive, and judicial powers, the Constitution tries to state as precisely as possible who has authority over a certain scope of objects."[8]

What changed? What changed is the Bill of Rights morphed into a tool for judicial ambition in the service of its own view of liberty against the democratic prerogatives of the states. Brutus, we can say, seems especially prescient, although his fears seemed like paranoid exaggerations for most of the history of our country. Hittinger observes this transformation in language from a rather consequential First Amendment case, *West Virginia v. Barnette* (1943). The case involved a requirement by the West Virginia state government that students should recite the pledge of allegiance. Justice Robert Jackson's opinion notes the following:

> These principles grew in soil which also produced a philosophy that the individual was the center of society, that his liberty was attainable through mere absence of governmental restraints, and that government should be entrusted with few controls and only the mildest supervision over men's affairs. We must transplant these rights to a soil in which the laissez-faire concept or principle of non-interference has withered at least as to economic affairs, and social advancements are increasingly sought through closer integration of society and through expanded and strengthened governmental controls.[9]

Not being able to find a particular constitutional text that could protect Jehovah Witness students in public school from participation in a flag ceremony, and having lost the confrontation to limit the powers of the government to what had been delegated, the "Court decided to limit power by a moral argument keyed to individual rights."

Jackson notes in this opinion that the Bill of Rights contains "majestic generalities." And that is precisely where the danger emerges for the rule of law. Once the judiciary has arrogated to itself the power of proclaiming new rights in the Constitution, it must then specify these rights, making itself their arbiter. But we might reason that a government that will not limit itself to the instructions it has already received in a written Constitution is even less likely to take advice on what it decides to consider as natural rights. Moreover, rights created by the judiciary are also subject to being discarded when the going gets tough. When governmental power clashes with these rights, and it inevitably will, then the rights will have to go. Majestic generalities soon invested judicial opinions themselves, and, as a result, the Bill of Rights was magnified by the Fourteenth Amendment, which incorporated and applied its provisions against every state and local government in the land.

INCORPORATION'S FOLLY

Amendments I–VIII of the Constitution, with most of these provisions being incorporated by the Fourteenth Amendment, have become the preeminent way we think about what the Constitution really protects, our rights, which we believe are absolute and absolutely devoted to securing individual autonomy as defined by the Supreme Court. Consider how we speak of the particular rights listed in the Bill of Rights where, for example, free speech has come to mean free expression inclusive of violent, masochistic video games, obscene speech, pornographic materials, and so on. In the 2011 case, *Brown v. Entertainment Merchants Association*, the Supreme Court ruled that a California law that banned the sale of violent video games to minors was unconstitutional under the Free Speech Clause of the First Amendment. This was despite the fact that the violence in many of these games involves the user in simulated acts of torture and sexual abuse, particularly of women. No matter, said the court, the law invaded a core right of free expression and had to be struck down.

Extending the Bill of Rights through the Fourteenth Amendment's incorporation of its provisions and applying these against the states has come through the Due Process Clause, the least likely candidate for such work. The champion for this was Justice Hugo Black. Black provided his wholesale theory for incorporation of the Bill of Rights against the states in his concurring opinion in *Duncan v. Louisiana* (1968): "'No State shall make or enforce any law which shall abridge the privileges or immunities of citizens of the United States' seem to me an eminently reasonable way of expressing the idea that, henceforth, the Bill of Rights shall apply to the States."[10]

Black first offered this rationale in a dissenting opinion in *Adamson v. California* nearly twenty years earlier, but here he observed its gradual progress to become the dominant position, one that fundamentally transformed the Bill of Rights into an instrument of judicial power against state governments. While Black's wholesale theory of incorporation was never formally approved as the rationale for incorporation—the selective theory of incorporation preferred by other justices, most notably Justice Brennan, became the accepted canon—even this latter model more or less equaled Black's wholesale notion of incorporation.[11] Brennan's selective theory, in fact, was dogged by lack of consistency owing to the lack of any real referent that would guide incorporation judgments. In practice Brennan's method amounted to a very personal reading of what seemed to be the right amendments to incorporate given his reading of the precise direction in which society needed to be pushed.[12]

One of the more convincing defenses of the historical legitimacy of the incorporation doctrine has come from Akhil Amar. Amar provocatively argues that there was no majestic moment of individual rights introduced by the 1791 Bill of Rights. Rather, these rights were geared toward the protection of majoritarian self-government in the states. The primary purpose was to pose a barrier to the federal government undermining the legitimacy of state governments. The amendments added to the Constitution are restrictions and further limits on the scope of enumerated federal powers.

As Steven Smith observes in his recent book, *The Rise and Decline of American Religious Freedom*, with regard to the religion clauses the congressional debate is so perfunctory that it would be foolish to conclude that we were given constitutional provisions that guaranteed pervasively secular government that remained strictly neutral between religion and secularism, as was later articulated by Chief Justice Earl Warren. Such philosophical commitment to strict separation of church and state as was instantiated by the Warren court in its insistence that it was recovering the true understanding of the religion clauses would have produced momentous debate in 1791. At the very least, the Northwest Ordinance would have needed to be amended, given that "religion, morality, and knowledge" were listed in the ordinance as "necessary to good government," and that schools would need to promote religion along with knowledge and learning. The real purpose, Smith observes, was merely to ensure that the federal government would not establish a national church that would prove injurious to the state governments, some of which had official churches. In this way, religious exercise would be protected.[13]

Amar concludes from observations such as this that if the 1791 Bill of Rights is geared primarily to insulating the majoritarian governing rights of states from intrusion by the national government, then the Fourteenth Amendment's Privileges or Immunities Clause becomes all the more powerful for its reworking of the Bill of Rights into a truly individualist set of rights that can be applied in a refined manner against the states. If the problem in 1791 was the need for additional limits on a newly empowered national government, the post–Civil War problem was protection from majority rule within the states against the freedmen. Thus, the Thirty-Ninth Congress that drafted and approved the Fourteenth Amendment clearly contemplates, Amar argues, protections for civil rights from the state governments, and it looks to the Bill of Rights for what constitutes these rights.

This helps us to rethink the charge, Amar argues, brought by opponents of incorporation that the wording itself of Section 1 of the Fourteenth Amendment should have stated objectively an intent to incorporate the Bill of Rights against the states. This is all the more significant given that the original allocation of power between the federal and state governments was to be redistributed in favor of the federal government under incorporation. Should not such a renegotiation have been clearly evident? But it's precisely because the first eight amendments were understood as barriers to federal incursions on the self-governing rights of states that wholesale incorporation could not work, Amar maintains. The rights would have to be "reconstructed" to become constitutional tools that would vindicate the private property and individual liberties of the freedmen and their political supporters.

Under Amar's approach of "refined incorporation" whereby select, really most, clauses of the Bill of Rights receive their transformation from devices to protect self-government in the states to clauses that protect individuals from majoritarian political outcomes, we see "outsiders" and dissidents now finding that they have national rights of citizenship. Amar notes that those who drafted the Fourteenth

Amendment were well aware of the state-sanctioned persecution by Southern states of abolitionists' and freedmen's political, religious, and civil rights. They sought to bring an end to this by a national "reconstruction of rights." Amar notes the powerful example of Samuel Hoar, who had been sent by the Massachusetts legislature in 1844 to vindicate the rights of free black sailors imprisoned in South Carolina without benefit of the writ of habeas corpus. For his efforts, Hoar was attacked by mobs seemingly approved of by the state legislature.[14] Closer in time to the Fourteenth Amendment was the August 1866 New Orleans race riot, where a white mob murdered forty-six freedmen who had assembled in a downtown New Orleans hotel to draft a new Louisiana constitution. Kurt Lash observes that this massacre resulted in a dramatic response by Republicans, who argued that the protections in the proposed amendment would secure these liberties from such wanton violation.

Acts such as these clearly revealed the need for national standards of free speech and assembly, among other civil rights in the first eight amendments. According to Amar, "The Reconstruction generation—not their Founding fathers or grandfathers—took a crumbling and somewhat obscure edifice, placed it on new, high ground, and remade it so that it truly would stand as a temple of liberty and justice for all."[15] The provocative thought in all of this is that our true debt is not to the founding generation for our liberties, but to those who drafted and ratified the Fourteenth Amendment, which has achieved for us a "new birth of freedom." Amar notes that we praise Jefferson and Madison for the Bill of Rights, but give shorter shrift to John Bingham, Frederick Douglass, and Harriet Beecher Stowe for their reinvention of American liberty in the aftermath of the Civil War. He means to reorder our historical memory on this point.

Against incorporation is Philip Hamburger's argument that, ultimately, the purpose of the Fourteenth Amendment was to establish a national standard of privileges or immunities of citizens rooted in the Comity Clause of Article IV, Section 2. As Hamburger notes, "the privileges or immunities of citizens of the United States" meant "Comity Clause rights, and the Fourteenth Amendment used this phrase to make clear that free blacks were entitled to such rights." The work the Privileges or Immunities Clause was doing related to the antebellum dispute whether free blacks were citizens of the United States and thus entitled to Comity Clause rights.[16]

The Fourteenth Amendment's famous and mysterious Privileges or Immunities Clause "echoed this anti-slavery interpretation of the Comity Clause and secured it in the Constitution itself."[17] Thus, the Fourteenth Amendment, Hamburger argues, was not concerned with incorporation, but with this more fundamental business of ensuring in the Constitution that blacks were citizens of the United States and entitled to the full scope of the privileges or immunities of citizens.

Amar's argument for the incorporation and transformation of the first eight amendments weakens, if not necessarily falling apart, if he's wrong on his first move that the Bill of Rights of 1791 provided little to no protections for individual rights against majority tyranny and was formulated exclusively for benefit of state governments' collective governing rights. There is obviously the fact that the federal government was constrained by the Bill of Rights in what it might impose on individual citizens. Those amendments offered enumerated protections to persons in the United States from certain actions by the federal government. We have the early example of the Alien and Sedition Acts (1798), which were perceived by Jeffersonian Republicans to threaten freedom of speech and freedom of assembly. While they mobilized their opposition through their state governments, that is, the Kentucky and Virginia Resolutions, and attempted to ground a constitutional right of state interposition, this does not detract from the fact that the rights being vindicated were, ultimately, individual rights.

Reviewing the debate between the Federalists and the Anti-Federalists over the need for a declaration or bill of rights to be added to the Constitution, we find evidence that protection of individual rights was clearly a concern voiced by both opponents and friends of the Constitution. Madison heeded such calls, as evidenced in his correspondence with Jefferson from 1787 to 1790, which discussed at length the arguments for a federal bill of rights. Madison relates "that among the advocates for the Constitution there are some who wish for further guards to public liberty and individual rights. As far as these may consist of a constitutional declaration of the most essential rights, it is probable they will be added."[18] Madison's correspondence with Jefferson evinces two lines of opposition to the Philadelphia Constitution of 1787: first, proposed amendments that would alter the nature of the powers of the Constitution and would require a second convention (a prospect Madison wanted to foreclose), and second, proposed amendments that would only add limitations to the powers granted in the Constitution but would not fundamentally reframe the document. This second line of opposition is the one that Madison indicates he can incorporate into the Constitution because it will not detract from the document and will secure the consent of the minority opposition.

We can turn Amar's argument around with regard to the purpose of the Bill of Rights by noting that it is to the individual liberties and rights listed in the state constitutions that Anti-Federalists appealed for a deeper vindication of rights in the Constitution. State constitutions of this period featured their own bills of rights or political, civil, and economic protections for their citizens. When these arguments are taken into account we see that the Anti-Federalists' arguments were the efficient cause for a federal bill of rights but that the rights actually ratified in 1791 were first contained in the state constitutions, eleven of which were amended, revised, and ratified in the crucial period between 1776 and 1780, when eleven of the thirteen states drafted new constitutions and provided, either prefatory to the body of their constitutions or in the documents themselves, a list of rights protecting individuals from government predation. We see that the states' so-called police power or general reserve power to regulate safety, morals, and health does not entail that the concept and practice of protecting individual rights was foreign to them.[19]

If we do, however, agree whole hog with Amar, we can wonder about the ultimate difference it makes. Few scholars seriously doubt incorporation anymore. Amar's work advocates for incorporating a redefined set of rights in the first eight amendments made more amenable to a nationalist rights republic. As we have shown, though, incorporating enumerated federal rights in the Constitution against the states did not entail the constitutional revolution that Amar articulates. The court was certainly not predetermined by the Fourteenth Amendment to enact the redefined rights found by the Warren and Burger courts in cases dealing with religion, speech, criminal defense rights, and sexual autonomy, among other gems of this period.

We can further note that the Supreme Court, in significant recent cases dealing with autonomy rights regarding abortion, assisted suicide, gay rights, and same-sex marriage, seems to have moved on from even considering the Bill of Rights via incorporation and makes pronouncements on new rights that, we are told, emanate from the term "liberty" in the Due Process Clause of the Fourteenth Amendment. In a string of cases, most notably *Planned Parenthood v. Casey*, *Lawrence v. Texas*, and *Obergefell v. Hodges*, the court has decided that its substantive due process jurisprudence has located the essence of the American founding in an individualist liberty that the court must unfold in a progressively liberating direction. From this we can conclude that the debate over incorporation not only was won by the Warren court, but achieved such a transformational understanding of what constitutes the privileges and responsibilities of citizenship in our republic that the contemporary court views Americans as individuals freed from relational responsibilities and duties. It follows that citizenship is that which facilitates the choices and plans of the individual, who must be unencumbered from both public and private constraints.

Our recovery should begin with getting right with the Due Process Clause.

As Michael McConnell and Nathan Chapman noted in their historical review of legal due process from the Magna Carta to Reconstruction, its purpose with regard to the legislature was to ensure that it exercised only legislative powers and not executive or judicial functions.[20] Most emphatically, McConnell and Chapman conclude that the Due Process Clause did not declare certain liberties to be fundamental rights that existed above the legislative process. McConnell notes that in the plurality opinion in *Casey* we are given the most extended justification for substantive due process: The opinion begins by acknowledging that the "literal reading of the Clause might suggest that it governs only the procedures by which a State may deprive persons of liberty."[21] As McConnell notes, "This is a considerable understatement." "The Court points to no linguistic ambiguities and offers no alternative readings, even nonliteral, under which the Clause might suggest anything else." Finally, the *Casey* opinion "makes no attempt to show that the history of the Clause, prior to its adoption against the federal government in 1791 or the states in 1868, supports any other reading."[22]

The court asserts in *Casey* that the path of judicial restraint is "tempting" but that it must rely on the precedent of earlier cases that are rooted in substantive due process. But as McConnell observes, the *Casey* court's judicial trip down the substantive due process lane cites cases that founded and culminated in the *economic* substantive due process doctrine of the infamous *Lochner v. New York* case.[23] *Lochner* has since been repudiated, along with its doctrine of economic substantive due process, but the court failed to mention this, intent as it was on showing the historical pedigree of substantive due process that stretched back into the nineteenth century.

Turning to the cases most typically thought to be relevant to unenumerated rights, *Griswold v. Connecticut*, *Eisenstadt v. Baird*, and *Roe v. Wade* are all notable for trying to avoid use of substantive due process and for the contradictory lines of reasoning used by the court to support its holdings.[24] Justice William Douglas prominently announces in the 1965 case *Griswold v. Connecticut* that a constitutional right of privacy was formed from the litany of rights listed in the First, Third, Fourth, and Ninth Amendments, which "suggest that specific guarantees in the Bill of Rights have penumbras, formed by emanations from those guarantees that help give them life and substance. Various guarantees create zones of privacy." That is, somehow the various rights in these amendments had combined, swirled, and multiplied with one another, and created a new right to privacy. The opinion was further thought to be limited by its resounding appeal to the sanctity of marriage and the inherent right of couples to be free of intrusive interference in their reproductive choices by the state. Finally, Justice Harlan writes in his concurring opinion that a national democratic consensus of access to contraception for married couples had emerged from state legislation seemingly ratifying the court's decision.[25]

This right, however, would then be extended seven years later in *Eisenstadt v. Baird*, to include contraception for individuals regardless of marital status. It was, the court said, wrong to make prohibitions on contraception based on marital status. The sanctity of the marriage bed from state regulation gave way to the privacy rights of mere individuals. Of course, the case we most remember in this vein of privacy jurisprudence is the 1973 case *Roe v. Wade*, which founded the constitutional right to abortion. Again, the court's opinion gave "a string of constitutional provisions, demonstrating little or no interest in which one to rely on for its decision."[26] As for Justice Harlan's argument of a privacy right emerging from national consensus in *Griswold*, the court ignored it. In both *Roe* and *Doe v. Bolton*, the court would strike down abortion restrictions in more than forty-five states without even commenting on the distinction this made compared with *Griswold*.[27]

Finally, in *Lawrence v. Texas* (2003) the court struck down Texas's ban on homosexual sodomy, penning telling lines that if "those who drew and ratified the Due Process Clauses of the Fifth Amendment or the Fourteenth Amendment [had] known the components of liberty in its manifold possibilities, they might have been more specific."[28] Where the court in *Casey* had stated that it was bound by precedent, the court in *Lawrence* ignored the directly applicable precedent in *Bowers* and launched into the deep mystery of incorporating libertarian philosophy to support its decision. There is nonetheless a straight line that leads from *Casey* to *Lawrence*. The problem with unenumerated rights discourse is its inherent tendency to create rights antithetical to the rule of law by formulating vague propositions about justice that fail to give clear instructions to government on the limitations of its powers. Here is Supreme Court Justice Kennedy in *Casey* dramatically making the absolute autonomy argument: "At the heart of liberty is the right to define one's own concept of existence, of meaning, of the universe, and of the mystery of human life. Beliefs about these matters could not define the attributes of personhood were they formed under compulsion of the State."[29] This claim is unlimited. It undercuts the very ground of justice by tying liberty to the shifting sands of individual sentiment rather than the truth of human dignity as the foundation of individual rights. The right announced by Justice Kennedy is unspecified and thus open to infinite interpretations, and, most dangerously, warrants the power of government to secure its unbounded claims. Rather than enlist in this project, and its perils, we do better to rearticulate that, however paradoxical it may seem, liberty flows out of the constraints in the very design of the Constitution. That road avoids the near certainty of the arrival of confusion and danger that flow from a judiciary creating and articulating rights by its own lights.

These opinions on their own offer little guidance on what substantive due process provides us other than the strongly held opinions of a majority of justices on the court. But if substantive due process jurisprudence has redefined in crucial respects the core of American self-understanding by a singular focus on autonomy, we must wonder exactly how stable and how limited it truly is if we are to preserve self-government, federalism, and separation of powers or what has been considered the authoritative meaning of American constitutionalism. That is, a jurisprudence of autonomy, which sees society itself as the occasion for ever stronger pronouncements of liberation, might finally end in the anarchical position, one that has completely removed the social and relational virtues from law. These are precisely the virtues that are needed to maintain republican government, which remains dependent on the objects we put in common as determined by the judgments and deliberations of rational and relational beings. But rational deliberation about public goods becomes increasingly foreign in a republic that views words as weapons used to secure various identities against perceived hostile structures of class, race, sex, and marriage. To do so, we need to look to substantive due process itself to grasp how the autonomy project slowly eclipses the possibility of self-government in a republic by removing the responsibilities of our relational obligations from the law. We need only analyze the Supreme Court's recent decision in *Obergefell v. Hodges* (2015), which made same-sex marriage a constitutional right under the Fourteenth Amendment's Due Process Clause.

3 · The Meaning of *Obergefell*

Now that the Supreme Court has ordered the states under the Fourteenth Amendment of the Constitution to recognize same-sex marriages, we are confronted with the question, does the right to marry persons of the same sex narrow the ability of particular institutions to freely exercise their religion? This chapter will attempt to state a rationale for why there should be a place in our civil society for genuinely countercultural religious expressions of marriage that embody the view that marriage is rooted in the conjugal reality of man and woman and the reproductive consequences that regularly issue from their union. What was once dismissed as slippery-slope delusion on the part of social conservatives is now almost expressly admitted as a future reality by no less than the former solicitor general Donald Verrilli. During oral arguments in *Obergefell*, Justice Alito inquired if the holding in *Bob Jones University v. United States* that a college was not entitled to tax exempt status if it opposed interracial marriage or interracial dating would also apply to a religious university or college if it opposed same-sex marriage in its policies. Verrilli replied: "It's certainly going to be an issue. I don't deny that."[1]

With *Obergefell*, the court's decision poses a new test of whether Americans can live freely with one another with different understandings of what marriage is. While there is much for advocates of limited government and the rule of law to deplore in *Obergefell*, there is also a deeper logic of the relational dignity invoked by the Kennedy Five that undergirds marriage but also inherently other practices and expressions of belonging in a liberal society. Most notable in this regard is the relational dignity of religious belief and expression that is never really individualistic or just private, but is done in groups in a context of corporate expression and belonging. It behooves those of us who believe that liberal society is more than humans and the state, or is rather constantly under threat to being reduced to those two densities, to consider if the majority opinion in *Obergefell* is capable of supporting the significant worth and vitality of the "little platoons" that give content and stability to the freedoms most of us choose to exercise.

To be sure, the loose construction in the opinion that relies so heavily on unenumerated "fundamental rights" to reach its conclusion, even to the point of dismissing the constraint placed on such jurisprudence, that is, that it recognize only "fundamental rights" with a long-established history and practice in the nation's institutions, is highly problematic. The "dignitary" concerns of same-sex couples are of such weight, the court's majority reasons, that "justice" demands the court order the states to recognize their unions as marriage. In this regard, worthy of consideration are the rather soaring paeans to the relational attributes of marriage found in the opinion. Also of note is the paucity of praise in the four dissenting opinions for the institution of marriage. Standing out here is Justice Scalia's deprecating remarks on Kennedy's observation that marriage leads, among other things, to greater freedom of expression for spouses. In response, Scalia states that whoever thinks marriage leads to greater expression must not have been married for very long because "long-lasting marriage . . . constricts, rather than expands, what one can prudently say."

Near the opinion's opening we read, "From their beginning to their most recent page, the annals of human history reveal the transcendent importance of marriage." Later in the opinion, Justice Kennedy writes, "Marriage responds to the universal fear that a lonely person might call out only to find no one there." Kennedy's analysis again hinges on the sempiternal: "Same-sex couples, too, may aspire to the transcendent purposes of marriage and seek fulfillment in its highest meaning." Has not Kennedy raised an extreme claim relative to the social-ordering purposes of civil marriage law, but one somewhat consistent with the Mormon theology of marriage, that the bonds of marriage may persist even at the end of biological life? If so, we can find a marker for a rather effusive support for the institution of marriage in the majority opinion, even if such praise comes as news to those hoping that the afterlife affords some sort of a break from a difficult spouse. And this also leaves unsaid what our singles may come to think of their situation in light of such reasoning. Perhaps singles will need to reconcile themselves to just being the forgotten. Call me lonely, maybe.

On this point of the dramatic support given to marriage, we note the relative absence of the duties and obligations that are necessary to give any relational institution abiding worth. If, in fact, marriage is of transcendent importance, indeed the answer one lonely soul might make to another, should not the state make divorce difficult, even slightly more so than the current no-fault standard? Should law not support the sexual virtues of chastity or fidelity, encourage procreation, or tie in any way the privileges of marriage with the performance of relational responsibilities? And it is precisely because of the sacrifices such duties demand from us that the truly transcendent quality of love is unlocked. Instead, the "reasoned judgment" in the opinion is that marriage confers a legal affirmation that then permits the couple to fill in the content. The emergence of such language on marriage can be understood as the latest stage of our "Lockeanization" of what marriage is and our detachment of the institution from any necessary connection with the raising of children, enduring fidelity, or sexual exclusivity.

Kennedy reiterates almost verbatim from *Lawrence v. Texas* that our Framers gave the word "liberty" in the Constitution no definite content, because they knew that they would be blinded by their time and place in seeing all its implications. So they meant it to be an instrument to be deployed by each generation of Americans for turning what was formerly regarded as necessary and proper into arbitrary oppression. That means that same-sex marriage did not used to be a right that was protected by the Constitution, but now it is. "The nature of injustice," we are told, "is that we may not always see it in our own times. When new insight reveals discord between the Constitution's central protections and a received legal stricture, a claim to liberty must be addressed." That our country has been characterized by this kind of evolution in the direction of individualism is undoubtedly true, and our shared understanding of what marriage is has been both evolving and deconstructing over time. The point of controversy Kennedy suppressed, however, is whether this evolution should have mainly been driven by legislative deliberation or judicial imposition.

But what about the beings who love not only with words but with bodies? In a point missed by many commentators, Kennedy treats with dignity the sanctity of marital sex protected by the court in *Griswold* from the forces of procreational envy that once prevented married couples from legally obtaining contraceptives. To return to *Griswold*'s "sacred precincts of the marital bedroom" in *Obergefell* seems to cast aspersions on the sex lives of singles, when the relevant teaching after *Eisenstadt* is that there is no difference between the sex of an unmarried or married couple. All are welcome. To be fair, though, Kennedy is not so much treating *Griswold* as live precedent, but rather he's appealing to it to underscore that marriage may be about sex, but it is really about love. *Griswold* is really in defense of that noble, transcendent relationalism of marriage. And here he answers critics who contend that dismissing the conjugal reality of marriage will make expressive individualism its core, thus emptying it of any enduring substance. Thus, we read, "The nature of marriage is that, through its enduring bond, two persons together can find other freedoms, such as expression, intimacy, and spirituality. This is true for all persons, whatever their sexual orientation." Then we are told that "the right to marry is fundamental because it supports a two-person union unlike any other in its importance to the committed individuals."

Kennedy's affirmance of marriage as love in these manifold aspects, but not procreative, however, comes with its price because he also wants the autonomy of *Eisenstadt*, it would seem. Liberties protected by the Due Process Clause extend to the most intimate choices individuals make, "including intimate choices that define identity and personal beliefs." Marriage may be of eternal worth to the contracting parties, but they are still autonomous individuals, the same individuals protected in *Eisenstadt*. The libertarian Justice Kennedy is ultimately unable to cross over from autonomy to the relational sacrifices that order and carry the load of marriage.

The empirically implausible part of the opinion is its contention that the changes that have transformed American marriage in recent decades have served to make marriage stronger. Without descending into controversial detail, we can say that marriage may be stronger in some ways, but it is undoubtedly weaker in others, especially with regard to the near majority of children growing up without both parents married. Moreover, it's hard to count as a gain the fact that many of our communities are full of lonely (often divorced or abandoned) single moms, and those seemingly superfluous "deadbeat" dads. The least we can say with all of the contradictory evidence before us is that we do not have any definitive insight into what marriage is in an age where there is little mediation between maintenance of responsible relational lives as social animals and our increasingly insistent claims for unfettered autonomy.

The argument that marriage is stronger because it has become more inclusive is stirring, and it makes sense to say that same-sex marriage—or the ability to live with complete openness as who you are—will attach those Americans more to their country and lead them to embrace more unreservedly the duties of citizens. And some candid gay writers acknowledge that marriage is on the rocks in America and offer us the hope that an infusion of same-sex marriages will shore up an institution in crisis.

Many libertarian originalists applaud the court's decision but find its argument dubious or worse. The case should have been resolved on the basis of the equal protection of individual rights. As Ilya Somin noted, the key is the equal protection of free individuals: we should all be free to marry the free individual we please—man or woman.[2] Kennedy might have proclaimed (as he had in the past) that distinctions rooted in sexual orientation should be accorded heightened scrutiny because they have become primarily rooted in irrational animosity. He had almost played that card in the past, but resisted going the implausible route of declaring that animosity had made said distinctions plainly and simply irrational.

Still, Kennedy might have declared "sexual orientation" a suspect category like race and gender, following some lower federal courts that thought they were faithfully adhering to his precedents in making such a ruling. One advantage of making a ruling on grounds of heightened or strict scrutiny is that arguments supporting the "traditional" view of marriage could be deemed rational, just not good enough to be "exceedingly persuasive" or beyond reasonable doubt. That means that religious institutions that continue to deploy them could be accorded the respect of being part of a dispute that really has two sides. And surely nobody could really believe that a religious community could be blamed for not reducing marriage to a matter of individual rights, even if our civil law has been moving in that direction for a long time.

A strange almost heretical thought is that this decision is actually an intramural Catholic dispute on the court about marriage and family. Justice Kennedy's homage to the dignity of marriage, coupled with the sharp tone of the dissents, is short on the legalistic responsibilities needed to maintain marriage, but understands marriage in a manner more enduring than the libertarian proclamation of rights-bearing individuals. Marriage has a transcendent purpose! And that is not to ignore that Kennedy's opinion falls short of a full comprehension of men and women who love with complementary bodies and whose conjugal reality cannot finally be dismissed, along with the permanence and exclusivity needed to bring forth new generations.

The problem facing us as citizens is the new version of history and progress that, purportedly, advances the claims of the autonomous individual against all forms of cultural and religious baggage impeding our true selves from emerging. Both technology and sexuality must be liberated from the claims of collectives, public or private. This unfolding is no longer a left-liberal force of big government and big bureaucracy conspiring against the free market and civil society, but is now a libertarian historical evolution. Being on the right side of history, accordingly, now means uncritical support for same-sex marriage. But the same objections remain to claims of inevitable historical progress, whether it's Hegel, Roosevelt, or Anthony Kennedy.

How reasonable is it to believe that history has brought us to some kind of "final solution" when it comes to all the basic human questions? Indeed, to make such claims is to be perched on the historical transcendent point of reference enabling certain seers to make authoritative observations on the meaning of progress. In short, both logic and justice require us to attend to the dissident thought of those who seem to be on the wrong side of history. One obvious method here is to assume that almost every form of change, especially those it's easy to generally agree on, has its corresponding form of regression. Most forms of innovative openness carry with them a corresponding new form of blindness. And every gain has its corresponding loss. This is countering "progressivism" in all its forms not quite with "relativism," but with a kind of judgmentalism that comes with selective nostalgia— or a disciplined appreciation of what used to be better.

The truthful, Socratic reason for opposing "totalitarian" claims such as "there aren't two sides" when it comes to issues such as same-sex marriage is that those opposing history might be right or partially right. We should be for the full understanding of the free exercise of religion because the churches (and other forms of organized religion) defend countercultural understandings of who we are that oppose the excesses of a country such as ours and its distortions that we may too readily embrace as liberation. Here, we do well to recall the uncritical embrace by therapeutic, academic, and legal elites decades ago of no-fault divorce laws that such elites said would lead to happier marriages, happier adults, and, most difficult of all to now accept, happier children who would no longer witness their parents constantly fighting. After the generational study by Judith Wallerstein and Julia Lewis, both of whom initially experienced professional stigmatization for their challenging findings, on the negative effects on children of the divorce revolution launched by such laws, we might hesitate, ever so slightly, before we categorically rule out those who dissent from Kennedy's same-sex marriage nationalism.

The purported conservatism of "marriage equality"—that stabilizing relational institution as a right of everyone—might depend too much on the sexual liberation that preceded it to be accepted uncritically as the characteristic of a sustainable institution. Love, all by itself, is a pretty ephemeral quality, and by itself not the foundation of an institution that Justice Kennedy (quoting Tocqueville!) claimed is indispensable for our social order. The court didn't talk about any legal responsibility or binding social custom that would work to keep our couples together; so Kennedy surely put too much weight on what he basically says is a government entitlement. He talked a lot about what marriage would do for the needy individual who wants to be rescued from loneliness, but not at all about the obligations that are required in return.

As long as we understand marriage as basically a duty-free conferral of dignity on a couple's love and nothing more, then the justice of same-sex marriage really cannot be denied. If we understand it as an institution requiring much more, as do many of our religious believers, then the argument for same-sex marriage is, to say the least, much more questionable—and in a way that's not intended to demean gays. While it's clear that a majority of Americans, at this point, are not going to be convinced by even the most eloquent and rational versions of that "thicker" marriage right now—at least as a civil institution—our more orthodox churches and synagogues and so forth are going to become more countercultural than ever. Is it really beyond consideration that we should embrace them as our friendly and genuinely helpful critics, critics who are really quite unlikely to be completely wrong, unless history has really come to an end?

On this score, we can note that Kennedy's relational approach, conceivably, could be used as a way to defend the free exercise of the church. Marriage is a form of relational belonging that responds to our natural longing for personal love, and under the Constitution it's to be affirmed as a kind of relational autonomy—the content of which is degraded or demeaned when denied by the state. But the free exercise of religion is not the right of the lonely conscience standing unmediated before God. It's a form of relational belonging in an organized body of thought and action—a loving community—often called the church.

Kennedy's concurring opinion in the *Hobby Lobby* case actually provides a promising response to Verrilli's barely concealed anticlericalism referenced earlier in this essay. Here Kennedy broached a high principle of religious freedom in America, when he argued that "in our constitutional tradition, freedom means that all persons have the right to believe or strive to believe in a divine creator and a divine law. For those who choose this course, free exercise is essential in preserving their own dignity and in striving for a self-definition shaped by their religious precepts." The pressing difficulty now is that dignity of religious belief for many may very well be denied after the court's momentous decision in *Obergefell*. Has Kennedy not given reasons in this concurrence for protecting, in addition to sexual relational autonomy, institutional religious autonomy? As Kennedy stated, religious belief is about more than just free belief, but also "the right to express those beliefs and to establish one's religious (or nonreligious) self-definition in the political, civic, and economic life of our larger community."

Here we do well to recall the court's ringing endorsement—joined by Kennedy—of the "ministerial exception" doctrine in the 2012 *Hosanna-Tabor* case. The court there affirmed that religious freedom would wither absent a certain institutional autonomy from civil rights laws. Although the case upheld a church's right to fire a minister for its own reasons, its wider application should include protecting the integrity of institutional religious expression in education, charitable, and medical missions from the ever-expanding state and its activist administrators. We could say that in 2012 the court affirmed this "Freedom of the Church" as the indispensable aspect of religious liberty. Likewise, after *Obergefell*, our nation's first freedom of religious exercise and the dignity it finds in corporate institutional expression should not be disregarded.

At this point, it's true, Kennedy didn't go far enough in identifying religious belonging as a component of relational self-definition. Kennedy's was an understanding of religion that is more of an isolated response to conscience that affects the way one participates in religious and nonreligious communities. He never took the logical next step of defining religion itself as a community with relational autonomy or the liberty to determine its own content. But there is no particular reason why other members of the court could not be led to see the inconsistency in regarding religious belonging as less a part of one's personal identity and personal dignity than other personal relationships, including, of course, those that have a strong and often quite temporary sexual dimension.

But organized religion, of course, is no less a form of community than political or economic life. It is, in fact, more of a community, more intimate and more deeply personal, less utilitarian or instrumental. Institutional religion is a body of thought and action and, no less than other intimate personal relationships, is degraded when its content is defined by government. Therefore, Kennedy's defense of the relational autonomy that is marriage, which might be understood to constrain the free exercise of religion, needs to be balanced by a defense of the form of relational autonomy that is the church and other forms of organized religion. From the consistent point of view that recognizes what should be his whole view of the person, religion cannot define marriage under our civil law, and the civil understanding of marriage cannot define the religious one.

The content of that belonging is determined by those participating in the relationship, and that relational autonomy is especially privileged under the Constitution against both the claims of legislative majorities and extremely individualistic distortions of what our Constitution means. Within the context of a religious form of belonging or observant community, marriage will necessarily be defined more dutifully than it will be under civil law. Religious belonging is obviously as least as transformative of personal psychology as marriage, and religion plus marriage understood as a sacrament might be the best antidote to democratic individualism. There are those who believe that marriage should center on being fruitful, multiplying, and caring for the bodies and souls of children. It's an unbreakable relational bond that includes the promise of sexual fidelity and standing together for better and worse. This tougher form of love inevitably involves judgmental relational premises opposed to prevailing legal views of autonomy.

We can say the church is, for many, a loving institution indispensable for human happiness that transforms the "lost" individual to someone more virtuous and even transcendent. It's not the job of government to determine who belongs to this or that church, and in our free country the free exercise of religion is about belonging and acting under a God who is not defined or controlled by the state. Our Constitution protects religion, finally, that's not civil religion. The institution of the church is demeaned or degraded when the government tries to give content to what is properly left to the relational autonomy of the believing community.

In defending the relational autonomy of the church, we defend the place where individualistic America has always received its most noble and even philosophical countercultural criticism. We defend the place where men and women find out that they are more than middle-class workers and individuals, and where they are inspired to be charitable caregivers in addition to productive individuals. We also defend the genuine moral and intellectual diversity that's the saving grace of our constitutional republic, whose very design evinces the belief that principled disagreement should be given institutional mechanisms for freedom of expression and belief. We will lose much that is true if we drag our religious institutions into the worldview vainly defined by the confidence that everyone should bow down to the way we believe history is going.

With the election of Trump, everything looks different, and conceivably better, when it comes to defending the diversity intrinsic to the whole truth about relational marriage. To be sure, there is no going back on the granting of the right to same-sex marriage. The court's way of doing so, however, even supporters of that right admit, was murky and even incredible, and one reason among many that the evolution of liberty on this front should have flowed from changes in public opinion reflected in state legislation is that it could have been done, as it was in some states, with appropriate accommodation for the free exercise of religion.

But still, one of the most memorable moments for one of us was driving back from Atlanta through heavily gay Midtown the weekend after *Obergefell* was announced. The gay flag was flying with the American flag on every storefront. A formerly marginalized group of Americans finally thought of themselves as accepted as full citizens. At the same time, however, many religious observant Americans—members of churches, synagogues, mosques, and so forth—thought that the next step would be their oppressive ostracism from citizenship if they remained faithful to their beliefs. The fear was for waves of persecution, accompanied by the sad thought that the American flag was no longer theirs.

Now, gays and lesbians are afraid that somehow history, against Justice Kennedy's confidence in liberty's evolution, has somehow been reversed with Trump's election. A right granted might be revoked, and political protection will be withdrawn from their form of relational autonomy. This fear, of course, is unreasonable if directed against the man Donald Trump, who said repeatedly that he's all for gay rights and has no interest in *Obergefell* being revisited, although it might be less paranoid in view of the animosity he has roused up among his most deplorable supporters, or in view of what his conceivably several court appointees might see fit to do to restore the Constitution's original meaning.

Meanwhile, concerns about the future of the free exercise of religion have been deferred for now. There seems to be little chance that the court will go beyond *Obergefell* in protecting relational autonomy, and the court will be less needed to protect free exercise against various administrative mandates.

Strangely enough, Trump has become president at a privileged moment when it comes to stabilizing relational liberty in our time. He can affirm the version of Justice Kennedy's understanding of liberty we've laid out here, one that protects both marriage and the church—two indispensable relational institutions for free persons—from political domination. The task today is to reconcile "marriage equality" as a civil matter with the churches' privilege and responsibility of saying what marriage is for their observant members. The churches have always dissented in a countercultural way to some extent or another on this score, and their motivation, until lately, hasn't been understood as arbitrary discrimination based on irrational animosity. It's not surprising that civil law, especially after the Fourteenth Amendment, will fall short of embodying the whole truth about who we are, but that's because even the original Constitution was all about free or desexed individuals, saying nothing at all about families or even the biological distinction between men and women.

Some originalists will insist that the court go ahead and overturn *Obergefell* as "judicial activism" or an elitist offense against democratic deliberation, and, as Brutus predicted, a capricious molding of the Constitution's spirit of liberty to undermine our Framers' intention to leave relational issues like marriage to the democratic deliberation of the states. Public opinion, to be sure, has shifted decisively in favor of same-sex marriage, tutored, in part, by the court. But the court, the reasoning goes, should always prefer the written Constitution to the "living Constitution" or trendy opinion. Still, there is a more prudential approach, one with a more modest view of the place of judicial review in our deliberative political order. And in turning to the more prudential approach, we give due deference to the fact that even "originalists" are divided on the right to same-sex marriage. Some, such as Somin and Randy Barnett and other libertarians and even conservatives, say that the right is implicit in the individualism of the original Constitution.

It's true enough that *Obergefell* was "judicial activism," but reversing it now would be equally so. It would disrupt the lives of people who have organized their lives in light of the new right, and it would produce the anxious uncertainty that comes with the perception that rights are given and taken away by 5-4 votes according to election returns. The reversal of *Obergefell* would be a huge stimulus package for the libertarian-liberal alliance against allegedly reactionary social or religious conservatives, and one in which the conservatives would not receive the support of Trump himself or many of his not-so-observant populists.

Now, you might say, that's the far-fetched reasoning that the court followed in *Planned Parenthood v. Casey* when it refused to reverse *Roe*, even if *Roe* had been wrongly decided. When it comes to such "watershed" decisions—the only other one being *Brown v. Board of Education*—only the "most compelling" (a higher standard than merely "compelling") evidence could justify a reversal. In *Casey* and *Brown*, the court meant to speak authoritatively to end a national controversy, and reversal under political pressure would undermine the legitimacy of the court. Not only that, in *Casey* women had organized their reproductive lives as free and equal economic and political beings with abortion as a backstop when contraception fails.

There are, it's easy to see, key differences between *Brown* and *Casey*. *Brown* was decided unanimously, and within a decade there was no respectable opposition to desegregation. In *Casey* and subsequent abortion decisions, the court is closely divided, reflecting a closely divided public opinion. Not only that, in *Casey*, the court was clearly suppressing legitimate dissent in the name of national unity, repressively marginalizing, from a constitutional view, those who continued to disagree.

Having said all that, the decision not to reverse *Obergefell* need not depend on any watershed status, but simply on the prudential judgment that reversal, at this time, would convulse the country without any corresponding benefit. For now, an understanding of citizenship inclusive enough to include both gays in the institution of marriage and the church as an organized and autonomous body of thought and action is a very conservative view of relational inclusiveness. On the question of marriage, the court shouldn't claim to have spoken once and for all, or to have expelled from respectable public discourse all who disagree.

And same-sex marriage and abortion should be separated as constitutional issues. Abortion is not just a question of the autonomy of women to define themselves as more or other than reproductive machines for the state. It involves the status of fetal or unborn life. The most inclusive view of citizenship would recognize the legitimate claims for the personal status of that life, and, as Scalia has repeatedly claimed, return deliberation about weighing those claims against those of women for liberty to legislatures. It is true enough that same-sex marriage isn't a matter of life and death, and it can exist in a genuinely moral and religious diverse country. But a country can't rest content with Justice Kennedy's easygoing view that our Constitution wasn't meant to accommodate people of differing views when it comes to abortion. And, in fact, it won't, whatever the court tries to do or say to bring the controversy to an end.

From the point of view of the Constitution in full, same-sex marriage is an outcome of the ongoing attempt to transform the relational institution of marriage in a Lockean, that is, individualistic direction. That transformation was and is in the interest of liberating the individual from all biological, relational imperatives and to free consent for every aspect of our life. So, when it comes to marriage, liberty has evolved in the direction of no-fault divorce, easing up on the demand for marital fidelity, the escape of an open sexual life from the confines of marriage (which includes easy access to contraception), the separation of parenthood from the expectation of marriage (as well as marriage from the expectation of parenthood), and so forth. Given all those reforms, the separation of the privilege of marriage from corresponding relational re-sponsibilities under the law, it was inevitable that same-sex-attracted Americans would start to wonder why the privilege was arbitrarily denied them.

The Fourteenth Amendment has resulted in the imposition of egalitarian and individualistic tendencies on relational institutions. This erodes the distinctions that constitute the life of a whole human person, those distinctions that can't be captured by the highly principled but unrealistically abstract Lockean view of the being with rights. But given that amendment, what's left for us to do is to protect relational diversity—our fractured moral life—from being emptied of its content by the replacement of prudential deliberation by principled imposition.

There is simply no right or wrong side to history, because its general tendency to expand the domain of individual liberty often has a relational cost. From this view, our Lockeanization of marriage is an experiment that may or may not succeed. The decline in birth rates—qualified as it is by the fruitful and multiplying behavior of so many of our observant believers—may or may not become a national security issue. It almost surely will stick us with an unwanted new birth of freedom that will be the truncation of our entitlements. Our individualism, in general, has been the source of a country with more old people than ever before, a blessing mitigated by the fact that we now have little idea what the old are for. And our individualism—having liberated women to be productive members of the work force just like men (in some cases, like it or not)—has reduced the amount of voluntary caregiving that was the special gift of our women. I could go on, but the point is that the future of marriage is open, and the court has no authoritative insight about the relationship between autonomy and what used to be called biological necessity or about the combination of privileges and responsibilities that gives weight and direction to both worthwhile work and relational love.

From this view, not only might the presidency of Trump be a privileged moment. So too might have been the composition of the court that decided *Obergefell*. Kennedy, the liberal Catholic, was opposed by the four dissents written by conservative Catholics. They shared a devotion for the relational institution of marriage, and even the relational institution of their church. The more radical individualists—those who would end up interpreting marriage itself out of existence as an offense to autonomy—stayed on the sidelines, thank God. Our Catholics showed us how much our interpretations of the written Constitution depend on our providential Constitution.

4 · The Republican Principle

Politically dominant at times, conservatives have never been able to secure the enduring majorities necessary to achieve the transformative constitutional changes they desire. Whether a President Trump and a Republican-led Congress can achieve such an outcome remains to be seen. Early returns appear doubtful, evidenced by striking failures of President Trump and congressional Republicans on health care policy, which have led President Trump to enter into agreements on spending and immigration policy with congressional Democrats. Conservatives now stand as merely one element in the Republican Party, and probably not the dominant one.

Under President Trump's leadership, the Republican Party has become animated by a hybrid populist nationalism that is less about limited and smaller government, devotion to the rule of law and to free markets, and more about employment of government on behalf of working and middle-class economic and status insecurities. This hybrid form centers on patriotism rooted in shared citizenship, increasing spending on the military, support for the current federal entitlements structure, trade protectionism, and foreign policy realism.

President Trump and his *yuge* personality magnified a form of nationalist politics that started with the failed presidential campaigns of Patrick Buchanan in 1992 and 1996. Former Arkansas governor Mike Huckabee in 2008 and former Pennsylvania senator Rick Santorum in 2012 attempted similar presidential appeals that found early success but were ultimately ended by factors that distracted voters from what Santorum called "blue-collar conservatism." Trump's wider appeal, in fact, came from his jettisoning from his movement much of the baggage of religious conservatism while retaining the allegiance of those who are deeply socially conservative. He widened the appeal to everyone who thought that a cultural and oligarchic elite was ruling with contemptuous indifference to the consent of the governed. President Trump, surprisingly, garnered more of the Latino and black vote than Mitt Romney did in the 2012 presidential election.

In the spirit of the populist/conservative coalition, let's begin with a legitimate concern conservatives and populists share: America has become very weak—flabby and out-of-shape—when it comes to self-government. This observation is particularly true for conservatives who blare populist rhetorical appeals but look to the federal judiciary or executive officials to vindicate some of their strongest political passions. We can recall the intense anger directed at Chief Justice John Roberts for not ruling against the Patient Protection and Affordable Care Act on two occasions: the first on its constitutionality and the second on the Obama administration's noncompliance with the law's statutory language by establishing federal exchange networks for patients, even though the most consistent reading of the statute countenanced only state networks. Making Congress look even weaker was the lawsuit it filed in *House v. Burwell* against the Obama administration for violating statutory language of the Affordable Care Act and paying health insurers funds that had not been appropriated by Congress. In a classic instance crying for Congress to use its constitutional weapons to uphold its prerogatives, the people's branch chose the courts for a resolution, one that was not likely to happen before the end of the Obama administration. The looming question is if the "institutional injury" here alleged by Congress in its suit against the executive branch will serve as a gateway for it to bring future claims against whoever occupies the White House as opposed to the aggressive deployment of its formidable power of the purse. In August of 2017, the Trump administration cited the failure of Congress to appropriate the funds and refused to continue paying the health insurance companies.

Whatever the shortcomings of his constitutional arguments, Chief Justice John Roberts was correct in his lead opinion in *National Federation of Independent Business v. Sebelius* that an issue concerning one-sixth of the economy should not be resolved 5-4 by the Court, when political means for rectifying any unconstitutional acts were clearly available. And nobody should rely on the Court to protect the free exercise of religion. The 5-4 *Hobby Lobby* decision, after all, depended on an expansive understanding of the free exercise of religion via the Religious Freedom and Restoration Act. But how long will the Court continue to rule in such a manner under various forms of executive and legislative assault? In his presidential campaign, Trump stated clearly that he would deploy the power of the presidency to repeal and replace Obamacare and protect the Free Exercise Clause against administrators and even courts. He shamed and outmaneuvered conservatives with his plainspoken effectiveness. Living up to his promises is another matter altogether.

Other more general causes can be adduced for conservative weakness: an administrative state that increasingly creates, defines, and enforces rules with only traces of accountability; judges who on sensitive social issues arrogate a legislative role to themselves; an inverted federalism where the center has co-opted the provinces with cash; and a detached political class; but one reason that stands out: the unresponsive extremism of party elites. That is, when both parties decline to incorporate the serious concerns of their voters on a range of issues including immigration, trade, foreign policy, and social and cultural issues, each party preferring instead its own consensus, one derived from a particular corridor of economic and cultural power, this creates openings for a populism that drips with disdain for those currently in office.

As the conservative historian Wilfred McClay noted in the *Weekly Standard*, "There is a saying, variously attributed, that when a political culture forbids respectable politicians from raising essential topics, the electorate will soon turn to 'unrespectable' ones. . . . The real problem is that . . . mainstream Republicans weren't respecting their own voters, and haven't been for a long time."[1] In this respect, the contending public philosophies of our day have proved inept at meeting this challenge of self-government. And this failure, more than any other, best explains how a real estate tycoon and reality TV star, with numerous public displays of reprehensible and indefensible behavior, was able to capture one of the major political parties in America and become the president. We also should not ignore that the Democrats barely survived a challenge by a hoary socialist from Vermont, one who had only recently joined the party, having referred to himself as a socialist most of his political career.

The basic political reality of 2016 was the huge success of the insurgencies of Senator Bernie Sanders (D-Vermont) and Trump, who, despite their huge differences, directed their fire at the complacent elitism of cosmopolitan liberalism. Two thousand sixteen was a terrible year for the conservative—or classical—understanding of liberty.

We then observed one of the most uninspiring presidential campaign clashes between two candidates who daily competed for who could be the most unpopular figure among American voters. Trump was nominated and elected despite being in way over his head and being the very opposite of a gentleman in matters public and intimate, because he was neither a conservative nor a "neoliberal." Comparatively speaking a gentleman, Sanders probably would have been elected more easily than Clinton. And Hillary Clinton lost to a hugely unqualified and repulsive character because so many had been tutored by Sanders in the perception that she was just another tool of Wall Street and the multinational capitalist elite.

Consider how quickly what was called our emerging libertarian political consensus has been overturned! The Democrats, it was said just a couple of years ago, had come to accept the more or less unmediated dynamic of the twenty-first-century global competitive marketplace, and so our leaders in Silicon Valley and on Wall Street had developed a cozy "crony capitalist" relationship with our government.

The Republicans, meanwhile, guided by their big donors, had surrendered concern for reactionary "social issues" and were focusing their attention pretty exclusively on pro-growth tax cutting, deregulation, entitlement reform, and other features of a new birth of freedom. Both parties, it seemed, were for a future in which individual autonomy flourished on all fronts, and even the Supreme Court would be on board in securing "the presumption of liberty." The libertarian combination of "social liberalism" and "economic conservatism" was winning! And that's the combination that was being lived by our "cognitive elite" and their corporate branders, and all that was left to do was "nudge" the rest of the country on board.

Only the most astute observers focused their attention on the most obvious problem. The "opportunity society" touted by Ronald Reagan and Jack Kemp was plausibly populist. Incentivizing the "job creators" through supply-side tax reform would raise up all Americans economically, if, inevitably, some much more than others. But now we can see that the "job creators" are more productive than ever, but with the creation of fewer and fewer jobs. Automation, robotization, and dazzling breakthroughs in making the division of labor more efficient have, in fact, been at the expense of the dignified relational lives led by many ordinary Americans. The gap between our classes has been widening, because, as Tyler Cowen put it, "average is over." Members of the middle class are either ascending into the cognitive elite or falling in the direction of proletarian subsistence (say, at Walmart). The political events of 2016 thus showed us, as they did the British with Brexit, the limits of "popular scripting" or manipulation by our cognitive elite. Who would have guessed that the loutish and ignorant Donald Trump could prevail in a contest in which every respectable part of our multifaceted establishment was allied against him?

Think, for a moment, about how clueless the more conservative candidates were during the 2016 Republican campaign for the presidential nomination. Senator Ted Cruz (R-Texas), for one, thought he could restore the Reagan coalition through a combination of Evangelical identity politics and an economic program that would cut taxes on the rich, take out government involvement in health care altogether, and truncate our entitlement programs. Why would a former steelworker from Steubenville, Ohio, support cutting taxes on the rich owners who laid him off and trimming the entitlements, not to mention his union, who provide some protection to him from becoming collateral damage in the new birth of freedom? Then there was the tendency of the Republicans—at least through their big donors and establishment public intellectuals—to treat citizenship as just another form of rent-seeking, and so to be for an immigration policy that doesn't distinguish between American workers and the workers of the world. Finally, we can't forget the conservatives' unwillingness to distance themselves from the sundry humanitarian interventions that used ordinary patriotic American warriors as cannon fodder for really ill-conceived and basically unwinnable wars. It's no wonder that they were seduced by Trump, who proclaimed that what we need is much better deals across the board with Americans first in mind. The Republicans, as much as President Obama himself, were styling themselves cosmopolitans—in that loose sense, citizens of the world—and not as men and women whose privileges are for responsible service to their fellow citizens who consented to their government. And even now, some conservatives have continued to believe that the Trump administration can be a vehicle for implementing the thoroughly repudiated economic vision of Paul Ryan.

A LIBERTARIAN DIAGNOSIS

The libertarian, or at least classically liberal, Charles Murray had in fact warned us that America was coming apart, that the "real family income of people in the bottom half of the income distribution hasn't increased since the late 1960s." Other factors of note include declining rates of workforce participation by working-class white men from 96 percent in 1968 to 79 percent in 2015.[2] So it's also not surprising that marriage rates for this same time period and among this same cohort have gone from 86 percent to 52 percent. Murray further adds to this set of observations the fact that millions of manufacturing jobs were sent out of the country during the last half century, at the same time that tens of millions of legal and illegal immigrants came into the country competing for the jobs that remained in the construction, trades, and crafts categories. Reflecting on the data, Murray in his book *Coming Apart* posits that the American idea of a middle-class country is moribund. One consequence, a shared claim of citizenship rooted in the rule of law, freedom, and individualism no longer claims the universal assent of the American people as it did only decades ago.

There have been, Murray also notes, a series of defections from the ideal in legal groupings of Americans into race, class, and gender differences and now economic and social stratification. This has left only certain prosperous middle- and upper-middle-class elements of the country still believing in our American ethos, while our *uber* rich don't really believe in it. Adding to our difficulties is that this same elite has cloistered itself in super-zips, insulating itself from many of the problems, social and economic, that have emerged in what is derisively referred to as flyover country over the last few decades. Here's Murray on this point: "The new upper class consists of the people who shape the country's economy, politics and culture. The new lower class consists of people who have dropped out of some of the most basic institutions of American civic culture, especially work and marriage. Both of these new classes have repudiated the American creed in practice, whatever lip service they may still pay to it."[3]

It would seem, at first, that it's the upper class that seceded in theory, while the lower class has seceded in practice. Members of our cognitive elite may mouth the words of sixties radicalism, supplemented by the newest discoveries about self-defined personal identity. But they live as the most competent of bourgeois conservatives, with increasingly stable and child-centered marriages. They're working harder than ever to balance the professional aspirations of both spouses with lovingly obsessive attention to the lives of their kids. They are officially "bourgeois bohemians," but their lives are more about being busy than taking time to enjoy the unbought goodness of being itself. Certainly they've repudiated in practice the romantic view of conjugal love, and they're very judgmental in practice about divorce, deadbeat dads, and all that among those of their kind.

The "in practice" repudiation of shared middle-class life by our cognitive elite is its secession from the shared experiences and responsibilities of citizenship. Military service and socioeconomically diverse public schools are no longer places that work against thinking of inequalities in wealth, education, and status as signifying inequalities in dignity and virtue. The problem with a cognitive meritocracy based on productivity is that people simply think they deserve what they have, and, unlike the aristocrats of old, they don't connect their privileges to civic responsibilities. Paternalism, in a way, remains, but it's all about scripting ordinary people to behave, not sharing with them the middle-class virtues that are the foundation of equal respect in a free country.

The lower class, in Murray's view, hasn't seceded in theory at all, insofar as it remains a more reliable source of "traditional values" that prize family and the attendant responsibilities. But the secession in practice comes when men and women no longer define themselves as beings who work for themselves and their own. Withdrawal from meaningful work inevitably takes a toll on relational love. People no longer possess the resources to live their values, and not only family but church and other local institutions no longer shape individual lives.

Murray errs in attributing too much of lower-class secession to welfare dependency, suggesting, incorrectly, that the withdrawal of the dole is the key to the restoration of middle-class country. He is right, however, that the upper class is happy enough, as Tocqueville predicted, to allow the government to manage the affairs of those not of their kind, just as he is right that our enlightened few are not about providing equal respect to ordinary white men who are comparatively unproductive and rooted in discredited tribalism or localism. Anyone who doesn't have what it takes to be a rootless role player in the global marketplace is on the wrong side of history.

Murray's portrait of a rescinded American ideal of citizenship is stark and depressing, but one that is difficult to deny. This same set of circumstances has led yet another libertarian, the economist and futurist Tyler Cowen, to muse on the rise of the "brutes" and the unsettling future for our politics and economics, thus abandoning his rather blasé contentedness displayed in his recent book, *Average Is Over*. There he rather coolly explained that the progress of the division of labor, combined with progress in the direction of globalism or cosmopolitanism, has and will continue to make life better for the top 20 percent or so of our population. They are the people who form our cognitive elite, who either work easily with genius machines or are adept at managing those nerds or marketing their innovative products. Cowen added that there is also a prosperous and otherwise promising place for those who provide the services—the amenities—for those who have all that money and power. In that service industry and in the workplace generally, the virtues now prized are being conscientious and being compliant, and he made the truthful—yet sexist—observation that those virtues are found far more commonly among women than among men. Meanwhile, many or most middle-class jobs have or will be downsized, and with good reason. The people who occupied them are not worth the money and perks they've been getting.

But Cowen, it appears, has finally been mugged enough by reality to have been awakened from his dogmatic slumber:

> Donald Trump may get the nuclear suitcase, a cranky "park bench" socialist took Hillary Clinton to the wire, many countries are becoming less free, and the neo-Nazi party came very close to assuming power in Austria. I could list more such events.
>
> Haven't you, like I, wondered what is up? What the hell is going on?

He gives us his hypothesis:

> The contemporary world is not very well built for a large chunk of males. The nature of current service jobs, coddled class time and homework-intensive schooling, a feminized culture allergic to most forms of violence, post-feminist gender relations, and egalitarian semi-cosmopolitanism just don't sit well with many . . . what shall I call them? Brutes?[4]

The world is now divided between the nice and the brutes. The nice includes educated men who do basically mental labor and most women. The nice either write scripts to be performed by those who are conscientious and compliant or revel in being conscientious and compliant. These are people who love homework, are "allergic to violence," and prefer a world in which sex has been displaced by gender.

Now, as philosophers such as Rousseau and Hobbes and, more recently, Allan Bloom in his American best seller explained, being nice isn't really being virtuous or even authentic. Nice people tend to deploy words to make social relations easier, not to tell the truth. Their cleverness serves the peace by pleasing customers. Their kind of manners aims at what Rousseau calls a "base and deceptive uniformity" through sacrificing controversy to public relations. Niceness levels out language by purging it, in part, of hateful prejudice, but also of its spirited, erotic, and deeply truthful content, of its real connection to human nature. Niceness is at war with the speech of free persons, of those who will not hesitate to sacrifice their lives and fortunes for the sacred honor it is to live in the truth.

The nice these days want to purge conversation of even microaggressions, to enforce a scripted political correctness that suppresses passionate animosity, and to marginalize those who speak their minds and are readily provoked to anger. The only way to take out all anger and what it abhors, after all, is to clamp down on love, too. That's why the nice disparage patriotism in favor of globalism; love of country too readily leads to war. And that's why they're against religion based on love of the real, personal, judgmental God. Niceness, in fact, replaces love and hate with indifference. Nobody really thinks that niceness has anything to do with coming to the aid of those in need. Atticus Finch and the Good Samaritan weren't nice!

Cowen, apparently, is just now starting to think through the implications of the fact that some people do better in a nice world than others. There really are winners and losers in a globalist market system. Those who love home and its simplicities, and will defend it in spirited ways, sense they are being replaced by nice people. When the world becomes more dominated by the nice, the brutes respond by being less nice, "if only in their voting behavior and perhaps internet harassment as well."[5] But that is just the beginning, and Cowen's subtext is the fear that even more brutish ones will emerge.

Cowen emphasizes that the explanatory factor isn't mainly economic. The labor market just wasn't bad enough to have generated the twin male insurgencies of Trump and Sanders. Cowen might be right that those he calls brutish might exaggerate how bad the economy and their economic condition is in the short term. But the long-term trends that make dignified relational life less possible for so many of our men can't be denied. It's not so much, after all, that there's some preference for work that's more brutish or involving physical strength and skill. There's less work that pays what it did and has the secure perks that the old union jobs did. The decline has something to do with money and status, but it has a lot to do with flourishing as a father, neighbor, and friend. Even brutes, after all, are gregarious animals, and, the Darwinians say, they find most of their happiness in loving and dutiful relations to others. The brutish voters are, in part, rebelling against the world in which life has, in fact, become more brutish for some, with the lives of many men detached from civilizing relational institutions.

That's why the so-called brutish voters are, as Trump understands, conservative in the precise sense. They want to protect what they have, including all the safety nets—both political and social—that appear to be fading away. They want to preserve Social Security and Medicare, precisely because they see that so many lives will become more brutish—or more lonely and detached—without them. For them, the abstracted, cosmopolitan role player with the flexible skills required to function in any and every place is, in fact, the inhuman opposite of the brute. It's the niceness of the role player that's in some large measure responsible for the degradation of so many particular persons and places in our country.

From one view, the most instructive part of Cowen's confusion about contemporary developments is his placing libertarianism and feminism on basically the same page. He alludes to the prospect of a government enforcement of feminine norms on men in a mode similar to certain of the Nordic countries, but Cowen also backs away from this suggestion, thinking it inadequate for the kinds of American men he's describing. In both cases, the point of human progress is to move free beings away from the "nasty, brutish, and short" natural condition Hobbes describes. Progress is understanding the social construction of gender to replace the natural relational division of our species into two biological sexes, thinking less in terms of men and women and friends and enemies than in terms of abstracted, cosmopolitan individuals, affirming the coming of a world where government, religion, the messiness of biological reproduction, and maybe even biological death wither away.

So the problem with the progress celebrated by our cognitive elite is that it's at the expense of the middle-class society based on consent of all the governed that's at the foundation of our Declaration of Independence. It's not about all humans being created equal by nature, but it aims at the overcoming of nature. It's not about the shared dignity of a nation of families, but the freedom of liberated beings disconnected from each other.

A RETURN TO NATURAL RIGHTS

Is it possible to return to the belief that the natural rights proclamations in the American founding provide the superior philosophical foundation for understanding the Constitution and the means of defending it against its principal detractors, the progressives? This position, mostly associated with Harry Jaffa and many of his former students, but more recently appealed to by Randy Barnett in a libertarian manner, heavily focuses on the Declaration of Independence's proclamation in the second paragraph: "We hold these truths to be self-evident, that all men are created equal, that they are endowed by their Creator with certain unalienable rights, that among these are the rights to life, liberty, and the pursuit of happiness."[6] From this core statement of the Declaration is derived the position that the equal and unchanging nature of man and of justice is the Euclidean bedrock of the American republic. It must, therefore, be at the heart of conservatism in America.[7]

Reviving interest in the teaching was the murderous chaos of the twentieth century, which led Leo Strauss to begin *Natural Right and History* by quoting from the Declaration's second paragraph, followed with this statement: Does this nation in its maturity still cherish the faith in which it was conceived and raised? Does it still hold those "truths to be self-evident"?[8]

Harry Jaffa, the movement's intellectual godfather, stated in the introduction to the fiftieth anniversary edition of his *Crisis of the House Divided*, that the book, first published in 1958, was an extended meditation and answer to Strauss's opening question. In this reasoning, Charles Kesler argues, the basics of American conservatism should be defined by "the rights of man under the laws of nature" and should "return to the natural rights doctrines of the American Founders in an intelligent way, to revive their moral and political enterprise and make it the heart and soul of a new American conservatism."[9]

The Declaration is a document of high purpose, one that announces the separation of a nascent political order from an empire, but it is also, like every great political document, one of context and place. An exclusive focus on natural rights as the exhaustive meaning of the Declaration, and, as such, the essence of the American founding, obscures as much as it clarifies what is distinctive about the founding and thus what American conservatism must be about. How exactly should we think about the Declaration? In *Crisis of the House Divided*, Jaffa argues that Abraham Lincoln politically sanctified the Declaration's principles in his monumental debates with Stephen Douglas in 1858 and in his prosecution of the Civil War—a war whose principles transcended the political order, Jaffa observes. Of significance is Jaffa's initial argument that the Declaration was an imperfect document, marred by Lockean self-interest, which served to atomize citizens and separate them from a proper concern for the order of justice.[10] Thus, the American Republic was imperfectly established on grounds of the need to protect interests that established minimal conditions for its maintenance and terminated it when these were no longer protected by the government. Lockean rights were really passions for things (interests) and were incapable of being "interrogated" or appealed to on the basis of what is right. Lincoln's fundamental contribution was to make the Declaration into a goal of equality as the guidepost of the American polity, as opposed to a Lockean contract that collapses because of oppressive conditions.[11] In this sense, Jaffa reasons, Lincoln connects the founding to the ground of justice by appealing to right as what is true and lifting it above the low ground of self-interest.

Jaffa's argument is really a devotional to political equality, one that is difficult to maintain on the purely rational terms of the second paragraph of the Declaration. For Jaffa, the absolute truth of the principles of the Declaration of Independence was in constant need of unironic or unexoteric political defense. That defense had to be authentically rational and authentically spirited. And his remedy was absolute dedication to political equality, a devotion that depends on an insight about irreducible personal significance that is, in fact, biblical. Political equality depends upon natural equality, on an unironic affirmation of the truth that all people are created equal. Jaffa's devotion to the Declaration's natural rights can, in the final analysis, only really be understood as arising from our Puritan biblicist heritage, which deposits in the American mind the equally created status of the human person. From their singular devotion to the Bible as the source and summit of Christian revelation, which was also to serve as the foundation of the Bible commonwealths they aimed to build in colonial America, emerges some of our best thinking and unwavering belief in the inviolability of the person. The elevated person of Puritan theological conviction, while constrained by a fanatical devotion to moral purity that was a part of their legal code, exists above a purely productive or technocratic understanding of personhood and is not reducible to these utilitarian meanings. For example, to the Puritans we owe the belief that education in America should not neglect the soul, even though it is largely about the instrumental preparation of students for productive lives in a capitalist democracy.

As Tocqueville tells us, a devotion to political equality that was both somewhat Aristotelian and very biblical was singularly characteristic of the original American Puritans. Tocqueville's criticism of the Puritans turned out to be that they weren't Christian enough—that is, that they were too focused on the legalism of Exodus, Leviticus, and Deuteronomy at the expense of the teaching of Jesus that was far from reducing even sin to a crime.[12] Jaffa, of course, was hardly as puritanical as the Puritans, but he, like Lincoln, owed them something. We also see this in Jaffa's unwavering defense of the family and sexual morality against the sexual revolution. His arguments for the family were based on its intrinsic moral worth but also on its standing at the center of the Republic.

In the end, the political philosophy of Harry Jaffa is vulnerable to the objection that his philosophic American Founding really, in all honesty, fails to give his moral dedication an adequate foundation. That, after all, is the objection that Lincoln himself may have had to the Founders—as is so memorably revealed in Jaffa's *Crisis of the House Divided*. Lincoln's refounding of our country as devotion to the proposition that all people are created equal depends on a Christian insight about human individuality that we received from the Puritans. And our common devotion—as we see today—recedes when we detach the individual from who he or she is as a unique and irreplaceable creature and citizen.

That's why it's ironic that the "natural rights republic" approach to our country now finds its most able defenders in our libertarian originalists like Randy Barnett who rely on the Declaration of Independence as foundational support for their own jurisprudence, which heavily emphasizes that because of natural rights, as buttressed by the Ninth Amendment and the Fourteenth Amendment's Privileges or Immunities Clause, all laws must pass, more or less, the presumption of liberty test, that is, a high-level scrutiny that federal judges should employ in evaluating the legitimacy of laws challenged for violating constitutional rights. The effectual truth of this constitutional theory is that the government is on the defense in every instance to prove that its laws do not offend the natural rights of citizens to live as they please. Barnett, unlike Jaffa, however, is short on citizenship and long on the boundless choices of individuals to define their own space.

As Randy Barnett explains, the Constitution, in light of the Declaration, creates a government that exists to serve the rights of individuals. In that respect, it's anti-democratic, insofar as pure democracy is majoritarian collectivism. Ours, Barnett says, is republican, not democratic, government. For the Founders, the distinction between republican and democratic is between a government that protects rights and one characterized by collectivist majority tyranny.

The difference between the late Justice Antonin Scalia and the more libertarian originalists is something like this: For Barnett, our Constitution creates a LIBERAL democracy, where democratic legislative outcomes are constantly being engaged by judges—and by the separation of powers in general—with liberty in mind. For Scalia, our Constitution creates a liberal DEMOCRACY, where democratic outcomes are given the benefit of the doubt unless they are contradicted by a specific constitutional text.

A COUNTRY FOR PERSONS

Most conservatives probably regard Barnett's interpretation as too theoretical, or theoretical at least in the wrong way. The conservative view is always fairly hostile to the unencumbered individualism of Locke and his state of nature that serves as the philosophical bedrock of Barnett's libertarian jurisprudence. Locke did well, and followed the Christian tradition, by regarding all human beings as free persons who deserved to be regarded as dignified "bottom lines." Locke's contribution to America is to have followed St. Augustine and the Anglo-American Protestant Christian tradition by freeing persons of the monism of classical civil theology and natural theology. One reason our Constitution is silent on God is to protect the City of God—which unites all nations and all creatures in, as St. Augustine memorably says, "a single pilgrim band"—from American politicization as a merely civic deity.[13]

But for conservatives, Locke is only half right. It's true that each of us is a free individual, but each of us is also an irreducible relational being with corresponding privileges and responsibilities. The danger of Locke's thought is that it seems to be about reconstructing all of human life with contract and consent in mind. The goal is to maximize individual freedom. The cost is the distortion of human institutions that are sustainable only if love and loyalty are more than illusions for suckers.

Because Locke is half-right, conservatives are generally in favor of the free, representative political institutions of the Constitution and of a national Constitution that, following both Augustine and Locke, doesn't distinguish between black and white and male and female and, more generally, doesn't understand persons as politically determined by categories such as social class and religion. They are also generally in favor of a free economy, while never neglecting the danger of the configuring of all human life according to the imperatives of technology or productivity. They aim to keep Locke in a "Locke box," mainly by understanding economic and political freedom as for the flourishing of citizens, creatures, parents, children, neighbors, and so forth. For them, America is only to a limited extent a nation of free individuals; the individual, in fact, is an abstraction deployed for beneficial economic and political purposes. America is a nation of real men and women who belong to families, churches, and particular states and a particular nation.

From this view, what's telling about Barnett's distinction between democratic and republican government is its simpleminded distinction between collectivism and individualism. According to the great tradition of the West, "republican individual" is, strictly speaking, an oxymoron. To be a republican citizen is to be loyally devoted to the way of life of a particular place devoted to a good citizens share in common. And republicanism is a source of egalitarianism. Whatever our differences in natural abilities or personal accomplishments, we are equal before the law with our fellow citizens, and we even owe them equal respect in dignity. Marx exaggerated when he said that, in modern commercial republics, civic equality is contradicted by the hell of the war of all against all that characterizes free or morally unfettered economic life. But Marx was certainly right that the social-contract/state-of-nature thinkers—Hobbes and Locke—regarded citizenship as an unreal abstraction and so too readily connected real dignity with productivity. For Americans, however, a country is really a country, and patriotism and civic loyalty are virtues that unite us all.

But that's collectivism, you say! And for the pure individualist, citizenship is just another form of rent-seeking. Consider this, however: the only place that universal rights are effectively enforced is by particular countries or nations. And those places are invariably "territorial," or citizens taking responsibility for a particular piece of earth. Borders in many ways define particular persons, and the real alternative to them is some abstract cosmopolitanism. To get a bit deeper, the real experiences people have of the universal truth we all share is in a particular community. Sure, Socrates transcended "the laws" of Athens by being a philosopher, but he also explained how dependent he was on Athens' relational familial and educational institutions to become all that he could be.

America's friendly admirer G. K. Chesterton said that the American romance of the citizen is about giving a home to the homeless.[14] All persons are equally homeless in this world, it's true. But their alienation is not so profound that they can't be at home with their homelessness in a particular place. From that view, the truth expressed by the Declaration with dogmatic lucidity is the equality of us all under God. Equality is more than merely civic equality, and the truth about all people being equally created is the foundation of our civic equality. The American nation is the universal truth secured in a particular political place.

Finally, what's wrong with Barnett is that he is too progressive himself! In his view, America is about the progress away from nature by liberated individuals, and so liberty itself expands over the generations, as relational life itself is increasingly perceived as oppressive. The "presumption of liberty" liberates marriage from biological imperatives, and then takes on the very existence of marriage itself. It's true enough that the old progressives—most radically, of course, the communists!—reduced the individual to mere history fodder. But the libertarian progressives—most radically, the transhumanists—lose the relational dignity of the person in a vision of abstract freedom with no real place for birth, love, dignified work, and death. Both the communists and the transhumanists point to the future imagined by John Lennon—and his Lennonists! What they ignore is that citizenship, religious practice, and the family are all parts of what it means to be a whole, free, and relational person. Our constitutionalism, therefore, must be freed from all forms of progressivism—both statist and secessionist—and embrace the full measure of the person's dignified relational content where life is measured by love, community, and work in the service of particular persons.

Considerations such as these should lead conservatives to deny that our Constitution can be adequately viewed through the theory of Locke that informs the Declaration of Independence. Orestes Brownson—and Russell Kirk, following his lead—say that our written Constitution should be interpreted through our providential constitution. Not even our great Founders created order out of nothing; they built with all the civilized resources with which they were provided. These included, of course, the politics of the Greeks and the religion of the Bible. Insofar as they thought they were guided by the theory of Locke, we can even say, following John Courtney Murray, that they built better than they thought they knew. They built not as theorists, but as statesmen, making prudential adjustments to their theory to accommodate the world—the civilization—they had been given.

Bringing these providential and anthropological understandings to bear on contemporary problems of our constitutional order exposes the false contest of our current battles that center on a conflict of individualism versus collectivism. Ignored by this formulation is that individualism and collectivism aren't really at loggerheads with one another, but rather reinforce each other. Collectivism does diminish family, free enterprise, local government, and the multiple associational contexts of our personhood that provide substance to individual liberty. Individualism, however, detracts in another way by endorsing a notion that we don't really have actual responsibilities to others save for what we contract to provide.

As these relational contexts such as family, religion, and various forms of associational life fade, the state inevitably steps in to fill the void. Left unsaid by advocates of restrained constitutionalism is that, if liberty is a blessing, its possession and exercise must be intrinsically beneficial to the relational person as a creature and a citizen. But the liberty of a citizen, if it is to be a blessing, must also require some account of its profitable use, that is, liberty must in some way be connected with the good, with self-limitation, and with justice, and that presupposes a consensus that "We the People" agree to beforehand.

THE PREAMBLE OF THE AMERICAN REPUBLIC

This means that America must be reaffirmed as a democratic republic organized by self-government to meet the fivefold ends of political life: freedom, justice, general welfare, civil unity, and security, as stated by the Constitution's Preamble, in order that the "blessings of liberty" might be secured. Frequently read as aspirational, the Preamble states the goals of our political order made possible in the deliberative republic. When these blessings are the object of constitutional deliberation, government's limited role is realized in support of its citizens reaching their highest ends of existence. We should say with Willmoore Kendall that "the issue is not whether the American system is or is not 'democratic,' but which of two competing definitions of 'democracy'—that which equates it with government by the 'deliberate sense' of the people, acting through their elected representatives, and that which equates it with direct majority rule and equality—should prevail."[15]

In this light, the task of those who wish to preserve and vindicate our constitutional order is to show that the constitutional consensus that rules our republican liberty is deeply consonant with relational personhood, one that differs mightily from an unbounded egalitarian temptation or an emancipated individualism.

We, therefore, should recover John Courtney Murray's notion that "civilization is formed by men locked together in argument," but argument that is not suffused with modern ideology that diminishes the richness of our relational lives by insisting on a Jacobin-type liberty of emancipated individuals ordered by a government bereft of any superintending limitations on its powers.[16] Institutions designed to lock representatives into argument need not ignore the play of factions and interests. On the contrary, these institutions can be a means of channeling factional conflict, along with ideological differences, into some kind of constructive engagement.

The components of Murray's fuller account are human dignity, constitutionalism as political sovereignty delegated by the people and limited by law, self-government as faith in citizens to exercise the duties of moral judgment in basic political decisions, and the constitutional consensus that serves as the basis for rational argument and the compromises that it forges. That much of this struggle is about interests and resources doesn't render moot the prior process of bringing various factions into contact with each other. And the institutional structure of that engagement, hopefully, means that the result is real politics, not a cynical game of power and money.

This is the deep background that enables "the deliberate sense of the community" wrought by our republican institutions to be reasonable. Murray's position, however, does not ignore the less than rational aspects that enter into civilization. The "formative soil of history" and a society's loyalties that are not necessarily logical, its "legends that go beyond the facts," and, as such, are "vehicles of truth," and its "materialisms of property and interest"—all of these, Murray notes, are components of the political order. However, the form of the "civil multitude," its "distinctive bond" is in reason, "or more exactly, that exercise of reason which is argument."[17]

We might ask, though, argument about what exactly? Murray's answer is threefold. First, citizens argue about those matters that are for the public advantage and require public decision and governmental action. Second, argument must also be about public affairs that fall in "decisive part" outside the scope of limited government. However, the effect of these affairs is that they come to shape the public order in a more foundational sense. Thus, the quintessential example for Murray is education in the primary school system and in higher education. Contained in Murray's example is the notion that the contents of a political society's various educations are part of its broader social and political goals and are a crucial means for realizing them. The third element is the constitutional consensus whereby a people obtains its identity and thus understands its purpose in history. The consensus is constitutional in that "its focus is the idea of law" that the people arrive at deliberatively by "reason reflecting on experience" and become a people in the process of coming to it. The consensus is "a structure of basic knowledge, an order of elementary affirmations that reflect realities inherent in the order of existence. It occupies an established position in society and excludes opinions alien or contrary to itself."[18] The consensus is the premise "of the people's action in history" that gives content to the "larger aims" of that action in domestic and foreign affairs.[19]

The larger point of Murray's consensus is its challenge to the notion that agreement ends rational argument. Murray's position is that the only disagreement worthwhile to political order is that which becomes possible because of prior agreement about the abiding consensus. Public argument, actually, is impossible without the consensus. If everything is an open question, if everything is in doubt for a political society, public argument cannot even begin; it is not possible. In that case, rational dialogue is displaced in favor of the nominalist's contention that words are weapons used to clear space and create power and extract benefits for the individual or the group.

How far can Murray take us with his account of men locked in rational, political argument as the formal principle of American political foundations? In an essay evaluating this question, "The True Sage of Woodstock," Willmoore Kendall asserted that Murray's account, even if questionable as to the actual origins of most civil communities, perfectly accords with the "origins and original character of . . . American political society." Was, Kendall asks, "American society formed by 'men locked in argument'? Answer: One could not imagine a better description of the Congress that produced the Declaration of Independence, the Convention that produced the Constitution, the state conventions that ratified it, and the First Congress that produced our Bill of Rights." Kendall also demonstrates other aspects of the Murray thesis that were realized at various points in these debates, arguments, and compromises of the founding documents. "Cohesiveness," he argues, was achieved as these moments were arguments that "got somewhere" and resolved disagreements. The record of the Philadelphia Convention demonstrates Kendall's point well, as framework plans for political order were presented, critiqued, compromised, and synthesized by the delegates. On the purely rational character of the delegates' arguments, Kendall answers in the negative, but Murray never claimed for political argument that it be purely rational. Kendall observes that loyalties, self-interest, passion, and prejudice, as well as legends, were operative in the Philadelphia Convention, as should be expected. However, these nonrational aspects "were subordinated to a 'distinctive bond,' recognizably that of 'the exercise of reason' which tied the delegates together."[20]

The final element of political argument for Murray is civic amity, which is held together by a motivation for justice, or that which the citizen can demand of the political order and the political order can demand of the citizen in his capacity as citizen. Kendall observes that justice for the Founders was an operative motivation, but its content was complex. The Founders used terms like "natural rights" and "happiness and prosperity of the people" interchangeably with the term "justice," and this usage is borne out in the records of these debates. So "the delegates seem to have used these phrases . . . thus tacitly assuming that if natural rights were made safe, that would *be* justice."[21] Murray's point was that the commitment of representatives to justice provided them with the motivation necessary to remain locked in argument until they arrived at a reasonable compromise. Therefore, reason is the definitive bond and the form of the political argument, but competing conceptions or aspects of justice provided the compelling force that ensures arguments find some resolution.

This process of compromise, animated by principles while also informed by property and interests, history and legends, can be seen in the arguments over the Declaration, the Constitution, the state constitutional ratification debates, and the debate in the First Congress over the content and wording of the Bill of Rights. These debates display the character of compromise and synthesis of the American constitutional tradition, and these foundational debates help achieve the constitutional consensus that can then be further debated and developed. The question haunting our tradition now is the partisan or ideological manner in which central questions are answered, and which institutional mechanisms (executive, legislative, judicial, or administrative) are chosen to implement them. Put differently, our politics is warlike, and the answers for difficult social and socioeconomic questions are seen as too significant to be settled by the deliberate sense of the community. Publius put matters quite differently with his belief in separation of powers that would provide deliberative government, requiring the interests, identities, and loyalties of a diverse citizenry to be locked together in "dry political" argument.

These are the foundational and dramatic instances of what Publius terms the "republican principle" at work in the formation of our constitutional law. But it surely did not end here in the laying of the fundamental law of the Republic. Rather it is the way of our politics, the politics of deliberation, whereby majority will prevails, but it does so through the seasoning and tutoring process of our intricately structured government. If the focus of much of our politics now turns on presidential elections, whereby the victor has the authority to enact mandates received from the voters with a compliant Congress doing the executive's bidding, what Kendall's scholarship returns us to is the constitutional morality that Publius elaborates in *The Federalist*. Put succinctly, this morality arises from the fact that majorities are to be restrained in our system not by the majority itself or by minority veto—the latter would defeat the whole purpose of republicanism by permanently hobbling majority rule—but through the inter-branch competitive process that, hopefully, ensures that temporary or indulgent or weak majorities are weeded out.

Those majorities that are able to capture Congress, the executive, and the federal courts are those that turn the country in their direction, perhaps decisively reshaping it. Moreover, it is the interplay of the federal branches that further protects minorities against being subject to mandates shoved down their throats, because the majority will, in most situations, be compelled to bargain, compromise, and trade on certain policies in order to obtain its more dear policy objectives. Of course, narrow majorities on the Supreme Court or regulators in executive branch agencies now frequently act apart from this deliberative process, the former through insisting that controversial accounts of unenumerated rights are to receive constitutional sanction, the latter by rewriting federal statutes through an informal rule-making process outside of even the Administrative Procedure Act. Kendall's republicanism opposes itself to both.

Kendall's scholarship on the republican principle reawakens us to the actual problems confronted by the Framers, which were not the problems, he says, of modern political scientists who concern themselves with voter preference measuring in the service of actual democratic outcomes. That is to say, the modern scientific model of democracy, one that studiously refrains from pronouncing on value, incoherently insists that measuring the preferences of an electorate is the only way to reliably provide for majority rule and democratic outcomes.[22] We might take note that the concerns of mid-twentieth-century political scientists on egalitarian preference weighing may now be superseded by our own legal academic mandarins, who have gone several steps beyond such theorizing and now openly embrace forms of illiberal executive rule in the name of giving the people what they need.[23] A regnant scholarly consensus presumes that the American constitutional order is positively set against majority rule, with its Framers having labored to make an antidemocratic system in the service of property rights and an array of oligarchic interests. Thus, its ability to weigh preferences has been stunted from the outset and requires various measures and techniques to be employed in order for democracy to be made real. It is a well-worn charge that the mainstream of political science makes, and Kendall's response to it remains worth considering fifty years later.

In his rebuttal of modern political science orthodoxy and its emphasis on the antidemocratic Constitution, Kendall underscores that the aims of the Philadelphia Convention of 1787 were not to act against the principle of majority will, but were to build a republican order that would be governed by the people through deliberation and compromise.[24] We might walk in their shoes, Kendall urges, and consider the problems they faced: schism within the country under the Articles of Confederation and the threat of breakaway states; mob rule in certain states that deliberately violated minority rights; and general crises of currency inflation and debts threatening to strangle the political order in its infancy.[25] Holding the country together in those circumstances was their chief problem, not to make war on majority rule in the name of preserving oligarchy. The Framers' aversion was not to majority rule as such, for surely they understood that in a republic the majority will have its way. Their aversion was to any manner of majority rule that encouraged division and oppression. Their hope was to find ways of forming majorities that encouraged restraint and forced the government to be responsive to the whole public. Thus the separation of powers, the federal government of enumerated powers, the equality of representation of the states in the US Senate, the electoral college, the states' power to set rules over voting and district maps for the House of Representatives—these are some of the vital ways in which the Constitution tries to form majority rule into the "deliberate sense of the people" such that majorities are ultimately engaged, shaped, limited, and informed by the whole of the represented public.

Thinking along these lines of deliberation immediately brings us to the diverse and extended country of *Federalist* No. 10, with its clashing interests that should represent a permanent challenge to unjust majorities by exposing their weaknesses and/or restraining their excesses. At the least, Kendall argued in a 1965 essay on "The Civil Rights Movement and the Coming Constitutional Crisis," those seeking drastic constitutional change are compelled by the logic of *Federalist* No. 10 to wait in the "ante-room" before they are "sanctioned either by a constitutional amendment or by consensus among the three branches."[26] Our constitutional structure makes it difficult to reshape the vast commercial republic that is America.

Another way of making this point, Kendall notes, is through the argument in *Federalist* No. 64, which concerns itself with the Senate needing to provide a two-thirds concurrence to ratify any international treaty. Publius argues that the "good of the whole can only be promoted by advancing the good of each of the parts or members which compose the whole."[27]

Even though Kendall was writing in 1960 about "The Two Majorities"—meaning the clashing representations of the two political branches of the federal government—he limns core political truths that connect with our self-government problem today.[28] He had taken up his pen in response to the position advanced by the legendary scholar Robert Dahl, who argued in his 1956 book, *Preface to Democratic Theory*, that the only legitimate majority is the presidential majority. That national majority expresses itself in quadrennial presidential elections that grant the winners a national mandate to make policy. But is there such a thing as a national majority, one that encompasses the country coast-to-coast, somehow above or at least apart from the "structured communities" of legislative districts and states represented in Congress? Kendall wonders what type of majority Dahl has in mind.

To be sure, says Kendall, a presidential majority does rise above parochial or more limited points of view found within many congressional districts on spending, immigration, foreign policy, trade, entitlements, and other issues. These political communities are often bounded and insular, but that means that when arguments about national policy are made, they become arguments about something concrete and particular that is refracted through existing communities with various interests. The appeals made to a national majority necessarily exist apart from actual communities. On the other hand, we might ask if such a thing as a national community can even properly exist—let alone an identifiable majority within it—or if what really emerges is a sense of how things should be ideally. Then the question becomes, of course, whose ideals shall prevail?

The arguments made on its behalf partake, Kendall observes, of ideals that have been formed by "faculty opinion" and more cosmopolitan sectors of society, and then amplified by media organs. Such appeals are then concretized into rules by those certified within the regulatory agencies. The president and the regulators in the federal bureaucracy are not in a position of congressional representatives who are beset with arguments, interests, and prejudices of many varieties as they go about representing a particular place.[29] Apparently the unlearned senators and representatives need to be educated by the national majority—or, what is really the same in Kendall's conception, elite opinion.

Considered from the perspective of the represented, though, how does one speak to a national constituency of the size, diversity, and complexity of America? Kendall observes that in the current situation of a domineering presidential politics, the country must be subject to the platitudes, maxims, and general statements of a candidate. The appeal is made to high-sounding principles, which provide authority to the newly elected president to pursue "mandate" politics fitting with the idealistic tenor of the campaign.[30] Thus, it seems, we argue about nothing in particular and everything in general. Presidential majorities, because they understand themselves to already represent the will of the whole, do not point in the direction of deliberation and therefore of compromise and moderation. And so we find ourselves with a politics of executive rule and administrative fiat. The presidential majority, left to itself, is hardly capable of doing otherwise or better.

We need to recover the mediated government of our republican political order. The surest way for us to reconnect with our roots is not in the originalist recovery of each clause of the Constitution but in congressional elections that are about something, shaped by communities of people who can argue with one another, and make a choice among themselves about what they concretely are prepared to favor, tolerate, or oppose. This decision is made in the form of a person who will represent the community and is accordingly sanctioned to deliberate on its behalf. These elections, Kendall notes, are the surest bridge we still have to the Founders' Constitution. Thus congressional elections turn not only on policies but on fitness of character; that is, the virtue of the person who is to represent a community and deliberate on its behalf is of greater significance. The judgment of character made by those represented as to who should represent them, then, is the often unstated premise to our institutions performing their constitutional functions. It is the virtue that our system requires to fulfill its constitutional end.

Kendall, though, makes the appropriate comparison and realistic judgment that as between presidential and congressional majorities, elite opinion favors the presidency. This is seen in the one-way process of cosmopolitan opinion educating the dark recesses of insular American communities reflected in congressional majorities. Here, we encounter coastal opinion versus the habits and practices of the Americans in flyover country. The crucial question remains: how are the latter represented in the federal government?

Does this group of Americans find only virtual representation in Congress, and is it effectively ruled by a federal rule-making apparatus composed of judicial and executive officials whose promulgations elude curtailment by Congress? What is needed is the authority to change the terms of the debate, which have remained similar, in certain respects, over the course of fifty years since Kendall's paper was published. What must happen is a new argument and framing of the contest. What type of country will we become and whose principles will dominate it through majority rule? Rather than teacher-president and pupil-Congress, we need a debate over how best to make real the principle of self-government, which permits relational persons to fulfill our responsibilities to one another. If this is secured, then we can build a future with reforms and innovations rooted in who we are as a constitutional people.

5 · A Constitution in Full: Written and Providential

Progressivism's powerful emergence in the closing decades of the late nineteenth century challenged federalism, separation of powers, and limited government as the essence of American constitutionalism. The abstract humanitarian ideal underlying progressivism is its commitment to the evolutionary ascent of human consciousness through elimination of the perceived hypercompetitive self-interested striving that dominates civil society and republican government within the classical liberal framework. Achieving a more wholesome development of humans has entailed a firm national superintendence of the supposed atavistic tendencies in civil society and government with an eye toward their gradual elimination. Eliminating the perceived negative externalities of a largely free and competitive social, political, and economic order has meant creating new fields of energy in government that reform the national spirit, moving citizens toward a grander, more consequential national telos.

More energy in government, however, was never really enough to affect the "reappraisal of values" that progressivism desires. Foremost in the progressive canon has been the denial that humans come to government with natural rights and liberties, the exercise of which perfects their being and leads to greater societal flourishing. Government becomes the author and guarantor of humans' fulfillment and must have unbounded discretion if it is to direct their latent potentiality. Specifically, progressive ideology has sought a plenary executive power that embodies the entire people, the evacuation of the deliberative form of the congressional branch in favor of the science of bureaucratic administration, the construction of positive rights to achieve "social justice," and an ideological insistence that American federal and state governments must embody democratic rather than republican forms.

Progressivism replaced these core understandings by issuing powerful alternatives of consolidated government power manifested in social welfare expenditures, spendthrift fiscal policy, extensive commercial regulations, and the co-opting of individual states as "partners" in diverse areas of federal policy, to name some of the more momentous transformations. Progressivism removes individuals from unproductive and harmful competition by opening to them higher realms of equality and self-fulfillment. This becomes the new constitution or the new deal with the American people. But progressivism is thoroughly American in its belief that reason can employ technology through state power to improve the future lives of citizens.

Progressivism's focus on equality as the measure of public policy is itself a legacy of a hyper-Protestant idealism regarding individual dignity as much as it also emerges from the historical philosophy of Hegel. Where the traditional American stress had been Lockean and supportive of business and capitalism to improve the future, progressives transferred this same spirit and desire to government, for it to employ new techniques to shape the social and political order. Progressivism is also an immense movement composed of numerous political goals and indeed different overall trajectories in its various stages of ideological growth. For example, comparing the progressive New Left of the 1960s, with its postmaterialist and authentic "lifestyles" philosophy, to the family wage and industrialist progressivism of the New Deal reveals a stark contrast in what government should mandate, regulate, and incentivize. Between these two opposing slices of progressivism rests the Great Society pickle of President Lyndon Johnson, which focused on national community development through promoting all manner of goals: environmental, educational, racial-equality, cultural, and social ideals that were nearly boundless in scope, resting on the proposition that scarcity of resources no longer plagued America as a country. History had moved beyond that limiting condition, and now a truly awesome national government could be built on America's postwar prosperity. Focusing on the New Deal itself, which we do later in this chapter, reveals the complexity within progressivism, but also, perhaps, its unifying threads.

That said, this chapter discusses how an American political philosophy that would successfully engage progressivism must stand on a basis much deeper than the classical liberalism and the natural rights theorizing that influenced much of the American founding, but that cannot provide a comprehensive grounding for the republicanism of our constitutional order. This entails a recovery of historical, philosophical, and religious materials that have shaped and continue to shape us as both citizens and relational persons and further reveals the possibility of transcending two opposite positions: collectivism and individualism. Once again we will bring Brownson to bear.

While the New Deal is largely understood as a dramatic expansion of federal power over the economy on behalf of labor, with redistribution of wealth a primary goal, funded by steeper taxes and borrowing, it also contains a significant pro-family element that should complicate efforts to pigeonhole it merely as an attempt to enthrone government at the expense of business and civil society. It was precisely to protect the autonomy of the family and ensure above-level replacement birthrates that a host of polices were erected during the New Deal with the goal of working fathers, stay-at-home mothers, and homes full of children. But what does this substantial intervention reveal to us about the original limiting principles of American constitutionalism and their perceived (particularly by conservatives) differences with the twentieth-century progressivism? Perhaps it reveals that while progressivism remains at odds with much of the fundamental ideas of our Constitution, its easy dismissal by advocates of the Founders' Constitution must be avoided. Indeed, progressivism can be seen as an emphatic response to difficulties that many citizens encounter in work, education, healthcare, environmental pollution, and the like that call for solutions of some kind not found in a politics of individualism. One concern is about the means and regards the type of policies that progressives propose: their desire to restructure the Constitution to facilitate more government or to create rules and regulations that steadily consume the independence of civil society to achieve their ends. But another concern is whether their stress on problems within a competitive and free economy reveals fractures that must be addressed by ideas that emphasize humans' social and relational nature, rather than ignoring it with a libertarian program or annihilating it with collectivist policies. In short, progressivism may shine a light on problems that can be easy to ignore until they issue in wide distress. But this is not necessarily to affirm their comprehensive statist solutions.

A number of approaches have been advanced against progressivism. The originalist position has typically stressed, with differing degrees of emphasis, core provisions of the written Constitution that must be understood anew and revived to ensure the reflourishing of liberty and self-government. Accordingly, textual "positivist" recovery should be sufficient to repel the collectivist occupiers of the federal government. A separate "natural right" methodology looks to the underlying philosophical foundations in negative rights that surround and protect the sovereign individual and are reflected in the Constitution's text, but are buried by the weight of the inverted, New Deal Constitution. Therefore, recovering the "Lost Constitution" becomes imperative for a rebirth of the constitutional experiment. Of course, neither the textual nor modern natural rights position needs be exclusive of the other. Both contend that the rights and structural protections encased in the written charter document are creatively reinterpreted or disregarded by progressive doctrine and practice.

Left unstated is that the Constitution itself requires a robust historical and philosophical grounding and explication if it is to endure. But the Constitution is now infrequently evaluated and defended in terms of its profound historical and philosophical fit to the unique circumstances, ideas, and cultures that formed the United States, much of which is still embedded in contemporary civil society and in the competitive federal structure of the Constitution. The reviving potential of such an argument was evoked by the nineteenth-century thinker Orestes Brownson in response to America's almost congenital difficulty in coming to terms with its political existence.

Born from what Brownson believed was a crisis of the American soul, his book, *The American Republic: Its Constitution, Tendencies, and Destiny*, published in 1865, ambitiously seeks to reground the American constitutional order in the aftermath of the Civil War. The central question engaged by Brownson is as follows: How does the constitutional order of America relate to the political system approved by the Philadelphia Convention of 1787?[1] His response to this question rests in two distinct concepts: territorial democracy and the unwritten constitution. Both ideas, Brownson thought, offer distinct opposition to their two principal constitutional rivals, the personal democracy of Jeffersonian Southerners and the national consolidation of power advocated by Northern humanitarians.

The concepts of territorial democracy and the unwritten constitution are both part of Brownson's larger effort to extricate modern democratic government from its basis in social-contract doctrine and to embed it in the solidified terrain of a republican political posture elevated by devotion to its foundational elements. Brownson was profoundly convinced that the location of political rule in the sovereign and solitary individual of Hobbesian and Lockean doctrine, or in the collective mass, as argued by nineteenth-century popular-sovereignty theorists, fails to respond to actual human beings. Thus, humans' relational nature and limitations entail a different set of conclusions for political sovereignty. Sovereignty is not given to persons or to a popular mass by natural right if they are unconnected to a particular jurisdiction. Rather, sovereignty follows only from the fact of holding territory; the fact has to precede the right. Given humans' limited condition, politics requires the circumscriptions of law, territory, and citizenship for it to be profitably ventured. Brownson affirmed that politics is a natural activity of humans, but one capable of deformation under the weight of ideological strictures promising its perfection (*vox populi est vox dei*) or its superfluousness by humanitarian progressives (and our own contemporary transnational progressives).

As the ordering element of a government's extant constitution, the unwritten constitution grounds the political constitution by limiting the range of potentialities that it can develop and manifest. Within a state's unwritten constitution are the facts of its unity as evidenced in its migrations, founding violence, religion and spirituality, and political documents. Deviation from it in the course of a state's development invites political demise. Written constitutions do not emerge ex nihilo, but must build on the various elements that provide guidance and limits to what statesmen may produce in the particular circumstances they confront. But these elements, as we have elsewhere noted, are not obstacles but "civilizational accomplishments" that enable the constitutional order to come primarily into being.[2] The unwritten constitution exists within a people's political culture, mores, customs, dispositions, and peculiar talents. The written constitution is made from this order and remains forever joined to it.[3] Thus, America's written constitution of 1787 has to be understood by the unwritten order of its common law heritage, unified colonial resistance to and independence from a monarchical empire, largely democratic emigration patterns, and commitment to religious pluralism.

Brownson's understanding of American constitutionalism offers a powerful corrective to abstract humanitarian ideals exalting national power against the liberty of both states and individuals to shape their futures as self-governing entities and persons. Brownson argued that the defeat of the Confederacy inflated the Northern humanitarians' quest for national power. While regarding the Southern states as constitutionally erroneous in their secessions from the Union, he also thought that their military defeat and perceived cultural humiliation emboldened certain politicians, clergy, and thinkers to engage in endless Jacobin-like political questing for national power in service of egalitarian ideals.

Brownson was uniquely situated to uncover and expound upon what he articulated as the true principles of the American Republic. Preceding and shaping this attempt were Brownson's myriad political and religious conversions that can best be understood in the positions he advanced in John Sullivan's *Democratic Review* and Brownson's own journal, *Brownson's Quarterly Review*. Having been an advocate for the rights of laborers and, in time, a proto-socialist, Brownson gradually moved away from his radical political positions through his own crisis of the soul.[4] Central to Brownson's rediscovery of classical political thought and reasoning is a deep investigation of constitutionalism, which he believes is misunderstood in the modern era, and, more specifically, within the country that claims to be its practitioner par excellence. The basic problem, according to Brownson, is understanding the constitutive truth of the republic, a truth that could contain and guide public argument toward legitimate political ends. In opposition to constitutional principles that insist upon the publicly negotiated trust responsibility of political obligations and liberties, social-contract theory, Brownson reasoned, has made power autonomous, inhering purely in the individual will.

The logical corollary to personal sovereignty is that the equality of individuals prevents one person from ruling another person, unless explicit consent is granted to such rule. Brownson analyzed that individuals, free and equal in a state of nature, could erect society only by a compact that "binds and can bind only those who voluntarily and deliberately enter into it." In this regard, Brownson found Thomas Jefferson's doctrine of generational consent as the more convincing application of social-contract theory, as opposed to the stretched fiction of tacit consent: "Mr. Jefferson saw this, and very consistently maintained that one generation has no power to bind another; and, as if this was not enough, he asserted the right of revolution, and gave it as his opinion that in every nation a revolution once in every generation is desirable, that is, according to his reckoning, once every nineteen years."[5] Of course, Brownson's purpose in interrogating social-contract theory is not to examine the claims of tacit versus express consent as its basis, but to underscore the fragility of any political order established by it. On this point, he stated, "The theory substitutes simple agency for government, and makes each individual its principal. It is an abuse of language to call this agency a government. It has no one feature or element of government. It has only an artificial unity, based on diversity; its authority is only personal, individual, and in no sense a public authority."[6]

We must now turn to territorial democracy to understand Brownson's account of republican government.

TERRITORIAL DEMOCRACY

In the aftermath of the Civil War, Brownson articulated that democratic popular rule, with its dual tendencies toward consolidation or centrifugal anarchy, should be informed by the real, though frequently misunderstood, principles of the Constitution. Brownson sought to explain the sovereignty of the United States by the term "territorial democracy," first coined by Benjamin Disraeli in his description of America. Sometimes seen as a defense of confederalism or even decentralized political rule, territorial democracy's true emphasis is on the territorial as opposed to the personal basis of power. Greece and Rome were exemplars of the term. Athens "introduced the principle of territorial democracy," and further subdivided power "into demes or wards," showing that territorial democracy was compatible with local rule, but the essential principle was the "loyalty of all citizens" to Athens, and not to a particular ruler or ruling group.[7]

In Rome, Brownson observed, the undifferentiated mass was organized into a body politic governed by the notion of public rule exercised by the senate body. Only those heads of households who were "tenants of the sacred territory of the city, which has been surveyed and marked by the god Terminus," were entitled to govern in the senate.[8] The head of a home held despotic authority over its affairs, but beyond familial association, claims to rule were formed by the Roman legal principle of land ownership. Brownson formulated that here was "the introduction of an element which is not patriarchal, and which transforms the patriarch or chief of a tribe into the city or state, and founds the civil order, or what is now called civilization. The city or state takes the place of the private proprietor, and territorial rights take the place of purely personal rights."[9]

Further explicating the Roman contribution, Brownson stated that with regard to the sacred territory, "the land owned the man."[10] To be a citizen with full political rights, it was first necessary to be "adopted" by this domain. This meant the following:

> The state is territorial, not personal, and that the citizen appertains to the state, not the state to the citizen. Under the patriarchal, the tribal, and the Asiatic monarchical systems, there is, properly speaking, no state, no citizens, and the organization is economical rather than political. Authority—even the nation itself—is personal, not territorial. The patriarch, the chief of the tribe, or the king, is the only proprietor. Under the Graeco-Roman system all this is transformed. The nation is territorial as well as personal, and the real proprietor is the city or state.[11]

This development, however, was not inevitable and had been lost in the aftermath of the Roman Empire. Feudalism's emergence was the bête noire of territorial democracy, because it predicated rule on the proprietorship of the nobles and the crown. Feudalism, reasoned Brownson, was a "barbaric constitution" where those who ruled did so for their private interests in exclusion of any notion of the res publica or the commonwealth. Nothing brought the competing interests into a coherent unity of liberty and authority, or as Brownson put it: "Under feudalism there are estates, but no state. The king governs as an estate, the nobles hold their power as an estate, and the commons are represented as an estate. The whole theory of power is that it is an estate; a private right, not a public trust."[12]

Territorial democracy is integral to American self-understanding and its habits of government because it distinguishes the republican form of government from modern political tendencies that claim to exemplify republicanism but ultimately are a slow return to barbaric political forms. As Brownson explained: "The most marked political tendency of the American people has been, since 1825, to interpret their government as a pure and simple democracy, and to shift it from a territorial to a purely popular basis, or from the people as the state, inseparably united to the national territory or domain, to the people as simply population, either as individuals or as the race." And this translates into changing "their constitution from a republican to a despotic, or from a civilized to a barbaric constitution."[13]

In some respects, Brownson's analysis of the importance of territorial democracy sounds almost banal. Yes, rights and liberties, obligations and penalties, attach only to those people who are citizens of the constituted state. To be outside the state is to be outside the benefits and burdens of the citizenship that it has authorized and guaranteed. However, Brownson saw within the development of modern democratic rule the complete lack of a limiting principle on either the claims that people can make against the state or vice versa. Modern democrats place sovereignty in either the individual or the collective, with the latter absorbing the individual into the human race, and then making its programmatic demands for humanitarian state action. A different approach is needed to better secure the liberty of the human person against the unbridled claims of the state and of fellow citizens.

Brownson's *via media*, which he found in America in preeminent form, is the notion of law, obligation, and right being fixed to the territory where sovereignty is exercised as a public trust. In this regard, Brownson observed, "The people of the United States are sovereign only within the territory or domain of the United States, and their sovereignty is a state, because fixed, attached, or limited to that specific territory. It is fixed to the soil, not nomadic."[14] America had completed this notion by its division of powers between and among the general and state governments, and the separation of the distinct acts of governing among the executive, legislative, and judicial branches. Thus the potential for democratic despotism, as was realized in the French Revolution, or in incipient form in the European liberationist efforts of 1848, is checked by devotion to the complicated concrete structures of political organization and rule in the United States.

Significant to this notion is Brownson's analysis of the "right to vote," which he insisted is not a right in the modern definition of right. The notion that it is a natural right is a crucial misunderstanding. All sovereignty rests on "domain" or "proprietorship." Under republican government, the domain is attached to and ordered by society, and power is exercised "for the common or public good of all." The "elective franchise" is accordingly a political right held from society, a civil right, and not a natural or personal right.[15] Thus, possession of the right to vote is a negotiated right exercised by its holders according to the needs and claims of the territorial domain, the original authorizer and guarantor of the right.

Brownson's rejection of a personal right to vote necessarily entails larger consequences for his political theory. Again, the territorial grounding of political legitimacy, in Brownson's argument, performs a limiting function on democratic excess. If the right is positive in origin, then its function is exercised on behalf of the republic. If it is the individual's personal right, then it would follow that the individual's personal promptings predominate in its use. Of course, Brownson's own writings indicate an awareness that territorial democracy is not a barrier to the pathologies plaguing representative government. But among the competing claimants for authority and liberty in modern republics, territorial democracy provided a better conceptual framework for reconciling the demands of individual liberty with state authority. Instead of leading with self-interest as a primary motivating factor, the individual learns citizenship historically from the framework of the republic and is expected to manifest this in political behavior.

Sovereignty's attachment to the territorially constituted people means that public deliberation and decisions have to adhere to the particular requirements of the polity. Moreover, the people do not possess sovereignty in the abstract, either as individuals or as a mass collection of individuals. Sovereignty consists only of the people attached to legally defined territory. In America, territorial democracy reaches its apogee in the functional division of powers provided for various levels of political opportunity, conflict, and compromise. Brownson maintained that the political teleology of America is "to realize that philosophical division of powers of government which distinguish it from both imperial and democratic centralism."[16] Brownson's basic formula is that general relations and interests are distinct from particular relations and interests. Thus, state and federal layers of government each have their own province of operations and hold authority in their separate spheres, while relying on the "interdependent" work of each government, state and federal, for the accomplishment of the full project of constitutional government.[17] As such, territorial democracy provides the architecture of devotion to federalism and the separation of powers in the American system.

Brownson's location of sovereignty in the *United* States further reveals his own original thought on America's constitutional authority. On this point, Brownson stated:

> As there is no domain without a lord or dominus, territory alone cannot possess any political rights or franchises, for it is not a domain. In the American system, the dominus or lord is not the particular State, but the United States, and the domain of the whole territory, whether erected into particular States or not, is in the United States alone. The United States do not part with the dominion of that portion of the national domain included within a particular State. The State holds the domain not separately but jointly, as inseparably one of the United States: separated, it has no dominion, is no State, and is no longer a joint sovereign at all, and the territory that it included falls into the condition of any other territory held by the United States not erected into one of the United States.[18]

Central to Brownson's thought is the idea that the United States hold power jointly and not severally. Therefore, Brownson attempted to avoid the error he thought informed both the John Calhoun and the Daniel Webster schools of political thought on America's constitutional origins. Calhoun argued that the sovereignty that inhered in the several states was retained by them even after ratification of the Constitution. Consequently, this allowed the states as principals to create the national government as their agent, whose authority they could restrict by acts of nullification and secession when constitutionally appropriate. Webster, for his part, thought that the states, while formerly sovereign entities, had ceded this sovereignty to the federal government during the course of constitutional ratification, and now exercised only reserved powers.[19] Brownson noted that both Calhoun and Webster failed to understand the curious character of sovereignty in the United States.

The distinction between Calhoun's compact theory and Webster's nationalist argument is, Brownson insisted, not as clear as it appears. Both men look to a social contract understanding for the origins of American political authority; that is, the states in convention had produced an overarching government in the same manner as individuals in a state of nature erected their own government. The distinction between Calhoun and Webster concerns only the degree of power reserved by the states. In truth, the states are not really sovereign, as Calhoun understood, nor are they mere appendages, or administrative counties to the national reach of the federal government, as Webster argued. Their sovereignty is held "jointly."

Brownson located the principles of the American founding in their historical and philosophical formation, in the fact and the right. The states are sovereign only in their unity. Citing John Quincy Adams, Brownson argued, "The States hold from the Union, not the Union from the States. The States without the Union cease to exist as political communities: the Union without the States ceases to be a Union, and becomes a vast centralized and consolidated state, ready to lapse from a civilized into a barbaric, from a republican to a despotic nation."[20] This was true, Brownson said, even during the colonial period, when the colonies existed under the British Crown and British common law, and in their formal act of separation and unified resistance to the English Empire. In short, the states had never been separate sovereign states.

In addressing the Declaration of Independence's appeal to the colonies as free and independent states, Brownson underscored that the Declaration also cited the "united States [*sic*]" and the "United Colonies" for the work of separation, resistance, and the establishment of a new country. Moreover, the states had also never exercised the full attributes of sovereignty: "They have had no flag—symbol of sovereignty—recognized by foreign powers, have made no foreign treaties, held no foreign relations, had no commerce foreign or interstate, coined no money, entered into no alliances or confederacies with foreign states or with one another."[21] As States United, governance of the continental republic was possible in both general and particular terms. Apart from the union, the several states could do nothing. To further understand this point, one must turn to Brownson's notion of the unwritten constitution.

THE UNWRITTEN CONSTITUTION

The unwritten constitution, or what Brownson also termed the providential constitution, expresses the notion that every constitution is twofold: (1) the constitution of the state or nation and (2) the constitution of the government. Brownson's basic observation is that the constitution of the government emerges out of and will always relate back to that constitution by which the nation is formed and is the source of its vitality and its destiny.[22] This emerges in Brownson's understanding of the unwritten constitution, which places stress on its providential element. Each state has its own unique founding given to it that must serve as the guide to the development of that state's political future. According to Brownson, "Every living nation has an idea given it by Providence to realize, and whose realization is its special work, mission, or destiny." But his ultimate concern is with finding the ground of political obligation that accords the most with reality and the human person. Here America is especially privileged, if properly understood.

Sovereignty, Brownson reasoned, has to exist "before it can act," and its existence presupposes the prior political organization of a people or nation. "The nation must exist, and exist as a political community, before it can give itself a constitution."[23] Herein rests Brownson's second objection to the contractual idea of state formation.

There is no such thing as the people or nation acting without some modicum of political form. If sovereignty inheres in the individual, or in entities like the American states, then sovereignty cannot simply be transferred to a new national government, previously nonexistent. Sovereignty can be ceded "only to something or somebody actually existing, for to cede to nothing and not to cede is one and the same thing."[24] Brownson's larger point is that the "sovereignty of the American Republic vests in the States, though in the states collectively, or united, not severally." This "original Providential constitution of the American state" avoids the pitfalls of "consolidation and disintegration."[25]

America's providential constitution restrains and informs democratic action by pointing to the "political destiny or mission of United States." The mission is to realize "that philosophical division of the powers of government which distinguish it from both imperial and democratic centralism on the one hand, and, on the other, from the checks and balances or organized antagonisms which seek to preserve liberty by obstructing the exercise of power."[26] Political modernity is characterized by the need for an abstract unity, "democratic centralism," over and against legitimate countervailing authorities in the government. Such unity is based on an ideological insistence for equality, sameness, and the reduction of human particularity to a common denominator. A countertendency in political modernity is individualism, with each element constantly fighting other elements for control. Checks and balances among classes has devolved in the British system, Brownson said, into a state "constituted to nobody's satisfaction." It is the American republic that is built on genuinely "catholic principles." The American system given "its division of the powers of government, between a General government and particular State governments," has the possibility to realize a dialectical whole of liberty and authority, the individual and the state.[27]

On this point, Brownson introduced the American Idea, which he argued is "liberty, indeed, but liberty with law, and law with liberty." But to realize liberty, properly understood, we must come to terms with "the true idea of the state, which secures at once the authority of the public and the freedom of the individual—the sovereignty of the people without social despotism, and individual freedom without anarchy." Authority and liberty are therefore in need of one another for their proper working, and that means that American constitutionalism must "bring out in its life the dialectic union of authority and liberty, of the natural rights of man and those of society."[28]

Nor are these the only apparent opposites that Brownson would see reconciled in the American republic. Federalism unites particular and universal in humans' political nature. But federalism needs better thinking. It needs to be understood in the light of a mediating principle that federalism opens to humans between the particularity and universality of political experience, which reflects the limitations and aspirations of political being. The American system attaches the individual's loyalty to the particular state of residency, thus making sense of our limited, finite nature and its inbuilt need for local loyalties and devotions. However, the American republic has also made provision for human equality in the Union itself, a union coterminous with the states, and has therefore a principled way to overcome local tyranny and inequality. "The Union and the States are coeval, born together, and can exist only together. . . . The Union is in each of the States, and each of the States is in the Union."

AMERICA'S LIMITED POLITICAL IMAGINATION

America's difficulty is its failure to understand its political origins, Brownson argued. "The great problem of our statesmen has been from the first, how to assert union without consolidation, and State rights without disintegration?" In answering this question, American statesmen, urged Brownson, "have confined their views to the written constitution, as if that constituted the American people a state or nation." The problem for statesmen is that "the American form of government has no prototype in any prior constitution." If the failure is in looking exclusively to the four corners of the written constitution to understand the American people, the solution rests in understanding how the Americans, prior to the Convention of 1787, understood themselves, and how this conception, in turn, formed the ratified constitution of the government. Brownson's investigation takes flight in the Preamble to the written Constitution, where the truth of the unwritten order is revealed.

The written Constitution, in its Preamble, professes to be ordained by "We, the people of the United States." But, Brownson asked, "Who are this people? How are they constituted, or what is the mode and conditions of their political existence? Are they the people of the States severally?" Brownson answered negatively because "they call themselves the people of the United States." Accordingly, the Americans are not merely a national people. Why? Because they do not exist outside and independently of their organization in "the United States." As Brownson concluded: "The key term is United States, which encapsulates the political organization of the country. In it there are no sovereign people without States, and no States without Union."

Brownson's notion that constitutions are generated is derivative of Joseph de Maistre's traditionalist account of national origins. Brownson's understanding differs from de Maistre's by incorporating human action in politics to a much greater degree. The quintessential monarchist, de Maistre stressed almost exclusively the divine givenness of a political order. America's providential constitution is different in that it is republican, built by the emigration of the "commons," and this means that political self-government defines the order. Politics and public conversation over the content and direction of the republic are themselves constitutive of American constitutionalism.

For any regime, change begins with the "congenital constitution," while the "reason and free-will" of the nation and its citizens determine the shape of the change. The development that occurs needs to interact with the elements that compose a nation's founding, or it will eventually cease to exist. Accordingly, America's political pathways were largely set by its foundational democratic and religious emigration patterns, its definitive commitment to religious pluralism, its initial unity under the Crown and common law, and the fact that such unity required first the colonies and then the states to sustain it. An opposite and detrimental form of development would stress, Brownson noted, hierarchical national rule that swallows states and persons, a failure to practice the unique notion of religious pluralism in America, and an insistence on the mutability of the written Constitution because it has no enduring supports other than public opinion. This, however, raises the issue that Brownson's work is anticipating: how does the citizen understand the American political order in the fact of its dissolution in the Civil War and, now, in its centralizing movements of the twentieth and twenty-first centuries?

Brownson's overt teaching is that unlimited volitional activity in politics is unreal and is ultimately state suicide when it divorces a nation's destiny from its unwritten charter.[29] Perhaps the salient point is to recall reverence and gratitude for America's republican condition. The unwritten constitution, as such, lifts the political order higher than partisan strife or ideological manipulation. There is something given in a nation's founding that transcends self-interest and public opinion.[30] A country that thrives and prospers looks to its congenital constitution for its estimable wisdom that has formed its path and that it can prudently rely on to meet contemporary challenges. The experience of a people territorially constituted, and the reflection on their formative moments and documents, entails that their future must be shaped in keeping with the past that, after all, led to the present.

The unwritten constitution serves the written Constitution by ensuring that in addition to being a framework through which the people govern, it is also a power that governs them and sets limits on their actions. On this point, Brownson reasoned: "Fit your shoes to your feet. The law of the governmental constitution is in that of the nation. The constitution of the government must grow out of the constitution of the state, and accord with the genius, the character, the habits, customs, and wants of the people." That is, "You must take the state as it is, and develop your governmental constitution from it, and harmonize it with it."[31]

Brownson further noted the contingency and limitations of the human person in his or her actions; therefore, the act of constituting a just government must incorporate the limitations to human choice as revealed and required by the political society humans already find themselves occupying. People must prudently discern the best form of government, rather than create it from theoretical or abstract conceptions. It follows that just law and just government realize the values inherent in the preexisting order.[32] On this point, Brownson added that if considered apart, a political convention's ratification of a written document "is no constitution, for it is extrinsic to the nation, not inherent and living in it—is, at best, legislative instead of constitutive."[33]

Behind Brownson's writings on the unwritten constitution is the same concern that sparked his theorizing for territorial democracy. Authority in modern representative government needs rehabilitation. Democracy unbound and limited by no higher authority than either individual or collective will represents a mortal threat to constitutional government. The difficulty, for Brownson, was that the prevailing forms of individualism, or, alternatively, self-righteous humanitarians, that is, abolitionists, had left unmoored the responsible use of power on behalf of constitutional objectives. As conceived by most modern democratic theorists, popular sovereignty eviscerates moral guaranties against state abuse where the people in "their own native right and might" are held to be sovereign. The immediate problem is that when "the will of the people, however expressed, is the criterion of right and wrong, just and unjust, true and false, is infallible and impeccable, and no moral right can be pleaded against it," then reasonable deliberation of the proper ends for state action loses its raison d'être.[34] Written constitutions are thin, "for they emanate from the people, who can disregard them, if they choose, and alter or revoke them at will."[35] Thus Brownson set himself in opposition to "the naïve view of the philosophers and statesmen of the eighteenth century that the tyranny of the majority could be restrained by a written constitution."[36]

BROWNSON'S CONSTITUTION AND PROGRESSIVISM

Brownson argued that the Civil War was fought to preserve the sovereignty of the American Union, which, as previously outlined, depended on state unity for its existence. If the Civil War was a war to preserve territorial democracy, as Brownson believed, its two chief rivals had been "personal democracy," or Jeffersonian democracy, and humanitarian democracy. "Jeffersonian democracy," Brownson held, was based on "individual sovereignty expressed by politicians when they call the electoral people, half seriously, half mockingly, 'the sovereigns.'"[37] Its home was in the South, where liberty was built on the strength and nobility displayed by those citizens possessing aristocratic excellence. This conception of political liberty, wrong because it dismisses the natural dignity of man, Brownson noted, was defeated by the federal army.

Humanitarian democracy moved the purpose of government beyond the limits of territorial democracy and the providential constitution. More than this was its diminution of humans in favor of a vague equality and sameness. Frequently referring to abolitionists and humanitarian democrats in the same terms, Brownson defined their ideology as follows: "The American Abolitionist is so engrossed with the unity that he loses the solidarity of the race, . . . and fails to see anything legitimate and authoritative in geographical divisions or territorial circumscriptions."[38]

Implicit in Brownson's prophetic insight was the anthropological reduction of humans by the humanitarian democrats to an egalitarian being requiring that the restrictions of the nation-state and citizenship be eliminated in favor of a universal commitment to equality. The humanitarian democrats of the North "exaggerate the social element: to overlook the territorial basis of the state and to disregard the rights of individuals." The humanitarian program was made even more effective by their apparent rarefied love for man.

Embracing humanity in its supposed purest form, they appeared more Christian than their opponents. Brownson said, "The humanitarians are more dangerous in principle than the egoists, for they have the appearance of building on a broader and deeper foundation, of being more Christian, more philosophic, more generous and philanthropic."[39] The restrictions inherent in territorial democracy and the unwritten constitution, not to mention federalism and the separation of powers, were not only false but positively harmful to man, they taught. Humanity is superior to the limiting requirements of citizenship and virtue. Property itself, Brownson warned, will come under scrutiny, given its inherent unequal possession among individuals, and in time, talent, achievement, all forms of personal distinction, even physical attractiveness, will come under the suspicious eye of the humanitarians.

Brownson's prescient understanding of the impending dangers to constitutionalism posed by humanitarian democracy was confirmed in the age of progressivism. While the rising humanitarians of Brownson's day wanted to emancipate people from the circumscriptions of territory, property, local law, and the requirements of republican citizenship, the progressive movement joined many of these ideas to a body of political thought that directly contradicted the historical and philosophical basis of the Constitution. Progressivism emphasized a consolidationist federal power that must, of necessity, supplant the individual and civil society, and to a large measure the states, if social justice was to be achieved. The competition in markets and in politics, particularly at the state and federal congressional levels of government, should be suppressed in service of a higher commitment to national progress.

Central to this ideal was a practically unlimited executive power and a rationalized administrative state that would secure the assent of the people by its efficient operation by disinterested civil servants. These latter, in their training and spirit, would stand higher than their fellow Americans and bring order to the inefficiencies and corruptions of capitalism and representative government. Woodrow Wilson, Theodore Roosevelt, and Herbert Croly argued emphatically that national power and enlightened public service must achieve a new progress in political purpose.

During his 1912 presidential campaign, Woodrow Wilson remarked, "The makers of our Federal Constitution read Montesquieu with true scientific enthusiasm. They were scientists in their way—the best way of their age."[40] Wilson thereby stigmatized the Founders' "new science of politics" as outdated. Making politics timely is Wilson's hope for the unbound constitution that is more "accountable to Darwin, not to Newton." Progressivism sees in the twin pillars of federalism and separation of powers unnatural and unscientific political limitations that enfeeble the pursuit of the rightful objects of government. Contra Brownson's attempt to discover the history and reason of a nation's unwritten constitution, the essence of progressivism is "to progress, or to move beyond, the political principles of the American founding."[41] Historicism makes us look forward in unlimited hope, rather than to the past, in gratitude, for instruction.

Progressivism's formal inability to limit government power emerges from its commitment to a nationalist and liberationist program of social welfare whose quest involves the construction of an egalitarian society through the distributional reordering of an ever-increasing array of goods. The progressive commitment to a pseudo-plebiscitary democracy parallels its belief in the presidential office sacramentally incorporating the people—the autonomous mass—and embodying their pure force against the deliberative and small-minded legislative branch. More productive of national well-being, Theodore Roosevelt argues, is the "New Nationalism [that] regards the executive power as the steward of the public welfare."[42]

Similarly, Woodrow Wilson argued that the Constitution's manifest failure to adequately provide for the executive leading the country to successful political outcomes should be overcome. Accordingly, for Wilson, "there can be no mistaking the fact that we . . . look to the President as the unifying force in our complex system, the leader both of his party and of the nation. . . . He is the representative of no constituency, but of the whole people. When he speaks in his true character, he speaks for no special interest."[43] Wilson's reasoning progressed by rejecting the Constitution's limitations on executive power, because it prevents the executive from elevating "the whole people." "The President is at liberty, both in law and conscience, to be as big a man as he can be, he can overwhelm congress if he has the force of the nation behind him."

The executive's political power is directly tied to the hypostasized union of the people and their leader in pursuit of the national good. Lost in Wilson's conception, and that of the progressives, is the responsibility of the sovereign to the constitutionally established forms of political rule in America. Rather, the focus switches to a national purpose realized in substantive equality. Brownson's observation that the humanitarian sees only "humanity, superior to individuals, superior to states, governments, and laws, and holds that he may trample on them all or give them to the winds at the call of humanity," correlates well with the progressive commitment to equality of outcome as a fundamental norm of politics.

In his "New Nationalism" speech, Theodore Roosevelt argued that the "New Nationalism puts the national need before sectional or personal advantage. It is impatient of the utter confusion that results from local legislatures attempting to treat national issues as local issues. It is still more impatient of the impotence which springs from overdivision of governmental powers." Sovereignty in the progressive dispensation is the people defined as a national whole, excluding in large measure the theory and practice of representative government and decentralized rule. Brownson's location of sovereignty in the States United, his notion that the Union was built on the states and national power existing coevally as the foundation of the Constitution's order, is excluded by devotion to national power on behalf of the people. Indeed, progressivism's heart-rending appeals for "the people" provide strong confirmation for Brownson's concern that humanitarian democracy would dismiss the division of powers because of its limits to political will.

Direct democracy is yet another attempt to overcome the "overdivision of governmental powers" by uniting the people and directing them to a deeper social and political union. Herbert Croly argued that the electoral devices of direct democracy (referendum and recall) are merely instrumental, and therefore, insufficient for its true purpose. The goal is to move beyond government by representation and negative restraint. It follows that there should be no formal delegation of power to a body of representatives. The one thing needful, Croly asserted, is "some method of representation which will be efficient and responsible enough to carry out a social policy, but which does not imply the delegation of its own ultimate discretionary power to any body of men or body of law."[44] In fact, advocates of democracy must recreate the unity of the people that had been fractured by the separation of powers.

Implicit in Croly's argument is the political alienation the citizen experiences in representative government. As a result, the individual must be permitted to gather in, as it were, the powers of deliberation, decision, and judgment that the individual had alienated to the legislative, executive, and judicial branches of government. Representative government must become less, and the people must become more. Only in this way, Croly counseled, would the true purposes of democracy become possible. Croly's larger point is that the citizens of representative government never fully exercise political power because they never realize the complete victory of their ideas or of their coalition. Even in victory, the opposition soon regroups and unites with injured elements in the current regime, threatens the ruling government, moderates its power, and typically replaces it in the future. To become one with political power and purpose means removing the separation of powers because its formalization of the judicial, deliberative, and willful powers of government compromises self-government. Croly desired the intense concentration of power in the people with no "auxiliary precautions," as articulated by Publius.

Brownson's observation about abolitionists' obsession with humanity explains well the animating purposes of American progressives in their incredible but quite successful attempts to remake American constitutionalism. "So engrossed" is the abolitionist, "with the unity that he loses the solidarity of the race, which supposes the unity of race and multiplicity of individuals; and fails to see anything legitimate and authoritative in geographical divisions or territorial circumscriptions."[45] If territorial democracy grounds responsibility in the people, attached to the specific bounded political territory, progressivism places political responsibility in liberation of the person from the rigors and filters of representative government and its necessary pillars.

Significant indication of this is provided by President Franklin D. Roosevelt's magisterial "Commonwealth Club Address," where a commitment to the installation of new economic rights "calls for a re-appraisal of values." According to Roosevelt, nothing less than the ideological transformation of the very soul of the constitutional republic will suffice. Included in this war is the right of "Every man" to "a comfortable living." "Every man," Roosevelt intoned, has the right to the means of happiness, with traditional rights of property bending in service of it. Territorial democracy's fundamental tie to the bounds of a particular state and its political subdivisions is inept because the lord should not be the territorially defined people but "every man." The use of the concept "every man" figures later into Roosevelt's 1944 State of the Union address, which calls for the provisioning of each citizen with a bevy of economic entitlement and distributional goods, the so-called Second Bill of Rights.

Roosevelt's deeper argument, realized during his successive administrations, is that the restraints of law, which created open space for civil society and commerce to flourish, need to be inverted. As such, the commerce of the Commerce Clause is no longer an opening up of the American people for trade with one another, as argued by Madison and protected for a century and a half by federal court decisions, but is now brought into the service of the social democratic and egalitarian project. Moreover, Roosevelt's requirements for every person are revealed in the access provided by the state to the means to happiness. Our duties as citizens must no longer be shaped by jealously preserving the rights of civil society, arguing public issues according to the rights and structure of the Constitution, but by placing the public treasury at the service of every man. Of course, by current transfer payments standards, Roosevelt's claims seem moderate, but theoretically no limits can be placed on his call for relief of every man's estate. America's limitless welfare state, as William Voegeli observed, began in progressivism's open-ended arguments for relief, comfort, and happiness.[46]

THE MATERNALISTS

A significant policy strain, known as the "maternalists," stands out within the progressive New Deal, and is worthy of comment for how it situates families within a comprehensive governmental welfare structure. The great historian of the American family Allan Carlson, in his work on the maternalists, states that this "reactionary New Deal social project aimed at rebuilding American families, albeit on a distinct model: breadwinning men married to homemaking women in free-standing, child-rich homes. Every significant New Deal domestic program assumed and reinforced this family type." The reality confronting them was quite bleak, owing to the Depression and its negative impact on marriage and birthrates. The Hoover years saw marriage and birth rates decline by an alarming 20 percent. If economic collapse had caused such frightful numbers, the aim was not only to reverse these trends, but to oppose ideas that had emerged in American life before the downturn of 1929 and had contributed to family decline: the industrialization and institutionalization of family life through women entering the workplace and their children being farmed out to day care and other forms of institutional care.

One adversary the maternalists faced was industrial America, which attempted to pass a host of policies based on the assumption that the family was to resemble a large suitcase, sharing space and emotional ties, but largely functionless in a centralized, industrial mass economy. Carlson notes that William Ogburn of the University of Chicago argued that "the factory had [irreversibly] displaced the home," making these "merely 'parking places' for parents and children who spend their active hours elsewhere." Ogburn said that because working mothers were to become the norm, provision should be made to move children en masse into collective care situations. The progressive sociologist pointed toward policy that would guide "the individualization of members of the family." In other words, the family as a thick intermediating reality with distinct obligations and rights would largely become a thing of the past.

The immediate opponents of the maternalists, however, were the equity feminists, with whom they had sparred over the Equal Rights Amendment, which, Carlson noted, was proposed for ratification in 1923 by the National Woman's Party, a group surreptitiously funded by the National Association of Manufacturers. Thus what we might characterize as one part of contemporary feminism, equal rights in the workplace, was known to the maternalists, and they rejected them soundly.[47] Instead, they aimed to protect and nurture the home as a place where men were primary earners, women were mothers who raised children, and a web of policies and welfare subsidies and entitlements reinforced this ideal family structure.[48] To do this meant the "family wage" became a key aspect of the New Deal. Mary Anderson, head of the Department of Labor's Women's Bureau, insisted that "if the [male] provider for the family got sufficient wages. Then married women would not be obliged to go to work," and the problems that many working women faced would be greatly limited. On the consequences produced by these policies, Carlson reports that for the first time in over 100 years, four things happened simultaneously in America: the marriage rate rose; the average age of first-marriage fell (indeed, to record lows, age 20 for women and 22 for men); the divorce rate declined; and fertility soared in the celebrated American "baby boom." Buoyed by VA and FHA mortgage guarantees, young Americans poured into the new suburbs and revolutionized American home-ownership patterns, creating a true ownership society. Feminism went into eclipse. . . . The American homemaker reigned, alongside her family-wage-earning husband. Children seemed to be everywhere and the construction of new churches and schools proceeded at a record pace.[49]

The undoing of the family wage and the model of the male breadwinner and stay-at-home mother would come about two decades later, as the federal apparatus that supported it was pulled apart piece by piece by economic, social, and cultural changes that proved far more powerful than the social conservative philosophy upholding New Deal maternalism.

But this reversal of the New Deal attempt to promote a conservative, deeply relational economic and social vision of the family proves, ultimately, that centralized progressive policy making is actually quite brittle and finally unable to maintain control of a dynamic commercial society. The undermining of New Deal family policy was effected largely by women seeking opportunities outside the home, buoyed by an expanding economy and social changes. Their restriction to the home, reinforced by policies that Carlson documented, might be seen as a sweeping dismissal of this particular aspect of progressivism as a socially confining nightmare.

Before we accept this received wisdom, we might think about what maternalism was attempting to overcome with its policies. Insofar as the maternalist vision enshrined an economic, social, and cultural vision of the family in the national government, it was a progressive one that believed the federal government should actively shape this most vital of intermediary institutions. The maternalists resisted the notion that a largely independent civil society and market could provide much of what was needed for family life. This more independent notion would have had government play a supportive role through favorable tax treatment or other devices, but would have refrained from integrating the family within a full network of federal welfare, labor, and economic policies.

In hindsight, the maternalist policy approach was destined for comprehensive failure. In limiting economic and social mobility for women, by relegating them to the home, rather than letting solutions for working families emerge privately, the failures were magnified by the centralized plan that had been implemented. The robust wealth produced during this period meant that the home ceased being a center of production and instead became a center of consumption. It was unavoidable that women would desire to participate in various ways in this prosperity, as much of the work in the home was replaced by affordable labor-saving devices, rendering homemaking more aesthetic than anything else. In short, the maternalists could not hold everything in place in order for their largely positive family vision to reign. But if a certain norm of family life had been propped up and held in place by national policy, then the fall of that norm would be equally dramatic and equally open to reconfiguration by national policy tools. History, however, doesn't move in a single emancipatory direction. We might notice here the persistence of households with stay-at-home mothers, particularly in the upper middle class and the knowledge elite. Polling data on working families evinces a desire in these homes for at least one spouse to be able to work less to permit more attention to their children. The emergence of the rapidly expanding home-school phenomenon is itself a reaction to the secularist individualism in the government schools, a reaction that recenters the home as the linchpin of community organization for these families.

We might also say that if the views of William Ogburn and the National Association of Manufacturers were truly emblematic of an altogether different vision for the family, with Big Business recreating it for their purposes, then the maternalists' policies are understandable. Their goal was a defense of the American family as a place separate from the competitive forces in society. Perhaps, though, the better place to focus on is an intermediate position between Ogburn's individualist view of the family and the family existing only as provided by the federal government. Was there a middle position that could have supported the American family with only limited forms of government support? That is, one who says A must say B. If government and the welfare state have been brought to bear in defense of the family with powerful affirming consequences, then it can also be brought to bear on behalf of alternative social views, ones that enthrone a range of individualisms. Better still is to have avoided such power conundrums altogether. Thus, even in progressivism's seeming conservatism it still reveals the fundamental weaknesses of an approach that attempts to master humans' relational existence rather than merely attempting to support its flourishing.

BROWNSON'S CONSTITUTION

As we said earlier, the Brownsonian teaching of an unwritten constitution providing intelligible guidance to political action is cast aside by progressive ideology. Political fidelity now is to the people collectively exercising power in new historical epochs, whose economic and scientific possibilities have outgrown and replaced those that prevailed during the formation of the original constitution. Indeed, utilizing the techniques of a Hegelian political science, the express purpose is to unlock the Constitution so that it serves the development of man's ongoing social, political, and economic ascent.

To Brownson's concern that endless revision of a nation's constitution invites state suicide, the progressives argue that the American Constitution, like any na-tion's charter document, must be a living thing that serves the march of humanity in history. The disdain for actual politics in favor of administrative prowess and executive branch power that is "more equal" than the other branches also reveals progressivism's deep-seated commitment to a rationalized scientific political order. Such development leaves behind what Brownson articulated as the real questions of politics, articulated in debates guided by interest and justice, jealousy and loyalty, weakness and courage, and citizenship in, and for, a particular place and order. People "locked into conversation" about the public responsibilities of government become strangely irrelevant under progressivism, as an all-encompassing equality, unmoored from America's historical and philosophical founding, gives political authority its goal.

What is political argument in the progressive view of government? New areas of equality, new measures toward it. Eschewed is a commitment to rigorous conversa-tion about the other political goods that the regime should support. Returning to the Wilsonian definition of living constitutionalism, the true charter is the collec-tion of milestones reached in social and economic rights. One would say that these become the constitutional touchstones reached not by consent but through the historical moment, ratified by evolving consciousness.

Social Security, Medicare, Medicaid, and various other welfare programs are sub-sequently lifted above debate in the public square. To even argue for the retrench-ment of the size and scope of these programs is to question the constitutional order itself. Consequently, domestic politics becomes warlike, as policy questions became all-or-nothing victories and defeats with little prospect for deliberation and compro-mise. How else to explain a politics that attempts to eliminate alcohol usage ("Prohi-bition"), poverty (the "War on Poverty"), and illegal drug trafficking and usage (the "War on Drugs"); names a federal education program "No Child Left Behind"; or, most recently, chooses to engage Islamic terrorism by invoking an open-ended "War against Terror"?

Ultimately, the unbounded nature of progressive rule fails to shape politics ac-cording to man's limited and relational nature. Progressivism's universal goals of equality and liberation have emasculated, in large detail, republican government in favor of governance by agencies, departments, and judicial officials who are functionally removed from the accountability of self-governing citizens. Politics and citizenship have been redefined as a clientele relationship between the individual who needs services and the state that dispenses them to the citizen. Of course, the ultimate undoing of this experiment will most likely come from necessity: America is short on the bodies and money needed to continue the project or for that matter pave a new road to serfdom.

Progressivism therefore will ultimately fail in its attempt to remake completely the American constitutional order. America has not, in Brownson's formulation, committed "state suicide," but now has an attenuated commitment to its political foundations. The return to the former constitutional consensus is now covered by over a century's worth of legislation, court decisions, program-driven constituencies, and bureaucratic rule making that obscure the Constitution in its full stature. The principles of our order, however, remain discoverable and teachable as Brownson understood in the wake of the Civil War. However, he also teaches us that notions of territorial democracy and the unwritten constitution must be grasped if the goods of federalism and separation of powers are to be regained.

6 · A Question of Loyalty

This chapter will consider the current troubles that exist in our great European and American republics through a deep investigation of the foundations of liberalism. The hope is that we will come to better terms with both the greatness and the weakness of liberalism. Our guide will be Orestes Brownson's mature political thought, which shores up the living tradition of liberalism by recalling its origins in Christian anthropology and the classical natural law. This is liberalism's sure ground for articulating a responsible freedom in an objective moral order that informs political decision-making. Brownson's theological and philosophical liberalism provides a realist understanding of liberal constitutionalism. In doing so, Brownson authentically connects such political orders to our nature as relational human persons who participate in a perennial order of social, political, economic, and religious goods. First, let us consider the sources of the roiling arguments threatening stability in Western countries.

At the beginning of the twenty-first century the democratic nation-state, in the words of many significant commentators, was to become less, as multilateral and transnational institutions became more. Where Francis Fukuyama had announced the end of history and the triumph of liberal democracy over totalitarianism, many went him one better and proclaimed the likely attenuation of political sovereignty itself. Borders and governments of these states would most likely remain, in this view, but the real action was in the transition to the globalist institutional architecture that would oversee trade, human rights, migrations, environmental standards, among other universals. These institutions, in turn, would be guided by numerous nongovernmental organizations (NGOs) that would represent the interests and concerns of a globalized humanity.

The proliferating varieties of international law in treaties, conventions, agreements, and customary international law, transnationalists argue, should be incorporated into domestic legal codes.[1] In this way a globalized middle class would be constructed by first removing peoples from living embodiments of past cultures, religions, and political orders. Taking the place of these for the new middle class of global scale was commerce and its attendant order of human rights that would marginalize the reminders of difference or separations of peoples along those old lines of nationality, religion, culture, gender, and so on. Humanity would move in the direction of an ahistorical, apolitical, and largely unmediated existence.

This is the idealist case for what many global business and political elites desire for individuals in our century, and obviously the biggest parts of it have not come to fruition. We now see emerging a decisive contest between advocates of nation-state sovereignty and the globalists on issues of free trade, immigration, the need for borders, and democratic accountability. Brexit is obviously part of this movement, as is the rising of nationalist politics in Hungary, Poland, Czech Republic, and Austria, to name a few countries who are rather stoutly challenging European Union rule. In fact, with regard to Europe, where the contemporary place of the nation-state has diminished greatly, we no longer hear as stridently or as frequently as we once did calls from EU leadership for "More Europe" and ever closer integration. Receiving only thin allegiance from most Europeans, the EU has proven almost incapable of decisive political action in the various financial, economic, demographic, and political crises that engulf the continent. Why? Perhaps the main structural reason owes to what law professor Michael Greve refers to as the Hamiltonian Proposition, that is, the EU can act upon and bargain only with member governments and cannot enforce measures on individual citizens. There is no fiscal policy of the Union. This was, Greve notes, the great weakness of the Articles of Confederation, which was reduced to impotence, ultimately, by not being able to act upon citizens directly, but only upon the states, who had the ability to put off or restrict the center's influence over its actions. Can the current European Union achieve its own Hamiltonian Proposition? It seems most unlikely.

America has warded off efforts, for the most part, to hedge it in by subsuming its domestic laws to guidance by transnational institutions. Well-known examples include the political resistance by the Senate during the Clinton administration and the Bush administration's refusal to implement the Kyoto Protocol, which, significantly, would have subjected US industrial production to international greenhouse gas rules. America shows little willingness to join the International Criminal Court. Still, ongoing efforts to implement more regularized methods for entangling American laws on criminal, civil, gender, economic, labor, and other subject areas have been documented by different legal scholars favorably and unfavorably. Jeremy Rabkin notes that "Proponents of 'global governance' have looked to courts to play a leading role in stitching together a transnational network of legal standards, committing national legal systems to a kind of global constitutional structure—largely judge-made."[2] This view has been stridently advanced in the scholarship of Harold Koh and Anne-Marie Slaughter, both of whom served in President Obama's State Department during his first term.

If America's political sovereignty is intact, despite various scholarly fulminations, the place of the nation-state in contemporary Europe has diminished greatly. French political theorist Pierre Manent, one of the most capable defenders of the nation-state, observes that the weakening of state sovereignty in Europe has not been succeeded by an actual political body of a common Europe. Manent's sobering conclusion is that "at least in Europe, the nation is discredited and delegitimized, but no other form is emerging. What is more, the reigning opinion, practically the sole available opinion, has been hammering into us for 20 years the idea that the future belongs to a delocalized and globalized process of civilization and that we do not need a political form."[3]

Forging a common, universalist Europe, Manent observes, requires that the unbridled principle of consent entails spiritual aspirations, which must involve shedding a predemocratic past whose means and principles produced the nation and provided a political body that consent operated in and with. That is to say, before there was consent, there was the sovereign nation-state made by blood, monarchy, and religion. This framework that consent operated in must now be dispensed with in the quest for universal European purity. Thus consent as the essence of modern European transnationalism does not want a body, does not want limits. Institutionally, the European Union desires to achieve an unmediated common existence. But the construction of a new Europe, a grand continental political project, has never really taken place. We can locate its failure in its inability to articulate its own identity and what it is organized politically to accomplish. That is, "for this body to become real . . . to produce and circumscribe an awareness of itself, it must have height, length, depth, and dimensions–that is, limits."[4] The objective political condition of the European Union has been left vacuous, precisely because limits look arbitrary. Politically translated, Europe has chosen to give itself "a body without limits."[5] But such lofty aims, guided as they are by a future order of humanitarianism, lead to practical problems that it cannot manage. In short, Manent wonders, why would Turkey be kept from membership, or for that matter, why Sweden over Morocco, a nation much more familiar with the French. Who belongs to Europe? Europe's political class cannot answer this question.

If unbounded consent is the principle of this aspirational Europe, the principle slighted is what Manent refers to as "communion," or the shared place where people "concretize their universal humanity" by putting in common their actions and reasons.[6] Here, we see that politics, even for democracy, so nobly conceived as it is by late-modern Europeans, requires a certain territory inhabited by a certain population. For law with liberty to order a society, loyalty to a defined territory is a prerequisite. It is loyalty to a territory that is theirs by right, the place where citizens belong, that undergirds the possibility of political consent. The body provides the framework for the governor and governed to be accountable to one another—territory, borders, and a distinct population—hence borders and a distinction between us and them, bearing as citizens their reciprocal rights and duties. This nation permits citizens to put speeches and deeds in common in building and developing their future.

The earthquake of Brexit has bent the inevitability thesis of the European Union. The supreme meaning of the British electorate's invocation of Article 50 of the Lisbon Treaty, which permits a member EU country to leave the union, is that one of the most significant countries in that body believes its fortunes as a genuinely sovereign nation-state outweigh the benefits of its partial surrender of its sovereignty to the European Union.

Many in Europe and in America now see political things in their actual form. But what some might call the return of history is really the inescapable reality of politics and the related need for territorial borders and for what they represent, that is, the ability to exercise power on behalf of a first person plural where the burdens of belonging receive the benefit of collective projects.

We need to return then to the foundation of liberalism and its development of our constitutional republics to inquire if there are resources that we could employ to, at the least, manage our contretemps.

THE SOCIAL CONTRACT

Orestes Brownson articulated that the modern project of social contract theory explicated by Thomas Hobbes, John Locke, and Jean Jacques Rousseau failed to understand the complex relationship between the nature of the human person and political order. Within the strictures of social contract theory we observe a scientific deconstruction of humans in order to provide for a new foundation of political sovereignty. The division of humans' being into manageable parts for political order is first hypothetical, and then made actual through its ability to reshape humans' understanding of themselves from a relational, created being to an individual whose purposes are defined by self-interested willing and choosing.

This, for Brownson, was not an item of idle philosophical speculation. Social contract theory, he observes, was the most consistent teaching among the American Founders for explaining their act of independence and forging of the Constitution. America accepted the theory as modified by asserting that the individual delegates instead of surrendering his rights to civil society, was generally adopted by the American people in the last century, and is still the more prevalent theory with those among them who happen to have any theory or opinion on the subject. It is the political tradition of the country. The state, as defined by the elder Adams, is held to be a voluntary association of individuals. Individuals create civil society, and may uncreate it when they judge advisable.[7]

Brownson quotes the Declaration of Independence to emphasize his point regarding the pervasiveness of the social contract theory within the American political tradition. Government "derives its just powers from the consent of the governed,"[8] Brownson observes as the centerpiece of the American Constitution. His qualified opposition to this concept emerges from his deep reading of the Western political tradition that had articulated the naturalness of political authority, our inbuilt need for society, and, from Christian revelation, the human's relational capacity and end in God, which gives human life a purpose beyond government, forever circumscribing its powers. This is not to say that he rejected the principle of consent outright, but that it operated on a background of tradition and inheritance.

Brownson's trenchant criticism of social contract theory focuses on its artificiality cloaked in its purportedly authentic articulation of a liberal political and economic order for enlightened individuals. Both Thomas Hobbes and John Locke confronted a world of persons defined by relationships and memberships. The individual their political science purported to demonstrate was certainly not a thick reality, but one they were dedicated to bringing into being. Alexis de Tocqueville gives a hint of this with his statement that "individualism is a recent expression arising from a new idea." Hobbes's *Leviathan* proceeds by reducing the person to the body, with the body then being reduced to matter in motion. Thus politics has a rationalist basis of individuals in motion, moved by pride and fear, using reason to calculate pleasures and pains that they are endlessly trying to achieve or avoid.

Social contract theory's foundational premise that politics is an artificial enterprise is in fundamental opposition to the notion that politics is a natural phenomenon of rational beings. What has been set free from any authority, that is, the autonomous human, must now be brought back under control by the state. Social contract theory entails the use of a negative fear of death, as in Thomas Hobbes, or of self-interest in property rights, in John Locke's account, to compel individuals into the political order and to maintain it. This understanding of humans in a prepolitical, if not prehistorical, state of nature was surely meant to challenge the Hellenic-Jewish-Christian anthropology of humans and its implications for politics and law.

The purpose of the state of nature, Brownson argues is to remove humans from authority, civilization, and religion. In this manner, the individual stood as a sovereign agent of the political order. Russell Hittinger observes that this appeal is "to no authority other than what is first in the mind . . . under the authority of no pope, prince, or scripture."[9] Thus does authority emerge from individuals making agreements on "what is (or seems) self-evident" apart from any higher order of law or obligation, save for what the contracting individual wills. So, we have "a secular substitute for the story of Genesis. Never a pure science of morality, it was rather a merely useful one, designed for the political purpose of unseating the traditional doctrine of natural law."[10]

For Brownson, the social contract theorists actually presuppose what they explicitly deny. Persons who roam the state of nature and finally calculate that it is in favor of their self-interest to consent to a contract that will found a political society must first have had a notion of the social setting to begin with. That is, to achieve political society requires an awareness of humans' social condition and dependency on others.[11] But, how, Brownson wonders, on its own terms, could the state of nature ever provide such knowledge? "The advocates of the theory deceive themselves by transporting into their imaginary state of nature their views, habits, and capacities of the civilized man. . . . But these are no representatives of the primitive man in the alleged state of nature. These primitive men have no experience, no knowledge, no conception even of civilized life, or of any state superior to that in which they have thus far lived."[12]

The "savage," Brownson holds, possesses at least rudiments of civilization, morals, and laws, but this is not true for the primitive denizen of the state of nature: "How is it possible for your primitive man to pass, by his own unassisted efforts, from the alleged state of nature to that of civilization, of which he has no conception, and towards which no innate desire, no divine inspiration pushes him?"[13] Brownson's lengthy interrogation of an actual basis for the state-of-nature teaching uncovers its sheer fictional character, placing before us its determined attempt to teach individuals how to be sovereigns who construct a politics that will permit the mastery of nature. Brownson's thorough criticisms see through to the bottom of their project.

The mastery of nature that comes by way of the social contract's construction of a liberal political order is given voice by John Locke's *Second Treatise of Civil Government*. Locke holds that the individual possesses a transformative power of labor that is able to turn the nearly worthless matter of nature into products of trade and consumption that perpetually lift humans' material condition.

> Nor is it so strange, as perhaps before consideration it may appear, that the property of labour should be able to over-balance the community of land: for

it is labour indeed that puts the difference of value on every thing; and let
any one consider what the difference is between an acre of land planted with
tobacco or sugar, sown with wheat or barley, and an acre of the same land
lying in common, without any husbandry upon it, and he will find, that the
improvement of labour makes the far greater part of the value. I think it will be
but a very modest computation to say, that of the products of the earth useful
to the life of man nine tenths are the effects of labour: nay, if we will rightly
estimate things as they come to our use, and cast up the several expences about
them, what in them is purely owing to nature, and what to labour, we shall
find, that in most of them ninety-nine hundredths are wholly to be put on the
account of labour.[14]

Thus, labor is almost the sovereign element of human existence that makes the
human the effectual author of everything with value. According to Locke, humans
find themselves in a preexistent, God-created reality, but the means to improve and
transform humans' estate, that is, property in labor, are singularly within humans'
province. The ramifications of this posture toward nature evince the sovereign individual as a godlike figure in the creation of property.

A deeper truth seems to rest in Locke's state-of-nature teaching when we com-
bine with it his observation that human labor is 99 percent of the input to property creation. If nature is virtually worthless, giving us the material that we fashion
according to our desires and creative efforts, then the human task is to continually
rise above any limits that nature might impose on us. The individual is on a jour-
ney of labor and productivity to prove his or her transformative mastery of nature,
harnessing and using it for his or her benefit. There is little that nature can give us,
and God seems far removed, if not eclipsed, by humans' self-willed horizons. Also
missing, it seems, are the virtues of gratitude, humility, and piety. If production and
property all come down to individual effort, then to what do you exercise gratitude?

The political sphere of Locke's economy is constructed by consenting individuals living in the state of nature who realize their need to protect their bodies and
property rights. Brownson observes that humans also stand as god to this political
order. Liberty, ostensibly, is its end, but it is a liberty of necessity to labor on behalf
of one's material self-interest. Albeit the promise is that scarcity will become a thing
of the past and necessity will be softened. The salutary promise is that government
will not pose undue interference to one's labor and its fruits.

A question that Brownson never directly asks regards the limits on the powers
of a regime that is devoted to self-preservation. He does note that Locke's conception of self-interest leading individuals into political society misses humans in their
fullest desires for order and loyalty. What moves humans, Brownson observes, are

their "affections, passions, instincts, and habits." Therefore, "Interest itself is powerless before their indolence, prejudice, habits, and usages." Those who believe that
"enlightened self interest" can "found and sustain the state" stand ignorant (and
impotent) before the facts of human passion, obedience, and command. Having
never known "the habits of obedience and habits of command," to believe that
such individuals "in a state of nature, without culture, without science, without any
of the arts, even the most simple and necessary, are infinitely superior to the men
formed under the most advanced civilization, is folly."[15]

Lockean self-ownership, which serves as the basis of labor, property, and the
government that protects these rights, is the anthropology of the regime. One can
also ask if self-interest is a sufficient basis for free government. If we assert that
self-preservation is the end of the political society, then how does this political
order summon the courage and sacrifice of its citizens, which will be required from
time to time, given that such acts might result in loss of property, limb, or life? The
government's very purpose for existence would be negated. If the state is unable to
provide an affirmative account of these virtues, then where will the true loyalties of
its citizens lie?

Self-interest is a thin reed, Brownson argues, for a government to rest on. What
he does not explicitly state is that the narrow conception of property rights and
bodily safety that Locke ties it to may, as a result, paradoxically lead to an unbounded notion of self-interest driving an equally unbound government. If the
state fences in private property and the bodies of its citizens from violent death so
well, then why not direct it to protect its citizens from a host of other unpleasant
outcomes: hunger, sickness, inequality and the resultant physical and psychological
burdens of poverty, environmental degradation, ignorance? Deepening this interrogation, we might note how a reduction of law and politics to bodily security and
property rights might over time be co-opted by those who are opposed to the liberal
founding goals of such a political order. The new regime, ostensibly, still serves
these old rights, but it almost imperceptibly loses touch with its founding spirit as
it posits new political values that must be constitutionally enshrined. Harvey Mansfield explains this possibility.

In his essay "On the Majesty of the Law," Mansfield frames the problem of such
a reduced conception of law: "Modern political science had a cure. . . . It was to
lower the horizon of law so that it covered only minimum human necessities, as
for example bodily security." Such a view meant that "law would no longer claim
to comprehend the whole of human life, or what you do with your secure body.
The law would merely free the citizen to do what he pleased, having satisfied the
demands of his and others' security of body." The real lesson was for "the soul and
its requirements" that now "would no longer be part of the law."[16]

Of course, not including the "larger matters" of "the soul and its requirements" means that the law is tied to what is useful. But what is useful? In the quest for utility it becomes a system engaged in the work of "empirical political theory."[17] But what results from formally neglecting possibilities for excellence or greatness in human action? Mansfield names this excellence as "the necessities of the human soul" or the desires to seek justice, excellence, to choose beauty over dullness, "greatness rather than pettiness." Is it the case that in forgoing these elements one has a surer, more certain route to liberty? Again, Mansfield critiques our comfortable modern political conclusions with the notion that property rights and bodily security do not constitute a whole but only a pediment, a base level of political agreement. Therefore, the body and property can be protected, as was initially promised, but "a society could change its beliefs and practices without touching its laws on the minimum necessities. Having no whole, it could change without changing the whole; it could experiment harmlessly, risking only bloodless revolutions."[18]

We can plausibly argue that the course Mansfield describes has been the way of progressivism in America. True, progressives may have lessened constitutional protections for property rights and inaugurated our modern regulatory state, but it is hard to maintain that we don't operate under a market economy, more or less free, one that affords many opportunities to be productive and compensated. Yet we also know that our society has departed in crucial ways from the goals of our founding. Moreover, the spirit of these changes is the continual effort to make American constitutionalism a quest to realize egalitarianism as the definitive form of our republic. Progressivism in all of its forms continually repurposes our regime, while not really eliminating the liberal goal of security in body and property. Indeed, it promises to realize these goods by providing for their more equal distribution. In doing so, progressivism lays claim to an Americanism that is more robust than that of its opponents because, it argues, it gives support to the market by transferring its goods to those citizens who are unable to benefit from it. Progressives promise to enrich our base-level agreement by inserting universal equality into the contract, making our society a just one. In this way, they attend well to the modern political soul. Do their opponents?

Mansfield's argument, then, illuminates a central problem that classical liberal constitutionalism confronts: how its form of rights might be protected, even as the political order adopts a largely egalitarian posture focused on making outcomes equal in virtually every instance of human endeavor. In this environment, the liberal insistence on property rights and the rule of law and limited government can be defended only on grounds that they promote socially desirable, that is, equal, outcomes. Something more substantial than the mere catalogue of rights must be put forward to defend liberal constitutionalism. Those speaking on behalf of liberal order must find and develop a language of the modern political soul, a language worthy of the drama of preserving such a society.

The language defending such constitutionalism must then speak to us of our relational personhood, which goes deeper than and is far more complex than modern ideologies of individualism, collectivism, materialism, secularist thought, and so on. A relational person exists with multiple dimensions: political, social, economic, and religious. A relational being understands that it is in cooperation (and competition) with others for essential goods that its personhood develops. This means that we care deeply about the truth and about what is good in our pursuits and actions with others. Thus our status in unwritten constitutional law as inviolable persons is in the service of our freely responding to what we hold as the truth that we come to know with others. But relational persons also recognize that we come to the good in part through our particular experiences and choices as historical beings. This entails our status as contingent beings who cannot help but be shaped and formed by the choices of those who have come before us. We do not create ourselves ex nihilo, and this holds for the political orders we inhabit, built on a long accumulation of politics, culture, religion, migrations, mores, and conflicts.

Thinking constitutionally about the relational person stresses that law is geared toward protecting the being who flourishes in a range of contexts and whose freedom is undergirded by a healthy separation of law and society. Such freedom is diminished when law intrudes on behalf of ideological goals into the differentiated societies of economics, religion, family, and education and when constitutional republicanism is eroded by an insistence on rule making by administrative or judicial officials who usurp legislating from representative bodies and arrogate it to themselves. Relational personhood insists on representative political institutions, because they more fully accord with human nature and the need to give and debate reasons for laws and to accept compromises and accountability, as opposed to receiving edicts from officials insulated from accountability to the represented people.

Politics, in Brownson's formulation, demands reflection on the human person as a whole.[19] To understand political life as a whole means that it cannot be separated from an understanding "that incorporates all aspects of human being."[20]

Brownson's understanding of constitutional government is, therefore, worth reflecting upon at some length. An important theme of liberty emerges here in Brownson's notion of communion, which supports the political order while fundamentally circumscribing its powers. The social, political, and economic orders provide a medium for persons to develop the relational aspects of personhood in communion with others. Political society is a medium of humans' relational nature, enabling their flourishing by facilitating social relationships, but it is not the originator of humans nor of its own existence. The material and spiritual aspects of relational personhood preexist government, thus limiting government to the temporal sphere. A human's highest end is above government and, thus, cannot be supplied by government. It follows that a life lived in the service and hope for its highest end requires that the person be free in conscience and in associative religious existence. The church must be free as an institution to teach and aid its members in this process of communion. Accordingly, Brownson clearly accords to religious liberty the status of first freedom, or that freedom which is authorized by one's obligation in concert with others, to understand the highest truths of one's own being.

Plato and Aristotle had posited that the order of the polis, its political health, was directly tied to the order of the citizen's soul within the polis. The polis and the soul have a profound analogical relationship to one another. Their classical teaching goes beyond any notion we might have that citizens must have good habits, virtues even, for a free society to maintain itself, and is instead a forceful insistence on the citizen's soul being expressed by the polis. Brownson's political teaching disrupts this linkage by affirming a higher freedom that lifts citizens and bids them to rise above the polis to find the truth of their existence. As such, the citizen is also a person who cannot be defined by the regime because his or her ultimate purpose is outside its proper sphere.

Brownson argues that humans' natural condition as embodied beings who must labor to sustain themselves firmly entails that they cannot be deprived of their labor and property without injury being done to their existence. Such activity is inherently relational and is conducted most efficiently when a high degree of trust pervades the social order. Property, its creation, trade, and ownership is, Brownson maintains, integral to human flourishing, both for persons and for the larger social and political order of which they are members. Thus a free economy is a significant dimension of the person's development of relational personhood.

LIBERTY AND COMMUNION

The limitations on government that come from humans' need for communion with God and other humans also provide it with a stable foundation and purpose, Brownson reasons. In confronting the abstractions of the social-contract theorists with observations grounded in history and the development of political life within Western civilization, Brownson begins by approvingly quoting Cicero that "every man is born in society and remains there" and "that everyone born into society contracts by that fact certain obligations to society, and society certain obligations."[21] As a result, a person as a citizen, born into society, "owes certain duties to society for the protection and assistance it affords him."[22] Government is necessary to our flourishing as persons, so we must be loyal to it.

The problem of political loyalty in the regime created and guaranteed by social contract was that it struggled for recognition and justification in a regime built on autonomy. Here, Brownson's point is similar to Hegel's trenchant objections to social contractualism put forward in his *Philosophy of Right*. Hegel argues that social contract liberalism is based on an enduring subjectivity that threatens the overall political realm. Creating a constitutional state on the basis of autonomy is deeply insufficient for the enterprise of maintaining liberty. How, ultimately, was a regime to avoid unending mutation, if not dissolution, when its basis was the calculating self-interested individual?

Brownson argued that in the liberal constitutionalism of Locke the personal truly was the political. If the political order is built on individual will, then the guaranties of the political realm ultimately return to the self-interest of individuals in maintaining it. A government created and guaranteed by consenting autonomous individuals for the purpose of protecting property rights struggles to understand political life because it is closed to the enduring questions of loyalty, sacrifice, and the common good.

The great difficulty, Brownson observes, is that political sovereignty based on such a conception permits for almost infinite volatility. Individuals can always withdraw their consent if the political realm fails to secure their particular interests. Because the regime itself is built only to protect personal rights, there is no natural grounding for the political order that elevates it as an entity that is above private calculation. That's why, Brownson notes, the most consistent Lockeans in the American tradition were its Southerners. They had rebelled on principle against a unitary conception of government (or so they believed) on behalf of political and economic liberty: home rule and property in slaves. Antebellum Southern leaders prominently argued that political liberty was meant for those who were big enough to enforce it for their interests. Such an aristocratic conception meant that liberty was not really natural; that is, it was not related to inbuilt features of the human person but was earned by those capable of self-command and of living life on terms other than dependence as propertied slaves or wage slaves. It followed that the *public* square was the domain of great propertied interests. As such, when the planter class believed that their property interests were under direct threat, it followed that the political order, wholly generated by and serving the rights in property held by free persons, should be dissolved and created anew on principles more in line with said interests.

The argument that the states were the sole principals of the federal union ultimately invokes the Lockean teaching that the self-interest of individuals makes and unmakes the political realm. How then, Brownson concludes, if one accepts this principle for the origin of American government, could the order ever be stable?

The end result was an endless fragmenting and breaking apart when powerful interests believed that they were no longer served by the Union. If the foundation of political power in the federal union rests with the sovereign states, who merely delegated certain limited authority to the national government, then what creates and legitimates power for a seceded state? If it is the consenting individual, then why is he or she not likewise able to rescind consent and engage in further withdrawals at local levels of government: county, town, and so on when the particular state fails to secure his or her interests?

Brownson never did favor the South, of course, nor did he dismiss or diminish the Northern effort in the Civil War. He held that it was essential that the war be fought and won by the federal army. However, his reasons for victory differ from those he labeled the humanitarians, that is, the abolitionists, who had ideologically supported the defeat of the South. Brownson favored a Northern victory so that the country could be reunited on what he calls proper constitutional principles. Therefore, he did not support the abolitionist position of imposing a monolithic democratic understanding of government and society on the reunited country. The real work consisted in the country practicing with greater specificity the constitutional government the United States had been given. The political failures that had contributed to the onset of the Civil War emerged from the inability of most American statesmen, Mr. Lincoln included, to locate the historical and philosophical sources of American constitutionalism.

Focusing on Brownson's theory of American constitutionalism must begin by further developing his treatment of sovereignty and the criticisms he poses to the centrifugal tendencies of our Lockean Declaration of Independence.

SOVEREIGNTY: REAL AND IMAGINED

Rather than personal agency as the first mover of government, Brownson goes in a strikingly different direction. Sovereignty vests in the people collectively, who are rooted in a territory, bounded by law, and not in individuals. Brownson's teaching, reminiscent of scholastic political thought, articulates a natural law understanding that proclaims the equality of persons before one another because they have been created by God. At first glance this proclamation seems to align with the natural-right teaching in the second paragraph of the Declaration of Independence. Of course, Jefferson and the Second Continental Congress drew from this teaching that just government must be created by the consent of the governed. Brownson, however, is proposing an alternative account that he believes is more in keeping with the reality of things.

Humans' fundamental equality is based on the fact of their creation by a personal God. As such, this equality entails that there is no right of any person to govern another. All are equal. Therefore, the exercise of government power is a trust from God mediated through the people to the rulers. Brownson's attempted correction of the American founding settlement that government derives its just powers from the consent of the governed implies that consent itself merely specifies the terms of a formerly preexisting political relationship.[23] Consent does not create political society from the wills of citizens who may later withdraw their consent and dissolve or overthrow the government. Consent properly understood designates "those certain obligations to society" that "every one born into society contracts."[24] On this point, Willmoore Kendall stated that "we must in any case distinguish between contracts understood as *creating* society, justice, law, and principles of right and wrong, and contracts understood as merely *specifying* society, justice, law, and principles of right and wrong in particular situations."[25] Kendall's argument brings out Brownson's understanding of the natural law that society, justice, and right, and also peoples, preexist governments. Kendall states, "The monarch is in any case subject to *law*; and that men do not create law, but rather *discover* it, either through reason or *revelation*."[26]

Brownson notes that his argument for sovereignty has a venerable intellectual tradition: "St. Augustine, St. Gregory Magnus, St. Thomas, Bellarmine, Suarez, and the theologians generally, hold that princes derive their power from God through the people, or that the people, though not the source, are the medium of all political authority, and therefore rulers are accountable for the use they make of their power to both God and the people."[27] The primary difference in Brownson's account of political sovereignty from social contract theory is that he does not derive sovereignty from the individual or the people in mass. Contracting individuals do not create government. Rather, all sovereignty is in God and is shared with the people who form a political society whose powers are held in trust before God and humans.

Brownson's corrective teaching on sovereignty also finds support in Jacques Maritain's significant mid-twentieth-century work of political thought, *Man and the State*. There, Maritain argues that sovereignty as a term should be dismissed from political discourse because it is "poison." The term's poison, however, fully emerges only when it is removed from the metaphysical sphere and made the law of politics. Sovereignty means that an entity stands apart from and over a lesser entity that is ruled absolutely by it. Maritain argues that its proper truth is in the metaphysical realm, where "God, the separate Whole, is Sovereign over the created world."[28] When applied to the state, "it vitiates" the freedoms of citizens and civil society. Independence and power that is separately and transcendently supreme, must, when applied to the body politic, be "superimposed" onto it or "absorb" it into itself because it is superior to that body. If the state is "absolutely supreme" or a power that is unquestionable and must be obeyed, the consequence is that pluralism is jettisoned and "centralism" replaces it at the level of principle.[29]

A better understanding than sovereignty, Maritain argues, is that the body politic has a right to full autonomy with respect to its internal governance and a right to external autonomy with "respect to the other bodies politic."[30] Internal autonomy implies that the state and its agencies serve the body politic in their topmost position of power "through which the whole governs itself." This autonomy "derives from its nature as a perfect or self-sufficient society." Here, Maritain uses the term "natural" to mean that a self-sufficient society cannot be forcibly deprived of this right of self-rule.[31] Sovereignty is not the source of the right of internal or external autonomy, unless one reduces it to this limited notion of rule. The body politic's "supreme independence and power are only comparatively or relatively supreme (as proper to this given whole with respect to its parts, and also with respect to the unorganized community of the other wholes)." The real element in sovereignty, "the *absolutely* or *transcendently* supreme character of independence and power, which in genuine Sovereignty are supreme *separately* from, and *above*, the whole ruled by the Sovereign," is absent from Maritain's conception of political autonomy. Like Brownson, Maritain affirms "that no human agency has by virtue of its own nature a right to govern men. Any right to power, in political society, is possessed by a man or a human agency in so far as he or it is in the body politic a part at the service of the common good."[32]

We can draw Brownson's teaching out even more by contrasting it not just with modern social contract theory but also with the divine right of kings theory of political sovereignty. Here, power is full because it is transferred directly from God to the king. Monarchs may have responsibilities before God for their rule, but to their subjects, who have no participation in debating the terms of political rule, there is only a demand for obedience to the power that God has bestowed. There is something crude, if not paradoxically modern, in this account of political sovereignty because it states that the power of the state is received unmediated from God with no account of human agency, or lacks the notion that human persons have freedom and responsibility before God in the ordering of their affairs.

Mediation—social, political, or otherwise—entails that humans exercise freedom and responsibility in a manner that makes sense of who they are as creatures. The divine right of kings forgoes this risky and unpredictable process and places certainty and obedience in political rule as the highest principle. In doing so, it must dismiss the debate in the public forum that proposes, reasons with, persuades, and compromises with fellow citizens. People's accountability to each other for the political decisions that are made is vanishingly thin within this regime type.

The observation that government's ultimate origin is in God but mediated through the people who entrust political rule to a set of rulers has significant implications for Brownson's idea of the natural-law origin of government. Natural law is the "law by which God governs the whole moral creation."[33] "The law of nature is not the order or rule of the divine action in nature" but is law "ordained by the Author of nature, as its sovereign and supreme Lawgiver, and binds all of his creatures who are endowed with reason and free-will." Its natural content owes to its promulgation "through the reason common to all men."[34] Natural law is not from nature, contrary to what many ancient and modern natural-right theorists articulate as the basis of just government. For Brownson, the just principles that found a government are ultimately located in the reasonable will of God.

Brownson's political philosophy, republican and Christian, poses a challenge to the American founding. The immediate effect of Brownson's account of government is that humans' obedience to government is heightened because its ultimate ground is God and not a self-sufficing nature. Brownson's controversial argument is that the personal God of Christianity is a superior foundation for political authority because it is first a superior ground for human freedom. We might fill in the Founders' thought as follows: The person subjectively experiences self as a free, relational being who must wonder if there is an ultimate foundation for personhood. The God of Aristotle is a principle, a what, ontologically incapable of concern or love for humans. But how do you derive a who, or a person, from a what, or a God that is a principle? How do you account in convincing fashion for a human freedom that exists within a finely honed universe of living things that live by natural impetus, with our personal knowledge that we seem to be the singular choosing and languaged exception in this universe? A fact that is spectacularly evidenced in our anxiety, war making, depression, and confusion about what we should choose with our choices. The human, it seems, is the being "prone to trouble as the sparks fly upward."

Brownson's commitment to republican principles is beyond dispute, and, as I have noted, he fundamentally rejects all aristocratic claims for a natural inequality. In fact, Brownson's belief in equality guides his unique understanding of the Declaration of Independence. However, Ralph Hancock also observes that Brownson's understanding of the origin of government is bound to offend republican and American sensibilities, which hinge on the secular and consensual founding of political authority. Here, Brownson must tread carefully as a friendly critic of his nation's political settlement. Much of his language, however, continues to rub democratic sensibilities the wrong way. He declares that "to every true philosopher there is something divine in the state. . . . Society stands nearer to God, and participates more immediately of the Divine essence, and the state is a more lively image of God, than the individual."[35]

This initially shocking observation is juxtaposed in *The American Republic*, however, with a discussion of the near-monolithic character of political authority as articulated in nineteenth-century political theory. This latter formulation departed from social-contract thinking and its individualism by transferring political sovereignty to the collective people. This meant that government's origins had been implanted in the people as a collective sovereign and need only be announced by them in mass.

Political authority finds a sturdier repose in this theory of sovereignty, says Brownson, even though it still rests in fundamental error. He compares it with social contract theory and notes that in collective sovereignty government now "ceases to be a mere agency . . . and becomes authority, which is one and imperative." The recovery of authority occurs because "the people taken collectively are society, and society is a living organism, not a mere aggregation of individuals. It does not, of course, exist without individuals, but it is something more than individuals, and has rights not derived from them, and which are paramount to theirs."[36] There was truth "of a higher order" in this theory, Brownson thinks, insofar as it moves in the direction of the naturalness of political authority. However, collective sovereignty posed a profound political problem. It attempted to vindicate both the state and the individual by fusing them together. The paradox, Brownson reasons, is that this purported advance in politics was really a return to Greek and Roman political theory, which was unable to distinguish the person from the state. "The state with Greece and Rome was a living reality, and loyalty a religion."[37]

Christian revelation of a personal God, however, had forever shattered the undifferentiated character of "ancient republicanism" because there was now an authority beyond the state. "Individual freedom before the state," Brownson argues, comes from "the Christian religion, which asserts the dignity and worth of every human soul, the accountability to God of each man for himself, and lays it down as law for every one that God is to be obeyed rather than men."[38] Elsewhere, Brownson argues, "conscience is accountable to God alone, and civil government, if it had only a natural or human origin, could not bind it."[39] Prior to this genuine political revolution, "there were rights of the state and rights of the citizen, but no rights of man, held independently of society."[40]

The paradox, as we said, is that collective sovereignty reverts to an unlimited conception of state power on behalf of the people. Sovereignty had been merely transferred from the divine monarch to the people who were now "people-king," if not "people-God." Many "European democrats recognize in the earth, in heaven, or in hell, no power superior to the people," Brownson observes "and say not only people-king, but people-God. They say absolutely, without any qualification, the voice of the people is the voice of God, and make their will the supreme law, not only in politics, but in religion, philosophy, morals, science, and the arts."[41]

The real problem was that collective sovereignty was yet another abstraction of

modern political theory that was unable on its own terms to account for the formation and existence of the modern nation. Borders, jurisdiction, and the authority
of laws all had to be determined in the process of constituting a nation. The sovereign people, whoever they were and wherever they were, "does not solve, or furnish
any means of solving" so concrete and detailed a problem, necessary for political
society.[42] The ideological core of its argument was that it places power without in-
dicating who the people are and without defined limits. This permits a constantly
revisable and liberating political program to proceed against any constituted authority: civil, social, religious, and political.

Returning to Brownson's notion that collective sovereignty was a regression in
the Western understanding of both authority and liberty, he states that if the people
"in their own native right and might" are sovereign, then "the people are ultimate,
and free to do whatever they please." It "transfers to society the sovereignty which
that asserted for the individual, and asserts social despotism, or the absolutism of
the state. It asserts with sufficient energy public authority, or the right of the people
to govern; but it leaves no space for individual rights, which society must recognize,
respect, and protect."[43] Brownson's counter to this new form of state absolutism
was to return to older sources of Western political liberty and authority. In doing
so, Brownson recovers a doctrine of sovereignty that government and the citizenry
participate in but do not impose or exercise on one another. Sovereignty is in God
alone, not government, whether deriving it from the solitary individual or from the
collective people.

THE LOYALTY OF ORDERED LIBERTY

Loyalty is the crucial element to understand Brownson's attempt to rehabilitate
political authority and liberty and also to circumscribe both. Authority, Brownson argues, is the basis for liberty. As Ralph Hancock notes, we are not given an
account of virtue in Brownson's *American Republic*, but we are given a profound
understanding of political loyalty.[44] The effect is to emphasize in the place of virtue,
which typically builds on a natural anthropology, an understanding of loyalty that
is regime specific. Excellence in human action, in part, emerges from and is shaped
by the political order. Social and cultural institutions within which citizens interact
with one another are inevitably formed by the regime.

The significance of loyalty rests in the earlier discussion of the providential
constitution. Government is a given reality of authority for humans. Each nation,
Brownson says, realizes a divine idea within history. To quote Hancock, "It is because our purpose is beyond nature that we must recognize this purpose in history."[45] Brownson describes the providential constitution as "The constitution of

the state . . . [that] is, in its origin at least, providential, given by God himself, operating through historical events or natural causes."[46] Humans in their capacity as citizens must respond affirmatively to this political order, given its definitive, authoritative role.

This entails that "the right to govern and the duty to obey are correlatives, and the one cannot exist or be conceived without the other. Hence loyalty is not an amiable sentiment, but a duty, a moral virtue." Also correlative, Brownson says, are law and loyalty. Remember that properly constituted nations are founded by the natural law, law that comes from the will of God, the true sovereign. The ultimate, metaphysical character of law, mediated by government in the temporal sphere, is the source of Brownson's demanding notion of political loyalty. "In general, Loyalty is the highest, noblest, and most generous of human virtues, and is the human element of that sublime love or charity which the inspired Apostle tells us is the fulfillment of the law. It has in it the principle of devotion, of self-sacrifice, and is, of all human virtues, that which renders man the most Godlike."[47] In this light, "civic virtues are themselves religious virtues," because we belong to "a given people and a given state" with a purpose to fulfill in history.[48] If "government cannot exist without the efficacious presence of God any more than man himself," then those who build government on "atheistical principles" build something less than "a castle in the air," Brownson argues.[49] The modern political spirit articulated by Hobbes and Locke fights against loyalty and denies that the duties of citizens are natural or in accordance with the will of a providential creator. The modern political spirit wars ultimately against not monarchy or aristocracy, but loyalty.[50]

"Civil rulers," he states, hold "their authority from God through the people, are accountable for it both to Him and to them." Brownson's search is for responsibility in the use of power by first understanding its origins, which also provides for its limitations. In opposition to Brownson are the "abstract principles" of modern times, which erect a state on the will of the people or the consent of the individual. His argument is that the "guaranty against tyranny, oppression, or bad government" is through the elevation of "the civic virtues to the rank of religious virtues, and making loyalty a matter of conscience."[51] This returns us to Brownson's stated desire of reconciling liberty and authority. The church and the state are truly distinct entities but are not separated; "both are from God, and both work to the same end," to aid humans in their communion with God. Thus it is that "men serve God in serving the state," or "he who dies on the battle-field fighting for his country ranks with him who dies at the stake for his faith."

Civil liberty finds its sure grounding in the moral right of government to govern. The right to govern, Brownson informs, cannot be conflated with despotism. "The assertion of government as lying in the moral order, defines civil liberty, and reconciles it with authority." Only on this basis can we understand the nature of tyranny, which cannot be equated with being prevented from merely following one's subjective will. "Tyranny or oppression is not in being subjected to authority, but in being subjected to usurped authority—to a power that has no right to command, or that commands what exceeds its right or its authority." The reconciliation of authority and liberty and, for that matter, obedience and despotism, occurs through "the moral right of authority, which involves the moral duty of obedience, [and] presents, then, the ground on which liberty and authority may meet in peace and operate to the same end."[52]

Brownson's aim is the reconciliation of liberty and authority in light of his prior argument that political society has been diminished by social contract theory and collective sovereignty theory. Participation and communion of humans with God and one another in the secondary order of causality are preeminent for Brownson with regard to government. "Like man himself," government "participates of the divine being, and, derived from God through the people, it at the same time participates of human reason and will, thus reconciling authority with freedom, and stability with progress."[53]

Brownson's intention, however, contrary to first impression, is not to sacralize politics. Rather he thinks it necessary, from a full reflection of humans, to vest political authority in a body of law that citizens as human persons participate in, reason about, and are responsible to in their acts as rulers and ruled in a state. Of course, "The nation may, indeed, err or do wrong," but by operating "with the clear understanding that all power is of God, that the political sovereignty is vested in the people . . . that the civil rulers hold from God through them and are responsible to him through them, and justiciable by them, there is all the guaranty against abuse . . . that the nature of the case admits."[54]

The notion of republican government as an exercise of trust by its elected officials is also an attempt by Brownson to provide moral guaranties for the use of authority and power. Recognizing that the state has immense prestige and that it holds "conscience, moral sentiment, interest, habit, and the *vis inertia* of the mass," Brownson states that the individual holds constitutional checks, which are really only "moral guaranties" against the abuse of power. Such guaranties will prove insufficient, but Brownson weighs them against the absolutism of collective sovereignty and its principled refusal to place limits on the democratic people. No limits, moral guaranties or otherwise, are found "where the people are held to be sovereign in their own native right and might, organized or unorganized, inside or outside of the constitution; . . . if so, the will of the people however expressed, is the criterion of right and wrong, just and unjust, true and false, is infallible and impeccable, and no moral right can ever be pleaded against it."[55]

Brownson also provides a powerful rebuke to the democratic humanitarians of his day and the transnational progressive elite of our own, who lead multinational corporations or aim for multinational governance and believe that actual nation-state government can and should be dispensed with. This salutary dismissal is owing to its diminished utility in a globalizing world, or in a related sense, it impedes the evolutionary growth of mankind by focusing our concerns on parochial national interests. Ever the skunk at the humanitarian garden party, Brownson proclaims that civic virtues, local devotions, and attachments reveal humans to themselves, allowing them to realize their freedom in concrete manifestations that build their love and loyalty to the social and political order of their birth. In fact, the failure to understand and practice a type of patriotism, pride in the laws of one's country, and gratitude for its continuity with its history and tradition might easily lead to confusing and slumbering actions abroad by those countries. The failure of a people to understand itself, to know what they are about as a political society, is the beginning of a nation's aimless path through history, slow-walking it to a collective suicide.

7 · Constitutional Thomism

Orestes Brownson begins with the proposition that to understand the American republic, the written Constitution has to be viewed in the context of the providential constitution. The providential constitution is what lies behind the written constitution that couldn't have emerged out of nothing, but is formed out of the political, cultural, philosophical, and religious elements that are given to statesmen and guide what they can do. These givens are achievements that make the written constitution and its political order possible.[1] And the givens are opportunities for development as well and do not form an unalterable straitjacket on a constituted people. The thought is that the written Constitution—especially read in light of the Declaration of Independence—might suggest a kind of political atheism. The sovereign will of individuals is unlimited by the will of God or even political loyalty, and we are bound together only contractually. If government is a contract signed out of personal convenience—even if that means making my natural rights more secure—then the contract can be broken at will. And that kind of "secessionism" undermines the entire web of relationships that constitutes the life of a whole human person.

But our Framers built as statesmen, not as theorists, and so on the basis of what they've been provided from the whole of Western thought, including Greek philosophy and politics and Christian theology. Even the Lockeanism of the Framers—the commitment to social contract thought—must be understood not as a rebellion against Christianity, but, at least in part, as part of their Christian inheritance. Not only that: in Brownson's eyes, the American republic received an indispensable aristocratic supplement from the experience of the Southerners, who excelled in personal greatness in comparison to the Puritan North, even at the expense of justice.[2] Our purpose here is to examine, elevate, and partly displace the view of America as a "natural rights republic" in the direction of a constitutional Thomism that can be firmly established on our country's providential constitution.

THE NATURAL RIGHTS REPUBLIC

Our country is often defended by classical liberals and libertarians, such as Randy Barnett and Michael Zuckert, as "the natural rights republic," as the country most securely rooted in the secular, universalistic, and individualistic principles of John Locke.[3] In Zuckert's most astute interpretation of our Declaration of Independence, what's most important, politically, is that all citizens hold the truth of the Declaration to be self-evident, but they need not grasp the true foundation of its "cognitive or theoretical status." That means that "the highest kind of statesmanship is the cultivation of the necessary right opinion," and "right opinion"—as opposed to genuinely, self-evidently true opinion—is the necessary foundation of our political life.[4]

In Zuckert's eyes, model American Christian preachers are the "Lockean Puritans" of the eighteenth century, who transformed the puritanical view of Christianity to harmonize it with natural rights political doctrine—political life oriented around the self-interested individual and not republican or Christian idealism. He recommends those preachers to us, in effect, for following the example of Locke himself, for reconfiguring biblical doctrine in light of what we can know about ourselves through unassisted reason. They taught people to believe in the revolutionary doctrine of natural rights as flowing from what they believe to be true about the will of the Creator.[5]

When America works best, Zuckert claims, our devotion to our natural rights republic receives "salutary aid from deep-flowing religious impulses." Salutary, of course, is to be distinguished from true. Religious impulses and their theological articulation add nothing real to what we can know about who we are. America works best, in other words, when religious and secular, individualistic impulses and arguments work "tensionlessly" or don't compromise our basically secular devotion. When they are in "disharmony and tension," as they often seem to be today, America becomes disoriented and needlessly contentious.[6]

Christianity, so understood, ought to be our civil theology—or a way of getting God or the gods behind our "regime." Locke "affirms Christianity as a civil religion in Varro's sense . . . [and] attempts to reinterpret it as to be more civil."[7] But Locke, Zuckert observes, never really solved the problem that natural rights civil theology is somewhat of an oxymoron. His civil religion is in the service of "transforming the dominant understanding held by men of the human situation in the world for the sake of improving that situation physically, politically, and morally."[8] That means, among other things, leading them to think of themselves less as either citizens or creatures—as grateful to God or country or as part of wholes beyond themselves.

Locke, Zuckert shows us, both presented "a powerful case for the necessity of civil religion" in the modern world and "contributed to creating a climate of opinion in which civil religion . . . is most difficult, if not impossible, to maintain."⁹ So we might criticize Locke for undermining even reformed Christianity's credibility by trying to civilize it in a context in which civil religion has been rendered incredible and degrading by Christianity. The "Lockean Puritans," from Tocqueville's view, were actually on the way to becoming transcendentalist believers in the natural religion of pantheism—a religion with no place for either divine or human individuality—for neither Creator nor creature, not to mention citizen or statesman.¹⁰

It's in defense of such an ambiguously Lockean transformation of Christianity that Zuckert dissents from Tocqueville's view that we Americans owe anything fundamental or deeply true to the Puritans. When he quotes what Tocqueville says about the Puritans with approval, it's the part when the Frenchman condemns their "ridiculous and tyrannical" laws. That just and severe criticism, in Zuckert's view, occurs in the midst of Tocqueville's abundant and unjustified praise of their political project on behalf of equality and liberty. Zuckert doesn't think Tocqueville appreciates properly that Puritan legislative tyranny flowed not from weaknesses in human nature but from "the specific character of Puritan principles and aspirations."¹¹

Zuckert's bottom line here is that the Puritans had a "presumption against liberty," and that religious or Christian presumption explains why "their legislation . . . has earned the censure of mankind as Puritanical."¹² For Zuckert, the individualistic liberal, there's nothing positive about being a Puritan. So his polemical intention is to read anything distinctively Puritan from our authoritative political tradition, from the core beliefs that identify us all as Americans. But is it really true that true Christianity is characterized by a presumption against liberty?

LOCKE AND THE GOD OF THE BIBLE

Zuckert presents Thomas Pangle's argument that our natural rights republic is in discontinuity with anything deeply Christian as more extreme or less nuanced than his own—and not, of course, without reason. But even Pangle admits, Zuckert reports, that the "belief in the sanctity of all human beings as such" that somehow grounds natural rights philosophy "would seem to be a legacy of the biblical social and political tradition rather than the classical one."¹³ That would seem to mean, from Pangle's view, that the insight into the unique irreplaceability of every human person is biblical—and so not reasonable. For Pangle far more than Zuckert, it would be historicism to believe that anything that essential or foundational and reasonable could not have been known to Plato (and Aristotle).

Now authentic Lockeans, such as Zuckert, sometimes emphasize how much Locke actually discovered—or at least thought he discovered—that Plato and Aristotle didn't know. And Locke, Zuckert properly reminds us, holds that "the Bible in fact depicts the fundamentals of the human experience far better and to a far higher degree than any other premodern awareness"—including, of course, that of premodern or "pre-Cartesian" philosophy.[14]

Locke denies, in fact, that any particular being can be reduced to or defined as essentially a member of the species. And we're the beings with enough self-consciousness or self-ownership to have a relatively stable and clear sense of who we are as particular, vulnerable, mortal (or embodied) beings. By thinking through all that is implied in self-ownership, Locke's best students, in particular Zuckert and Lee Ward, show why Locke believed "he had discovered a new mental continent, a hitherto unexamined realm of subjectivity and interiority."[15] He had relocated being itself in the particular experiences of personal identity.

Locke, like the Bible, "sees man's differentia in terms of freedom." And at least it's unclear whether Descartes and Locke could have grasped that true insight about the true inwardness of each of us without knowledge of the Bible. According to Locke, it's freely creating man who created the freely creating God—or the opposite of what the Bible tells us. But the Bible—unlike other premodern texts—still shows who God should be if truly created in humans' image. Humans, alone among the animals, are partly and indefinitely free from nature.[16] To say otherwise, Zuckert says in criticism of the Darwinian Larry Arnhart, is to succumb to "biologism."[17]

Locke sides with the Christians against the classical thinkers and the Darwinians concerning free personal identity. From that personal view, even philosophy is not learning how to die; it's not forgetting about one's personal needs or personal contingency and mortality. For Locke, like the Christians, we might be able to say that our deepest longings are in some sense personal, for a sort of happiness compatible with the real experiences of personal identity. That's surely why Locke believed that his discovery of the "realm of subjectivity and interiority . . . surpassed in significance the discoveries" of the explorers, scientists, and so forth "in the terrestrial realm."[18] That would mean Locke is a post-Christian thinker, not an anti-Christian one. He absorbed much of what is true about the Christian criticism of classical philosophy and politics.

LOCKE AS A POST-CHRISTIAN THINKER

Before Locke, according to Jefferson, there was tyrannical "monkish ignorance and superstition," and the despotic world of Christendom was a decline from the world of the classical Greeks and Romans. For a helpfully extreme corrective to that misleading view, we can turn to David Bentley Hart's *Atheistic Delusions* (2009). Hart describes a pre-Christian world that was cruel and capricious—reminding us forcefully of the torture and murder that ancient paganism tolerated as a matter of course, precisely because it regarded particular persons as unreal. The impersonal truth was best seen by the philosopher who became dead to himself, who resigned himself to the ephemeral insignificance of his particular existence. Christianity was, in a way, the slave revolt Nietzsche described: a cosmic rebellion against the enslavement of each of us to natural and political necessity. Christ, the Christians claimed, freed us from the limitations of our merely biological natures through his perfect reconciliation of God's nature and human's nature. He was, the Nicene fathers concluded, fully God and fully human, and his redemption was to divinize every person.

It is barely too strong to say that, for Hart, Christ transformed each of us from being nobody to being somebody, a somebody of infinite value. None of us is destined to be a slave, and death has been overcome. We are no longer defined by our merely biological natures, because our nature is now to be both human and divine. From one view, there is no empirical evidence that death has been overcome for each particular human being. From another, there's abundant evidence in the unprecedented virtue flowing from the unconditional love present among the early Christians and that virtue's indirect, historical transformation of the broader social and political world. The change in who we are is the result of a deepened human inwardness or self-consciousness: Christ made each of us irreducibly deeper by infusing divinity in every part of our natures. In our loving relationships with other persons and the personal God, we don't surrender what we know about our own irreducible personal identity.

Many of the features of the personal liberation praised by Lockeans, Hart even claims, came into the world in Christian communities. Even the Stoics didn't approach the Christians in their indifference to a person's social status. The Christians were the first to be completely opposed to slavery; the first for raising women to equality in marriage and elsewhere; the first for faithfulness in monogamous marriage; the first for the egalitarian brotherhood of all humans. For the Christians, the community of personal love wasn't some otherworldly hope. Rather, that community was formed by obligations given to divinized beings here and now. Our divinization through Christ includes what is called life after death, but we can live lovingly liberated from death even before we die.

THE ROOTS OF WESTERN POLITICAL FREEDOM

So, as St. Augustine made most clear, personal liberation is most of all about a theological revolution. Christianity freed the person from the enslavement of civil theology (which understood each human being to be most fundamentally a citizen or merely part of a city) and the enslavement of natural theology (which understood each human being to be merely a part of nature fundamentally indifferent to personal existence). Christianity freed us from the lies that we're meant to be either "city fodder" or, as we say today, "species fodder." It has also protected us—witness the anticommunist dissidents Solzhenitsyn and Havel—from the more recent lie that we're "history fodder." Only the personal theology of the Christians can account for the longings of the whole human person, the free, relational, and truthful being who preserves his or her personal identity in loving relationship with a personal God.

There's nothing in Augustine that corresponds to the Socratic image of the cave. The wise philosopher-king—in touch with the whole truth about nature—constructs civil theological images with which he perfectly controls the lives of the citizens for whom he has taken responsibility. The exceedingly rare perfect liberation of the philosopher becomes the condition of the "cave" (or the civil-theological fantasy in which most people necessarily live) being his creation. The free mind—unencumbered, apparently, by any bodily or other limitations—takes charge of the world that citizens mistake for freedom. That mind, of course, views ruling as an unpleasant necessity that has nothing to do with any care or concern—much less love—for fellow citizens or fellow persons.

Augustine's good, empirical news about personal liberation begins with the thought that the cave—the city or regime—itself is a vain philosophic illusion, and personal, relational (and so not autonomous) freedom is equally the destiny of us all under a personal, loving God. There's not a word in Augustine's truthful teaching that suggests that God is personally concerned with the fate of any particular city, but God is equally concerned with the fate of every particular person. The truth about God is accessible to each of us, and it is so morally elevating that it can be conveyed without noble lies.

For Locke, God remains a free person with an irreducible personal identity, and so does each of us. This means that Locke sides with the Christians against the classical claims of civil and natural theology. The Lockean "law of nature" is all about persons—being both rational and industrious—employing their freedom to escape from their miserable natural condition and to remake the world in the image of their freedom. Nature's indifference to persons is to be inventively displaced by free assertions of personal significance. As a person, for Locke, I don't exist for my species or my country (as a citizen), I exist for myself. My body is my own property—to be employed for my own security and convenience. The Lockean radicalizes—on a Christian foundation—the claim for personal freedom. I'm not a part of some whole greater than myself. I'm not bound to others—including God—through love.

God doesn't simply disappear in Locke because the mystery of the human person—irreducibly self-conscious and relentlessly particular personal identity—

remains. So there's some connection, at least, between Locke and Pascal on the mysterious hiddenness of the Being who is the source of our self-consciousness, our freedom, and our uneasiness or restlessness in his absence. For all practical purposes, Locke teaches, that mysterious God is dead to us, and the good and bad news is that he left us free persons on our own. He encouraged us, in that way, to think of ourselves as on the way to replacing him.

Lockeans, from this view, are a kind of post-Christian who believe, without any belief in personal salvation, that they were born to be free. They believe that all persons are equally not nothing and are equally not completely determined by the impersonal laws of nature. But the Lockean lacks any loving sense of a God who has freed us from death and necessity for love. So our freedom is to be used to win, by our own efforts, what the Christian God had promised to provide. Each of us is not nobody, but it's up to each of us to make self into somebody, to create value and sustainability for our personal identity.

We are not, by nature, divine beings: there's no evidence for that without faith. But perhaps we can employ our freedom to make ourselves more and more divine— freer from the impersonal limits of our biological natures. The modern Lockean thought is that faith in a personal Creator can be replaced by a more reasonable faith in the unprecedented historical future, faith in what I can do for myself in a world basically indifferent to my personal being. Locke and Lockeans, as Zuckert shows, tell tale after tale of our self-won or inventive, historical liberation from nature.[19] Generally speaking, Lockean America is distinguished by a "progressive attitude toward politics and society," one "open to indefinite improvement" and regarding all limits to what we can do for ourselves as provisional.[20] Those who contrast our Founders (good) with the progressives (evil), in this view, are to some extent piously fooling themselves. Progressivism is actually a dialectical working out of our Lockean adherence to technological perfection of human beings. Its twist is that it is government who should become the primary agent in this quest.

But the Lockean stands with the Christians against the later, or more rigorously, historical—and so now opposed to individualistic or personal faith. Free persons, for both the Lockean and the Christian, can't be reduced to merely part of history or anything else, and so my rights today can't be sacrificed for a better tomorrow for others. The future must be constructed with me—my personal identity—in mind. The Christians and Lockeans readily allied against the Marxists by being clear that not anything might be done in the name of progress, by remaining focused on what's best for the particular persons around these days. In that sense, the Lockeans and the Christians are united against the progressive privileging of History (with a capital H) over the unique and irreplaceable person.

CAN LOCKE DISPENSE WITH ONLY PART OF CHRISTIAN TRUTH?

Still, without some Christian, or loving, or relational help, modern thought, Tocqueville explains, morphs in the direction of individualistic indifference. I can recognize your equal freedom, but that recognition is, if anything, compromised by my loving or paternalistic care for you. The Lockean or "past-tense" God doesn't care about or even know each of us in our personal identity, and each of us imitates him when it comes to other persons in pursuit of his or her personal freedom.[21] It's true that we know that each of us is equally not nothing, or equally distinguished from everything else that exists. We also know that personal identity—or avoiding not being—is somehow the bottom line of each of our existences.

Tocqueville was wrong to suggest that indifference could ever come to mean, in a Lockean world, indifference to me, or my surrender of concern for my own, singular future.[22] Lockeanism will never become nihilism because I will always know that I'm not nothing. Individualism means my surrendering any concern for you, based on the judgment that both love and hate are more trouble than they're worth, and getting my mind off what's really important in life.[23] From the beginning, as Sara Henary explains, the Lockean conception of self-ownership can't be expected to generate "an active, attentive concern for the other." So Henary concludes that even a Lockean defense of equality can't dispense with "a willingness to argue publicly from specifically Christian premises."[24] And a true defense of equality might defend those premises as being in some fundamental sense true.

Fortunately, with the help of Zuckert and Ward, we can see that Locke gives more independence to religion and the genuinely Christian point of view than it first appears. Locke holds that it's Christianity that discredited the idea of civil theology. He observes that "prior to Christianity, political control of religion was the natural human condition." It was "the ancient pagans" who reduced religion to "simply the encouragement of superstition and empty rituals by priests who served their political masters by employing religion to serve civil law."[25] Locke stands with the Christians against politicized superstition and ritual.

Locke holds that "it is only with the coming of Christ that the principle of separating of religion and politics first appeared."[26] It's only with the Incarnation of Christ, as Saint Augustine claimed, that popular religion can become something other than civil or political theology—or an instrument of the "cave" or "regime."[27] It is, similarly, only with the coming of Christianity that religion also can't be reduced to natural theology—or a way of expressing the impersonal truth about nature discovered by the philosophers. Because the human difference is freedom, religion that does justice to who each of us is as a person must understand each of us as more than merely or even essentially a citizen or part of nature. Religion must do justice to what each of us can know about his or her irreducible interiority or personal identity. Religion must be in some sense personal.

Remi Brague, in *The Law of God*, explains better than anyone why the separation of church and state—or the separation of human law and divine law—necessarily depends on this Christian view of personal freedom.[28] If, according to the pre-Christian or classical philosophers, the truth about the impersonal logos of nature is equivalent to divinity truthfully understood, then human beings need illusions about providential divinity to sustain their illusions about their own freedom or personal significance. The task of the political philosopher is to protect the tension between the truth about impersonal divine "law" and the moral or political dogmas that support human law. That means that civil theology is indispensable but merely salutary, and true or natural religion is philosophical liberation from personal concerns. That understanding of civil rheology, to repeat, couldn't be Lockean.

Insofar as our Darwinians share that view of the impersonal, species-oriented truth about the logos of nature, then religion still makes sense as a way of supporting those same beneficial communal illusions. Neither Aristotelians nor Darwinians can, however, make sense of the freedom from political/divine law that we all believe human beings to possess. Freedom from political/divine law must be for personal/divine law for beings who are in some sense created in the image of a personal God. In that way, limited government must be for both personal freedom and freedom of the church.[29]

In light of this, Locke can easily claim that "the notion of a national church is problematic both theologically and logically."[30] Some Christians, of course, have been for using the state to encourage true religion, but in that case the state is subordinate to the church. It's virtuous for Saint Augustine's Christian emperor to use his power to spread true religion, but that's in an idealized context where all political power is ministerial to virtue freed up from political utility.[31]

That's not to say, of course, that the nation's political life does not have its own goals, which, for the Augustinian Christian, are peace and religious liberty. Christians are called to do their duty to their country—without the solace of sharing in its civil religious illusions. Augustinian Christians, deeply unmoved by even the glory that was Rome, are most deeply aliens or pilgrims in their political home. The Augustinians and the Lockeans agree that we are not naturally political beings (Thomists would affirm politics as natural) and that government is instituted in response to the neediness of free beings; it is one of the merely necessary consequences of sinful—or passionately self-interested and domineering—personal identity.

That's why at least the Augustinian Christian agrees with the Lockean that political goals—even political expansion—should be pursued through contract and consent and without war—which is good only for glory—whenever possible. And the Christians and the Lockeans agree that differences in forms of government are to be evaluated according to a standard of personal liberty that's not, most deeply, political liberty. The form of government, in that sense, is not to be confused with some Platonic "regime." The personal Christian alien—in apolitical, cosmopolitan detachment—is not so different from the Lockean person.

No Christian, Locke is right to say, sounds properly Christian when speaking of "religion established by law."[32] Locke's attack on using political coercion to enforce religious belief and practice is aimed at both pagan and premodern Christian religious practice. Both, we might say, can be criticized as a violation of natural rights and genuinely biblical personal insight. Both Locke and true Christians are about articulating a universal ethics available to all free persons, and both agree that to be free—and moral—is not to be fundamentally political or deeply or merely philosophical.[33]

Ward emphasizes that "Locke's toleration argument presupposes that the churches are institutions with a vital role to play in a free society." He actually mentions two roles. The churches will provide "a support for the moral foundation of a free society," and they will be "a salutary counter-weight to the potentially overweening claims of the state and political sovereignty." In neither case, of course, will the role of the church be civil theological. In order to be a "salutary counterweight," the church has to be an organized body of thought and action with the freedom to teach what it thinks best about who we are and what we're supposed to do, and on that score "Locke insists that churches enjoy complete autonomy."[34]

The solitary person can't resist the power of the state—either in thought or in action—alone. Inwardness or subjectivity, to be real and genuinely democratic, can't be too lonely. That means, of course, that Locke doesn't actually share the anti-ecclesiasticism of Madison's "Memorial and Remonstrance," which is very extreme in portraying one's conscientious right to discovering one's duty to one's creator as a solitary or lonely activity. The true difference between the revolutionary American and French Constitutions, John Courtney Murray points out, is that our freedom for the exercise of religion is, in part, freedom of the church, an indispensable condition of the conscientious freedom of the more-than-political person.[35] That's why Ward says that the "church is meant to assist the cause of freedom by serving as an independent source of moral authority to which the individual and larger community can refer on matters of conflicting principles."[36] It's the revolutionary French who, by denying the autonomy of the churches, made democracy "totalitarian" and religion merely civil-theological.

"In the absence of the right of conscience," Ward goes on, "it is certainly possible to imagine a society directed to the Lockean goals of promoting economic industry and productivity that would allow such a massive system of coercion as to be unrecognizably liberal."[37] These days, we obviously don't have a massive system of political coercion, but times are still particularly bad for secure personal identity or the effective exercise of the right of conscience. Persons have a harder time than ever finding a secure point of view to resist impersonal public opinion or fashionable conformity and the reductionism of popularized science. We have a hard time defending genuine autonomy from the demands of productivity. We also see, of course, that it's the religiously observant—or socially and morally "churched"— Americans who most readily resist fashionable conformism, as well as the aimless restlessness of an undirected pursuit of happiness.[38]

We can conclude that Zuckert's and Ward's revelation of Locke's view of personal identity is far from free from Christian premises, and it depends on Christian support that's not merely salutary. The relationship between the indispensable churches and the secular state in even a Lockean regime shouldn't really be tensionless. The churches should be relatively countercultural proponents of a more deeply social and so more genuinely personal account of who we are, one that generates generous and charitable duties that go far beyond the domain of rights. Locke's attempt to turn God into a past-tense, unprovidential, unjudgmental, uncaring, basically impersonal being is at odds with his project of securing a free society based on secure personal identity. It's also at odds, perhaps, with what he recognizes as true about the free, willful, and caring biblical Creator—a "who," not some natural "what."[39]

THE AMERICAN COMPROMISE

America at its best is a kind of genuine compromise between wholly Lockean and, in a way, theocratically Christian (meaning Puritan or Calvinist) views of who we are. We can find one account of the magnificence of the American spirit of compromise in Tocqueville. Both the North and the South—New England and Virginia—began with extreme views of what human liberty is. Tocqueville could affirm neither as what's "true and just," although both have elements of truth and justice. America at its political best is a compromise between colonial North and South, between New England and Virginia, between meddlesome political idealists and vulgarly self-indulgent, morally indifferent pirates.

Virginia, Tocqueville reports, was founded by "old seekers," "rest-less and turbulent spirits," solitary adventurers out to get rich quick. They were England's "lower classes," people "without resources" or virtuous habits, people incapable of being animated by "noble thought" or some "immaterial scheme." They had no sense of home and no sense of having the paternalistic, magnanimous responsibilities of class. They weren't even ennobled by any bourgeois devotion to the virtue of worthwhile work well done.[40] They, like the middle-class Americans Tocqueville elsewhere describes, loved money, but, unlike the properly middle class, they weren't at all devoted to the just principle that it should be the reward of one's own honest industry. The Virginians were in every crucial respect uncivilized.

Tocqueville goes on to observe that the Puritans established colonies without lords or masters—without, in fact, economic classes. They weren't out to get rich or even improve their economic condition; they were in no way driven by material necessity. They "belonged to the well-to-do-classes of the mother country" and would have been better off in the most obvious ways staying home. Their lives were structured by resources and by morality; they came to America as family men, bringing their wives and children. They were models of social virtue. They were also extremely educated men—on the cutting edge, in many ways, of European enlightenment. They were, Tocqueville observes, animated by "a purely intellectual need." They aimed "to make an idea triumph" in this world. The Puritans were as civilized as the Virginians were not, and they devoted themselves to a kind of egalitarian idealism aimed at educating or elevating free beings with souls.[41]

The Puritans can be criticized as hypermoralistic despots in some ways, but the Virginians were amoral despots in others. For the Virginian, in effect, every man is the despot, and his point of living is to make himself wealthy and powerful, even at the expense of others. That view, truth to tell, is even present in the Lockeanism of our founding Virginians, who regarded every man as a sovereign who consents to government only for his personal convenience.[42] And it's the individualism or emotional solitude that is the product of that Lockeanism that paves the way to the soft despotism Tocqueville feared far more than any Puritan excess. The American religious and political, localist, familial, egalitarian, and intellectually idealistic ways of combating individualism, Tocqueville makes it quite clear, are our most fortunate Puritan legacies, ones indispensable for combating individualism on behalf of civilization.[43]

What was wrong with the Puritans, from Tocqueville's view, is that they weren't civilized enough. A Puritan enigma is how "the legislation of a rude and half-civilized people," that is, the people portrayed in "the texts of Deuteronomy, Exodus, and Leviticus," could have found its way "into the heart of a society whose spirit was enlightened and mores mild." The people of those books weren't much like the highly educated and civilized Puritans. That contradiction resulted in laws full of death as the penalty for violating all sorts of moral lapses, and severe penalties even for kissing, laziness, and the use of tobacco. But those barbarous penalties were, in fact, rarely enforced against the guilty, and the truth is that such legislation couldn't hope to be made effective for long among an enlightened and peaceful people.[44]

The Puritans could have learned even from the Virginians and the Europeans of their time much about respecting the liberty of conscience. They eventually learned that respect, in part, from Locke, as Zuckert explains. But, for Tocqueville, they also could have learned it by being more consistently Christian. The Puritans weren't Christian enough! Jesus, in Tocqueville's view, showed little interest in enforcing religious morality through political legislation, and that's why Christianity, in fact, has been compatible with a variety of political arrangements. It's not the Gospels—which "speak only of the general relations of men to God and among themselves"—that were the inspiration of the Puritan dedication to criminalizing every sin.[45] But it was the Gospels—more than anything in the books of the Old Testament—that devoted them so extremely to the equality of all moral creatures. The Puritans' tyrannical idealism came from being inconsistently Christian; their dead-serious political utopianism came from attributing to the state what was properly the job of the church. That means, to a point, the Lockean/Jeffersonian criticism of our Puritans is Christian!

The truth, as Brownson explains, is somewhere between Virginia and New England: The Virginians were uncivilized criminals; there was no order or direction to their freedom. But the Puritans criminalized sin. They didn't see the limits of political life as a source of civilization and personal elevation. However, they were right to say that equality in freedom must be civilized, aiming to elevate every soul.

We see this spirit of compromise between Virginia and New England in our Declaration, in which the influence of the Virginian Jefferson was equally as a prudent statesman and as principled theorist. The Lockean theoretical core of the Declaration is all about inalienable rights and not about the personal God of the Bible. "Nature's God" is a past-tense Creator, and the guidance God provides humans now is questionable, insofar as they institute government and many other inventions to move as far away from being governed by nature as possible. But thanks to the insistence of members of Congress who were more under the influence of Christian Calvinism than Jefferson and Franklin, God also became, near the Declaration's end, providential and judgmental, or present-tense and personal.

Zuckert acknowledges that the "appeals to God" found "at the very end of the Declaration . . . appear much closer to the biblical religions than to the natural theology dominant elsewhere in the document." And he acknowledges that "it is no accident" that these changes came from Congress, not the Lockean Jefferson or Franklin. They were part of a legislative compromise. Zuckert dismisses any claim that this compromise changed the essential teaching of the Declaration; the providential and judgmental God "acts to enforce the very order of the 'God of nature' affirmed in the Declaration."[46] But someone might respond that God coming to life as a personal being has to have huge consequences for understanding who we

are. That change in our Declaration might even be thought of as removing a contradiction in Jefferson's Lockean draft: he incoherently attempts to ground personal
identity in an impersonal or absent God. Chesterton, for one, was inspired by our
Declaration precisely because it secures the equal personal significance of us all with
a center of personal significance.[47]

Probably the most nuanced or balanced judgment on the significance of our Declaration comes from R. L. Bruckberger in *Images of America*. Bruckberger, another
of our friendly French critics, took what Tocqueville said about our Puritans about
as seriously as anyone, and maybe surpassed Tocqueville in seeing more clearly the
connection between the Puritans and the Calvinist believers who helped to shape
our founding documents. "The greatest luck of all for the Declaration," Bruckberger
explains, "was precisely the divergence and the compromise between the Puritan tradition and what Jefferson wrote." A "strictly Puritan" Declaration, of course, "would
probably not have managed to avoid an aftertaste of theocracy and religious fanaticism." But if it had "been written from the standpoint of the . . . philosophy of that
day, it would have been a-religious, if not actually offensive to Christians."[48]

The Declaration as a whole, Bruckberger concludes, might even be viewed "as a
more profound accomplishment," one of "the great master-pieces of art, in which
luck is strangely fused with genius." The combination of American Lockeanism and
American Puritanism/Calvinism produced something like an accidental American
Thomism. It's that fact that led the American Catholic John Courtney Murray in
We Hold These Truths to praise our political Fathers for building better than they
knew, although even Murray didn't acknowledge properly the Puritan contribution to what our political Fathers built. As Bruckberger says, "The Declaration
was superior to the men who signed it," just as our Founders were better "than the
[Lockean] philosophy of their day."[49] There are few more Brownsonian observations
than those!

Arguably, the Declaration as compromise is a better guide for Americans than
the intentions of either of the parties to the compromise. God is personal, but
that fact supports rather than negates the equal right to freedom all human beings
have. Properly understood, in Tocqueville's eyes, that understanding of equality
unites the teaching of Jesus and the teaching of Locke, while both Locke and Jesus
distance religious idealism from the requirements of good government. But it's still
the idealism of Jesus that turns equality into more than a principle of calculation
or self-interested consent, into the Puritans' beautiful idea or an undeniable moral
proposition that leads us to do good even at the risk of our lives. We can speculate
that one reason Tocqueville doesn't discuss the Declaration as America's "creed" is
that he regarded it as more Lockean and less Christian than it really is. And Brownson, it seems to me, too often made that same error.

In the case of James Madison, there's the same divergence between his theoretical view—which was more anti-ecclesiastical than that of Locke himself—and what he achieved as a statesman, a member of Congress, in putting together the First Amendment. According to John Courtney Murray, Madison, like "Locke, his master," understood religion as a "personal, private, interior matter," or of no relevance to public or even institutional life. His personal view was that freedom of religion is for "religion without a church."[50] But Madison, in pursuing legislative compromise with the more Christian members of Congress, was only about achieving a kind of nonestablishment that was subordinate to free exercise, the nonpreferential equality of churches as institutions. The free exercise of religion is the freedom of churches as organized bodies of thought and action, as authoritative relational institutions within their nonpolitical, or better, transpolitical, sphere. In that respect, the Constitution's distinction is between "state and society," and the church is a relatively autonomous society. Madison the statesman, it turns out, works his way to a kind of Christian practical wisdom shared by Locke himself.

Against the classical liberals, we can see that the theoretical will of the largely Lockean Jefferson and Madison was moderated—or better, enlarged—by the necessities they faced as statesmen operating in a somewhat Christian social order. Both in the Continental Congress and the First Congress that composed the religion clauses of the First Amendment, they did not, as Murray observes, "erect atheism as a political principle."[51] Even if they were privately unbelievers in the specific faith-claims of Christianity, their disbelief—which didn't, after all, extend to skepticism about the reality of individual liberty—has no public status in our country. Because our founding compromises not only accommodated Christian concerns but affirmed Christian truth, they aren't even post-Christian, but parts of the Christian tradition. The person whose rights are protected by the Constitution, Murray claims, "is, whether he knows it or not, a Christian man."[52] Well, to be sure, such persons are more than an Augustinian man, insofar as they understand themselves as more than alien pilgrims in their country. But that means their understanding of their personal dignity as Thomistic, as persons born to work for themselves and their own, to enjoy social life, to have a gratitude to their government that inspires the dutiful loyalty of a citizen, and to come to know God as a rational and loving person. This person is born to be civilized man or woman in full.

DEMOCRACY AS AN END

It's neither good nor truthful to believe Locke tells us all we need to know about who we are, and a tensionless America—a perfectly principled or uncompromised America—would, in fact, be a free but empty and so unsustainable one. Locke doesn't tell the whole truth about who we are as social, personal, erotic beings; the unique and irreplaceable person is a lot more than the being with rights. That doesn't mean that we shouldn't be grateful to Locke for the contributions our economic and political freedom make to our personal security and happiness. All in all, I'd rather be living in a largely—but not completely—natural-rights republic, one which has plenty of room for the countercultural influence of churches.

Today's rigorous Lockean George Will argues that American politics is divided between conservatives, "who take their bearings from the individual's right to a capacious, indeed indefinite, realm of freedom," and progressives, "whose fundamental value is the right of the majority to have its way in making rules about which specified liberties shall be respected."[53] For Will, real conservatives favor an activist judiciary that will aggressively defend our "capacious, indeed indefinite realm of freedom" from the majority. For Will, individual liberty triumphs over every form of egalitarian moralism.

The distinction here, as the late Carey McWilliams explained, is between those who regard democracy as a means and those who regard it as an end. Yet McWilliams tells a very different story about this distinction. America, from the beginning, has been in dialectical tension between the democratic and libertarian "voices." The dominant voice, which we hear in *The Federalist*, is about securing the conditions of liberty for the free and self-interested individual. The second voice, which originates with our Puritans, is about participatory, egalitarian idealism rooted in the Christian insight about the dignified equality of all creatures.[54]

We see Lincoln (who is a "progressive" only to hyperlibertarians), McWilliams reminds us, as correcting an excess of the dominant voice of our founding in the Gettysburg Address: "The Declaration of Independence asserts that we are created equal and that government exists to secure rights; Lincoln argued that the Union, conceived in liberty, is dedicated to equality."[55]

The democratic citizen, McWilliams goes on, "measures contribution by the quality of human devotion."[56] And the effort to abolish slavery and end segregation in our country depended not only on Lockean calculation of rights but on what can only be called religious devotion. Jefferson spoke eloquently against the violence slavery did to natural rights, but he wasn't inspired to do much about it. He certainly didn't think much of the neo-puritanical abolitionists who refused to compromise when it comes to personal freedom. Lincoln thought highly of Jefferson's principles but not of his indifference to taking even modest risks on behalf of justice. In the same way, Martin Luther King Jr.—who mixed perfectly Christian and individualistic themes—didn't think much of the "white moderate" who knew what was right but lacked the idealism to act now.[57] So America, at its best, is about people who somehow see democratic citizenship as both a means and an end, and so it avoids the extremes of endlessly meddlesome democratic tyranny and apolitical libertarian indifference to the souls of their fellow citizens and creatures.

THE SOUTH'S CONTRIBUTION

Returning to Brownson, McWilliams acknowledges that the two relational anti-dotes in our country to unfettered individualism are the Puritan Christians and the Southern aristocrats. They are, in their ways, both extremes, but they both, if you think about it, are about preserving the greatness of the human person against the leveling atomism of the individualism that morphs into pantheism. When Tocque-ville praises the Puritans' Sunday, it's about the way it raises the individual above rodent-like materialism to take self seriously as an immortal being with a singular origin and destiny. And Tocqueville makes it clear that his praise is in a classical mode: Christianity, the most aristocratic form of egalitarianism—the one that pre-serves the whole truth about each person—flourishes in democracy.

The Puritan and the American aristocrat are, when it comes to justice and moral legislation, opposite extremes. But they unite in opposing the materialism of the solitary "I" or self-obsessed individual that is the purely middle-class American. They were clear on who they are and what they're supposed to do as members of a class or community. And they agreed that education is, most of all, about the soul—for the cultivation of a being not determined by the surrounding impersonal forces or defined merely by the requirements of earning a living. The Puritans and the Southerners were about, in different ways, civilization. Restlessly opposed to civilizing influences, Tocqueville shows, were middle-class Americans who thought of education as merely indispensable for acquiring technical skills and who identi-fied philosophy and science with technology, or the transformation of nature with bodily need in mind. The American individualist is constantly running from civ-ilization to some solitary place on the frontier. Individualistic or emotionally self-absorbed Americans, on their own, resist having their hearts and souls enlarged by a particular "city" or political and religious society.

The thought that the South might make an enduring contribution to curbing American pop Cartesianism, it seems, couldn't be taken seriously until after the Civil War. The South, we might say, is liberated to make that contribution by being freed of the monstrous task of defending slavery in thought and deed. Brownson might have been the first to notice, immediately after the war, that the true interpre-tation of the American Constitution, the one that does justice to the whole truth about the material, political, and spiritual dimensions of being human, combines Southern particularity with Northern universality.[58] The South was all about the as-sertion of the particular individual—by itself a tyrannical assertion—but an assertion that displays emphatically part of the greatness of who each of us is. The South was, in this sense, too personal.

The North—both in its materialism and in the fanaticism of Puritan abolition-ism—is too universal or general or destructive of human distinctiveness. The par-ticular individual is dissolved into a kind of abstract humanitarianism—a seductive doctrine that preys upon the weakness of the displaced "I" in an anonymous world. Northern abolitionism, in Brownson's expansive understanding, culminates in the homogeneity of both materialism and pantheism.[59] But the North, of course, is also strong on the universal principles of justice, on not exempting proud individuals from the social and political responsibilities we all share.

Brownson suggests, thinking along lines remarkably similar to Tocqueville, that the proper combination of Southern particularity, or its concern for particular per-sons and places, with Northern universality, especially at its highest levels of coming to terms with our shared embodiment and equality under God, is the real truth about who we are as whole human beings.[60] In this sense, Brownson concludes, America is the most Catholic of nations. I say this only in passing because his ad-mirably subtle philosophic and poetic attempt to convince Americans of that fact didn't catch on anywhere. I do say it in passing to show that a strongly antislavery, Yankee, very deep, and fairly astute thinker could say that the aristocratic South was partly right in its criticism of the emptiness of American Cartesianism. Surely Tocqueville writing later would have done the same.

We know, of course, that the Southern aristocrats returned to power for a while after the Civil War. They lost the war, but through what amounted to a successful terrorist movement forced the Union troops out of their states and restored "white rule." The Southern Stoics viewed themselves as ruling the blacks and ordinary whites paternalistically, as gentlemen who by nature and education deserved to rule. Their class was displaced in the early twentieth century by more "populist" or angrily racist and vulgarly democratic political leaders, and the Stoic self-consciousness mor-phed into being members of an honorable class that had ruled responsibly, fought nobly against overwhelming force in a great war, and been involved in a futile effort to resist its inevitable decline and fall in a democratized world where there would be no place for them. Freed from having to defend slavery, their literary efforts turned to the articulation of the experience of sustaining oneself in a world where one had been morally and politically dispossessed. It became a criticism of a world in which those in charge were incapable of recognizing who they are. It's these dispossessed Stoics—such as Will Percy—who achieved the greatest self-consciousness about who they are, writing, as did Tocqueville, at a privileged moment after the incomplete fall of aristocracy and just before the full rise of democracy.

TOCQUEVILLE AND WALKER PERCY IN RELATION
TO WILL PERCY: THE FRIENDLY CRITICISM OF
BOTH ARISTOCRACY AND DEMOCRACY

The Southern Stoic, as presented by the Percys, is not so different from Tocqueville himself. They're both open to the possibility that being human is some kind of cosmic accident, and they identify the loneliness of being lost in the cosmos as a truthful insight. Will Percy aside, most Southern Stoics, like Percy's characters in his novels, divert themselves through the pride that comes from knowing their place and doing their duties. They, like Tocqueville, experience the political plea-sure that comes from ruling oneself and others; Tocqueville's high opinion of him-self is confirmed by what he actually does. True individuality—true greatness—comes through the development of character, through the acquisition of the virtues that make easygoing, confident self-respect possible.

Walker Percy, we can say, wrote not on behalf of political liberty, but to examine the predicament of the heir of the dispossessed Stoic, the being who, as "the last gentleman," experiences life as pure possibility.[61] He thinks he can't be a Stoic, but he knows enough from the Stoics to be aware that the pop Cartesian expert doesn't offer him even a clue about what a being like himself is supposed to do.[62] Still, many of the differences that separate Tocqueville from the aristocrats he describes apply to Walker Percy too. They are both touched by the Christian, egalitarian claim for justice, and so they don't join the Stoics in viewing progress toward democracy as nothing but decline. Democratic progress, in truth, makes the world better in some ways and worse in others. There's more promise and more greatness in ordinary lives than the Stoic aristocrats suggest. And so Southern Stoicism failed, most of all, in mistaking the clamor for equal rights of the civil rights movement as ungrateful insolence.

Walker Percy comes close to Tocqueville in his balanced and quite political ac-count of the strengths and weaknesses of the political dimension of his uncle's singular version of Southern Stoicism.[63] He begins by noting, as Tocqueville does, that aristocrats are typically willfully naive about the injustice or exploitation that accompanies any form of paternalism. Uncle Will wrote, as Tocqueville would have also noticed, as if he was too noble to think about his self-interest, but it was in his interest, after all, to regard his sharecroppers as beings unfit to care for their own interests.[64] The aristocratic doctrine of noble self-forgetfulness had its use as an ideology, which doesn't mean it was completely untrue.

It's true, after all, that terms like "noblesse oblige" refer not to privilege but to magnanimous and generous duty. It certainly couldn't have been wrong for the Southern Stoic—such as Will Percy or Atticus Finch—to believe that his position in society entails a responsibility to others—to the poor, the vulnerable, and the otherwise needy. Walker compares Will's real-life courageous confrontation with the Klan on behalf of endangered blacks (see also, of course, *To Kill a Mockingbird*) with a fearful and otherwise emotionally stunted individual in a democratic city closing the blinds rather than getting involved with a neighbor being murdered.[65] It's true enough that Uncle Will or Atticus Finch was wrong not to believe black people or poor whites could rule themselves, and their relationship with their inferiors had nothing to do with love or rights. But justice understood simply as the protection of rights wouldn't have inspired their undeniably noble and indispensable deeds.

Percy, in that spirit, provocatively suggests that paternalism "might even beat welfare."[66] Welfare seems better because the individual is not treated as a child by being degraded by a particular person. But it's really worse precisely because it's so impersonal or unresponsive to the person's real needs. Worse than the aristocratic form of aristocratic injustice (except racially based slavery), in Tocqueville's eyes, is the soft despotism of the bureaucratic control of every feature of our lives that would be the logical culmination of our creeping individualism.[67] Equality would be preserved insofar as people wouldn't think of themselves as dominated by anyone in particular, but the result might be that we'd all be reduced to less than we're really meant to be as free and relational persons. Better than paternalism, Percy suggests, would be a world that's both egalitarian and personal, a world governed by charity.[68] But his search for that Christian solution began with the Southern, Stoic criticism of the impersonality that comes from a world full of equally contentless democratic "I's." That Northerners have a loving concern for humanity and Southerners for particular people is a criticism that is equally aristocratic and Christian.

Tocqueville was, compared to Percy, a little weak on Christian charity and personal love, just as he was a bit too much about the anxiety of the wonderer and wanderer and not enough about the corresponding joy. He didn't really seem to believe, with Pascal, that the true explanation of our homelessness—our wandering—is that our true home is somewhere else. Still, he did what he could to reconcile aristocratic greatness with democratic justice by trying to see with the eyes of the Creator. Aristocrats, he says, see things too particularly, and so they miss what's true and good about what all of us share in general. Democrats think too generally, and so they miss what distinguishes one human being from another; they miss the particular content that is the source of irreducible personal significance.[69] God, Tocqueville sees, doesn't need general ideas or "theories." God sees each of us as we really are in our unique particularity, in how we are alike and how we are distinguished.[70] Democracy that does justice to human particularity, it seems to me, can be grounded only in a Christianity that preserves what's true about aristocracy.

The first form of that mending—but not ending—of the aristocratic account of personal significance can be found in Thomas Aquinas's realistic correction of Aristotle's description of the classical virtue of magnanimity. Tocqueville and Percy continue that great tradition of Christian realism, which, in our time, mends democratic tendencies toward personal emptiness and disorientation through elevation in the direction of our true greatness.

There are, as it turns out, two routes to American Thomism. The first is the amended Declaration's correction of the Lockean past-tense unrelational by transforming the "Nature's God" into a providential and relational being. The insight of the Declaration is that to be personal is to be relational, and the God who created each of us as a free being must be a relational being who made us in his image.[71] The other is the Southern correction of middle-class individualism in the direction of the high and proud relational virtues of generosity and magnanimity, a correction that, when truthfully American, is not at the expense of the egalitarian justice cherished by our Puritans.

Our Southern Catholic philosopher/novelist was, in fact, a homegrown American Thomist. He accepted the aristocratic criticism of clueless middle-class vulgarity, and he accepted the Christian criticism of the aristocrat's injustice and contempt for the lives of ordinary people. He assimilated what's true about the noncondescending egalitarianism of our Puritans and neo-Puritans, while rejecting the endlessly intrusive "abolitionism" and "prohibitionism" that is characteristic of Puritan—and, in its secular version, humanitarian or progressive—political reform. He preserved the Christian insight about inwardness—our predicament of seeking and searching—given to every human soul, while reconciling that "wandering" with the wondering of the Greek philosophers in the mode of Thomas Aquinas. But searching and searching in no way releases us from the responsibilities to be loyal citizens, loving spouses and parents, and good friends. That's American providential constitutionalism in full!

Epilogue

Throughout the 2016 general-election campaign, just as throughout that election year's Republican primaries, most of the people who follow politics for a living spent their time thinking about how things would be after Donald Trump lost. Politicians and strategists tried to position themselves just right for a post-Trump world. Journalists wondered how Republicans would come back. And conservative writers and thinkers, especially those who were implacably opposed to Trump, sought the best ways to learn lessons from his failure.

But Trump won because he was a little more, rather than less, than a conservative Republican. Trump won—unlike Republicans recently—in Wisconsin, Michigan, and Pennsylvania, because a significant number of voters (mainly from union households) who had voted for Obama flipped. They were perfectly fine with voting for the African American president who had their backs against the oligarchic, union-busting, entitlement-trimming Romney Republicans. But this time, they (tutored by Bernie Sanders, in part) thought Hillary Clinton was the more oligarchic candidate, the one taking orders from Wall Street, and she didn't waste any of her campaign on the Rust Belt voters and their concerns. Trump, meanwhile, spent lots of time speaking directly to them in his huge rallies, promising to protect what they have—their industrial jobs, their unions, even their Social Security and Medicare—while restoring at least some of what they've lost.

Trump ultimately did not prove to be exceptionally popular. He entered office as the least-popular elected president since the invention of polling—and he actually lost the popular vote. But the huge number of voters repulsed by both Clinton and Trump ended up breaking in the direction of change where it mattered.

So what was the status quo the Trump voters opposed? Until early 2016, many of the experts were writing about a convergence of our two political parties. The Democrats were getting more comfortable with the free market and less devoted to resisting the dynamic of the twenty-first-century global competitive marketplace.

146

And the Republicans were obsessing less about the "social issues," accepting, for example, their inevitable defeat on same-sex marriage and adjusting themselves to various demands for personal autonomy. The convergence was around a kind of soft libertarianism found among our elites and in our multinational corporations—one that, on balance, benefited the Democrats more than the Republicans, insofar as our "cognitive" elite now places itself complacently among the more sophisticated Democrats.

We now know that this convergence among "the masters of the universe" was simply too "liberal"—too indifferent to the relational dignity of ordinary Americans left behind by history—to prevail in our (or any) democracy. The "populist" insurgency occurred in both parties. The socialist Bernie Sanders (who isn't about the workers of the world but the workers of America) was barely defeated by Clinton, although he won in most of what turned out to be the key states in the general election. And the nationalist Donald Trump actually captured the Republican nomination with surprising (if not embarrassing) ease, and despite—not because of—his low character and degrading words, he was the change half of the country wanted in November. Two thousand sixteen was the year of the populist rebellion against liberalism understood as liberated—or displaced, and so unencumbered—individualism.

The party with a future, we should hope, is the one that best builds a coalition that preserves its principled devotion to liberty while acknowledging and accommodating the legitimate demands—for both economic security and personal dignity—of the populists. Both parties are destined to suffer defeat if they slight our new populism or have nothing but contempt for it. There's a lot to be learned from Trump's success about the true relationship between liberty and equality in our country and about the threats to both that come from our complacency in the face of the coming apart of our middle-class country, as it diverges into two increasingly distant classes. The relationship between liberty and democracy in our country right now remains confused, among both most liberals and most conservatives, because we think about them both too abstractly and unrelationally.

THE AGE OF IRRESPONSIBILITY

One view, shared, after all, by so many of our techno-libertarians, is that human history is the freeing of consciousness from the constraints of the uncontrollable or alien machine. Machines, all of nature, become increasingly subject to conscious manipulation. Life as a result gets longer, more comfortable, and more about choice and less about chance. Life also gets less cruel. Nature itself is, from the point of view of the free human person, a cruel and random mother, with no respect for particular human lives. The liberation from nature also causes human beings to surrender their own cruel impulses, most of which can be rooted in revenge against a nature that does not, in fact, provide what we most need. People, for example, get less religious, and their religious identity is no longer capable of inspiring either violence or charity. People become more cosmopolitan, liberated from the tribalism that inspires wars rooted in monstrous combinations of love and hate. The global marketplace, as Marx predicted, tears down the walls that separated one people from another, creating a world without borders.

The obvious objection to calling this progress genuinely human progress, Marx tells us, is that the many are reduced to machines manipulated by the infinitely productive few. It is true, after all, that the coming apart of the classes means that one thinks of the other less in terms of relational responsibility and more in terms of scripting and nudging—gentle but increasingly intrusive modes of controlling. Alexis de Tocqueville cautioned us that if aristocracy were to return to the world in democratic times, it would be a cold or unfeeling class that gets smarter as those it manipulates gets stupider. This new aristocracy, unlike the old ones, wouldn't connect its privileges to responsibilities, because its members would be convinced that they deserved what they have. We can't help but think here, of course, of the technocracy emerging from Silicon Valley, just as we can't help but think of the British elite during the Brexit campaign of 2016, which was so confident that it could use big data to convince the people that the developing EU—even with the surrender of political sovereignty and any meaningful sense of the consent of the governed—was in its economic self-interest.

Now Marx was wrong to think that the great mass of people could be reduced to machines devoid of all human content. They would revolt, Marx predicted, because for them freedom would be just another word for nothing left to lose. The complaint about ordinary Americans today is that they're increasingly incompetent. Families are pathological, schools are worthless, and generally we no longer have the social capital required to produce reliable cogs.

Marx also didn't predict that the mechanized members of the proletariat would actually be replaced by machines—by robots and so forth. And, as Tocqueville predicted, the new aristocracy would deploy government entitlements to keep those who have become, at best, marginally productive from revolution, assisted, as Tyler Cowen adds, by all the enjoyments to which all Americans—from billionaires to the chronically unemployed—have equal access through the screen. No one really fears a revolutionary uprising today, and critics such as Joel Kotkin exaggerate (but only exaggerate) when they write about the proletarianization of the middle class.

Still, it's the libertarian (or classical liberal) social critic Charles Murray, as previously noted, who has most ably chronicled the "coming apart" of Americans into a cognitive elite living in its bubble and a class that lacks the wherewithal—productive and relational—to live a dignified life. What's fading away are the intermediary institutions shared by all Americans, from the church to citizenship to the public schools to the workplace. One way of thinking of the "middle" is the mixture of mind and body that produces the relational person, the person able to think in terms of his responsibilities, not only to those in his immediate circle, but to all his fellow citizens and creatures.

As Murray points out, both of our classes are now irresponsible. The members of our cognitive elite, it's true, have deployed their resources to live sensible lives in child-centered marriages that produce stable families. Their irresponsibility is their indifference to the lives of their fellow citizens. That includes, in Murray's eyes, their condescending conclusion that they have no right to expect all Americans to share middle-class values—those of the self-sufficient being who works to take care of his own. It also includes their abandonment of those values in their liberationist promotion of nonjudgmental autonomy. Their sixties talk is contradicted, in effect, by their fifties lives (with fewer children, to be sure). But what the intellectual class says, after all, still sets the tone for society as a whole. It is certainly setting the tone for what is taught in our schools, which has little to do with the rights and duties shared by American citizens and all free beings who work, much less all children of God.

This elitist irresponsibility Tocqueville called individualism. Individualism, for Tocqueville, is a kind of "heart disease" or an emotional deficit. The individual is locked up in a bubble or gated community of his immediate family and friends and is indifferent to or experiences no real connection with the larger world of citizens and creatures. For the individualist, religion, for example, becomes a kind of nonjudgmental spirituality that detaches "me" from real concern with particular people; the duties of personal charity are dissolved into an amorphous empathy. For our cognitive elite, individualism might be best explained as generated by the complacent thought that earned privileges—those of the hugely productive—don't generate corresponding responsibilities.

The aristocrats of old, by contrast, were "paternalistically" oriented toward those over whom they assumed responsibility; that relationship veiled exploitation in some large measure, of course, but it also meant that human beings were linked together in more than a contractual or "cash nexus" way. Our elitist indifference, we might also say, is rooted in part in a failure of higher education to be about more than competency and diversity, and in the replacement of virtue with niceness.

Still, those Americans living less than middle-class lives are also irresponsible. There are way too many single moms and deadbeat dads, as way too many young men are lost to the virtual world of the screen. There are too many who have concluded that the jobs available to them aren't worth their effort. Murray's thought is that the way to restore responsibility in the country is to replace our complex system of entitlements with a guaranteed minimum income. The goal is to allow people to live as they please, but fully accepting the consequences of their fecklessness and personal failures.

One problem with this conclusion is that it really is true that many jobs currently available to ordinary Americans don't pay enough to make dignified relational life possible. Doubtless this trend, as the libertarian Brink Lindsey contends, can be countered to some extent with job training that makes employees more techno-competent and with "diversity" training that makes people less tribal and better at being abstracted role players. But it is also true that making work less "brutal" in one way makes it, in a more subtle sense, more brutal in another, or more suited to what C. S. Lewis called "men without chests." Many employees, after all, now are required to be nicer than ever. They can't say, for example, the edgy "no problem" when confronted with an unreasonable request of a client or customer, they're scripted to say the more masochistic "my pleasure." And it just might be that the one reason most Trump voters were men is that men suffer disproportionally in a world where the faking of pleasure is a condition of employment.

All in all, the proper correction to Murray's analysis is that it's the techno-progress of the division of labor as much as the culture of dependency that's responsible for the coming apart of Americans. And for many people, the progress of the global marketplace in our time produces experiences of loss. It's easy to go on to talk about the atrophying of all the "safety nets"—both governmental and relational—that have cushioned lives from the unmediated rigors of the marketplace. And our churches are doing increasingly less well in ministering unto relationally displaced persons—such as the chronically unemployed, the divorced, and especially the allegedly deadbeat dads (who, after all, remain children of God and sinners like us all).

BETWEEN INDIVIDUALS AND MAJORITIES

Let us return, then, to the movement in American politics that has disoriented so many libertarians and conservatives: the one from the basically bourgeois Tea Party to the populist Trump voters. The Tea Party is or was all about rolling back aspects of the welfare state to protect the relational lives of ordinary Americans. It was about deploying libertarian means to protect the right of families, Christians, and so forth to live as they please as dignified relational beings.

There is no denying that the Tea Party has been overwhelmed by the populism of Trump. Trump has displayed no interest in rolling back entitlements, and he feeds into the perception that "the new birth of freedom" generated by the competitive marketplace has been at the expense of the greatness of American citizens, creatures, and family members. His is a different view about how to protect the embattled relational lives of ordinary Americans, one that has a huge role for government and its capacity to provide security and make good deals for Americans. The decline of the Tea Party movement, as many of its members easily shifted into Trump mode, indicates that most of what they were about was fear of big government in the hands of progressive ideologues, that is, the Obama administration, and not opposition to big government simply.

Still, the fear that some libertarian and conservative writers experienced in the face of all those Trump and Sanders voters wasn't misplaced and might be salutary. For one thing, if Trump were better at being "not a gentleman"—or being a really effective demagogue on behalf of America and Americans—he would have won more easily. And if his message were a little less tribal and more about an edifying civic identity, he might have attracted even more Sanders voters.

Rethinking conservatism begins with revising Randy Barnett's view that the American Constitution is all about protecting individual rights from majoritarian collectivism. The place between individualism and collectivism is the relational world in which people find the significance that makes life worth living. And majority rule doesn't have to mean some kind of mob rule. It was the view of our Framers, in fact, that ordinary Americans would have majority rule, but the majority would be formed by the process of deliberation and compromise. The American majority, as Publius explains, would not be a majority faction—a unified collectivity all about violating the rights of others—but a majority coalition of diverse interests and inclinations.

Restoring the world of egalitarian citizenship, in which Americans enter with their relational concerns and compete with inevitably controversial opinions, is the indispensable beginning for ameliorating or, better, mediating the "world split apart" (to borrow Aleksandr Solzhenitsyn's phrase) that our country has increasingly become. Liberty means, in part, the freedom of the people to choose, not simply freedom from our common life to live however you please as an unencumbered (and implicitly disembodied) individual. Consent of the governed means, in part, not having elitist institutions tell us what our rights are from some detached perspective or undisclosed location. It doesn't mean "pure consciousness" dictating to free persons as if they were mere machines.

Neither being nice nor being brutal is being virtuous. And moral virtue is, after all, the foundation of the common life shared by all political beings inhabiting a particular part of the world. Both niceness and brutality are forms of domination and control. Both work against the consent of the governed who rule and are ruled in turn. We should, in fact, expect all Americans to be ladies and gentlemen, and to treat each other with a dignified equality free from condescension and contempt.

That means, if you think about it, that our courts and our bureaucrats should do less, and our legislatures should do more. The meddlesome soft despotism promoted by the experts driving our administrative state can be checked most effectively, of course, by majority vote. And the majority—in the name of virtue and dignified relational life—should be about resisting the experts both public and private who think of ordinary people as less than they really are. The idea that the nice should rule over the brutish is what, in fact, links together too much libertarian and progressivist thought about being on the "right side of history" and all that. That form of manipulation, thank God, is bound to fail them in the end.

It's true enough that we have, in our country, those who think of themselves as more cosmopolitan and those who are more nationalist, and those who think of themselves more as free individuals and those who think of themselves more as observant creatures of God. The consent of the governed means beginning with trying to discover the truth in each point of view, truth that is neither nice nor brutish. We're not going back to the fifties and sixties, nor to our country's dominance of the global economy that made strong unions possible. And thank God we're not going to dispense with the progress we've made on behalf of women, blacks, gays, and so forth as free and equal individuals and citizens in both the marketplace and the political arena. We're not really moving to a world without borders, and we're stuck, more than ever, with being a morally and intellectually diverse country—differences we should cherish rather than aim to obliterate in the service of a uniformly degrading niceness.

Technological progress almost always has relational costs, and these days economic growth by itself is not going to eradicate the disparate impact of those costs on the diverse forms of American life. So, as the reform conservatives say, government needs sometimes to think of people as more than free individuals and members of historically marginalized groups but as parents and children and citizens and creatures. Religious freedom, both our liberals and libertarians often don't understand, is freedom for the mediating relational institution often called the church. It's not quite the same as freedom of conscience or intellectual freedom, although even the latter flourishes in communities often called colleges, which inevitably have diverse missions that aim higher than niceness and mere competency.

It is, after all, easy to understand why Evangelical voters—especially those concerned with preserving the integrity of their institutions—were attracted to Trump as the guy strong enough to protect them from our courts, bureaucrats, and foundations. It's easy to understand, in particular, why they don't want to trust the courts. Contrary to Barnett, it's easy to see that our conservative future depends on trusting the people more and all our elitist institutions, including the courts, less. Trusting the people means, of course, restoring the place of dialogue to our political life, over, for example, perplexing relational issues that are the collateral damage of the progress of the twenty-first-century global competitive marketplace.

FINDING OUR BALANCE AGAIN

One clear takeaway from Trump—and from the populism that has always, in some measure, been a part of our governing coalition—is the return of spirited people versus the administrative experts. And this fits nicely with our overall approach, which heavily supports the relational person loving and trusting their country because it is accountable to them. We always say that the human experience of universal truth— which is the truth, among other things, about each of us as a relational person— always occurs within the context of a particular community. True cosmopolitanism isn't abstract cosmopolitanism. Even Socrates didn't think he could understand himself or do his life's work without his indebtedness to a particular political community.

What could make our country less split?

We end then where we began, with the limited political unity of our country defined as the United States. That is to say, we are not a centralized nation without room for authentic self-government in the states and the localities; it is also to remind our latter-day Jeffersonian saints that our states are rooted and can only exist as united entities, a continental-union if you will. And that is to see in our constitutional form a recognition of the profound political truth of subsidiarity and solidarity that accords our existence as citizens and as creatures fundamental respect. Our political order permits through limited and compound government the development of citizenship at the national and state levels. We are permitted to be citizens more fully attentive to our local communities. And here our citizenship is most directly about developing government in accordance with closely held meanings of the good life. The federal level of government is, when properly understood, about those general concerns of defense for the country, fiscal policy that provides measured taxation and spending in service of national welfare and prosperity, and commercial policy that enables each American to put his or her goods and services on offer. But the truth remains that our complex citizenship, national, state, and local, allows of no ideological answers, nothing that can stand as a transpolitical template. In politics we deal in the here-and-now, and it remains an endless source of debate over meaning and purpose.

But this should not obscure a more general understanding that there are modes to American citizenship and a recognition of thinner and thicker realms of politics found in the federal and state level. We need both badly. But in our time we have lost, it seems, even the tools to understand the genius of our constitutional system and its delicate synthesis of subsidiarity and solidarity. What we should recover is this living synthesis of American citizenship, in a manner that recognizes the general competency of the federal government, but that is quickly drained of precision and accuracy the more it attempts to govern in particular areas remote from what any general body of rulers can accomplish. This is hardly a novel insight and has been announced powerfully by an array of thinkers both right and left. In our time we have seen Peter Schuck, James Buckley, Christopher DeMuth, John Di-Iulio, and William Voegeli underscore that an expansive federal government is an ineffectual one.

The states then must achieve a newfound growth in their freedoms and responsibilities. True, there is a legacy to overcome, which is too much subsidiarity (racism) in their past, particularly for our native region, the South. Today, however, the South is running full tilt economically, and we can say that much of the region is too busy to hate. Moreover, the federal government is incapable, as Peter Schuck notes in *Why Government Fails So Often*, of having most of its policies pass a simple cost-benefits test. Born under the weight of its lethargy could be a state-based recovery of self-government that simply must be set free to emerge. This is somewhat optimistic; still, it isn't for nothing that a system of competitive federalism can emerge when limits on the federal government are once again acknowledged and the states themselves, owing to their prosperity, again seek to block each other from undoing their gains. A political gift would be to recognize this measure of the rights of states to be self-governing, even in controversial social ways, even as the federal government provides in general terms the measure of defense, fiscal policy, and entitlements that our citizens most desire. We can keep hope alive if we find the mean between nationalism and cosmopolitanism that keeps "Americanism" from degenerating into tribalism. Let us hope the country as a whole finds that mean for itself.

Notes

A Brownsonian Prologue

1. Orestes Brownson, *The American Republic* (1865; rprt., Wilmington, DE: ISI Books, 2003), 76.

2. Brownson, *The American Republic*, 142.

3. Orestes Brownson, *The Works of Orestes A. Brownson*, vol. 17, *The Federal Constitution* (New York: AMS Press, 1966), 499.

Chapter 1. What Distinguishes America?

1. Orestes Brownson, *The American Republic* (1865; rprt., Wilmington, DE: ISI Books, 2003), 221.

2. Brownson, *The American Republic*, 225.

3. Brownson, *The American Republic*, 236.

4. Richard M. Reinsch II, ed., *Seeking the Truth: An Orestes Brownson Anthology* (Washington, DC: Catholic University of America Press, 2016), "Civil and Religious Freedom," 388.

5. Orestes Brownson, "Union of Church and State," in *The Works of Orestes Brownson* (Detroit: H. F. Brownson, 1900), 13:127–145.

6. Orestes Brownson, "The Church and the Republic," "The Day-Star of Freedom," "The Church and Modern Civilization," "Rights of the Temporal," and "Separation of Church and State," in *The Works of Orestes Brownson*, 12:1–32, 103–116, 117–135, 376–405, 406–438; "Temporal and Spiritual," "The Spiritual Not for the Temporal," "The Spiritual Order Supreme," "Temporal Power of the Popes," and "Mission of America," 13:1–94, 137–164, 551–584.

7. Richard M. Reinsch II, "Orestes Brownson's Freedom of the Church," *Logos* 20, no. 4 (Fall 2017): 112–123.

8. Reinsch, *Seeking the Truth*, 399–416.

9. Alexis de Tocqueville, *Democracy in America* (1840; rprt., Indianapolis, IN: Liberty

Fund, 2010), "What Makes the Minds of Democratic Peoples Incline toward Pantheism," 3:757–758.

10. Tocqueville, *Democracy in America* (2010), "Why the Study of Greek and Latin Literature Is Particularly Useful in Democratic Societies," 3:815–816.

11. Alexis de Tocqueville, *Democracy in America* (London: Penguin Books, 2003), appendix E, 827–830.

12. Tocqueville, *Democracy in America* (2010), "Social-State of the Anglo-Americans," 1:74–90, 87.

13. Tocqueville, *Democracy in America* (2010), "Social-State of the Anglo-Americans," 1:74–90, 88.

14. Tocqueville, *Democracy in America* (2010), 1:87.

15. Tocqueville, *Democracy in America* (2010), 1:87.

16. Tocqueville, *Democracy in America* (2010), 1:87.

17. Tocqueville, *Democracy in America* (2010), "Literary Physiognomy," 3:808.

18. Tocqueville, *Democracy in America* (2010), "How from Time to Time Religious Beliefs Divert the Soul of the Americans toward Non-material Enjoyments," 3:954–962.

19. Brownson, *The American Republic*, 257–266.

20. Brownson, *The American Republic*, 11, 55, 81–83.

21. Brownson, *The American Republic*, 55.

22. Christopher Lasch, *The True and Only Heaven: Progress and Its Critics* (New York: Norton, 1991), 184–188.

23. Pope Benedict XVI, *Deus Caritas Est* (Washington, DC: United States Conference of Catholic Bishops, 2006), No. 9.

24. Brownson, *The American Republic*, 221–240.

25. Reinsch, *Seeking the Truth*, 402.

26. Reinsch, *Seeking the Truth*, 411.

27. Reinsch, *Seeking the Truth*, 414.

28. Reinsch, *Seeking the Truth*, 411.

29. Brownson, *The American Republic*, 244.

30. Reinsch, *Seeking the Truth*, 403.

31. Reinsch, *Seeking the Truth*, 408.

32. Reinsch, *Seeking the Truth*, 408–409.

33. Reinsch, *Seeking the Truth*, 407.

34. Reinsch, *Seeking the Truth*, 385.

35. Reinsch, *Seeking the Truth*, 403.

36. Brownson, *The American Republic*, 224.

37. Brownson, *The American Republic*, 225.

38. Reinsch, *Seeking the Truth*, 389.

39. Orestes Brownson, "Nature and Grace," in *The Works of Orestes Brownson* (Detroit: H. F. Brownson, 1900), 3:371.

40. Reinsch, *Seeking the Truth*, 389.

41. Brownson, *The American Republic*, 176.

42. Reinsch, *Seeking the Truth*, 408.

43. Reinsch, *Seeking the Truth*, 406–407.

Chapter 2. *The Privileges and Responsibilities of American Constitutionalism*

1. Alexander Hamilton, John Jay, and James Madison, *The Federalist*, ed. and intro. by George W. Carey, James McClellan (Indianapolis: Liberty Fund, 2001) [hereafter *The Federalist*], 442–451.

2. Gordon Lloyd, *Law & Liberty*, "The Constitutional Liberty of the Anti-Federalists," March 2013, accessed October 29, 2018, http://www.libertylawsite.org/liberty-forum /the-constitutional-liberty-of-the-antifederalists/.

3. *The Federalist*, No. 84, 445.

4. *The Federalist*, No. 84, 445.

5. *The Federalist*, No. 84, 445.

6. *The Federalist*, No. 84, 446.

7. *The Federalist*, No. 84, 445.

8. Russell Hittinger, *The First Grace: Rediscovering the Natural Law in a Post-Christian World* (Wilmington, DE: ISI Books, 2003), 115–134, 122.

9. *West Virginia State Board of Education v. Barnette*, 319 U.S. 624, 639 (1943).

10. *Duncan v. Louisiana*, 391 U.S. 145, 166 (1968). Scholarship on the incorporation of the first eight amendments in the Constitution through the Fourteenth Amendment's Due Process or Privileges or Immunities Clauses is voluminous. Some of the scholarship in support of incorporation includes the following: Kurt T. Lash, *The Fourteenth Amendment and the Privileges and Immunities of American Citizenship* (New York: Cambridge University Press, 2014); Akhil Reed Amar, *The Bill of Rights: Creation and Reconstruction* (New Haven, CT: Yale University Press, 1998); "The Bill of Rights and the Fourteenth Amendment," *Yale Law Journal* 101, no. 6 (April 1992): 1193–1284; and Michael Kent Curtis, *No State Shall Abridge: The Fourteenth Amendment and the Bill of Rights* (Durham, NC: Duke University Press, 1986).

Scholarship in opposition to incorporation includes the following: "Does the Fourteenth Amendment Incorporate the Bill of Rights? The Original Understanding," *Stanford Law Review* 2, no. 1 (1949): 5–139; Raoul Berger, *The Fourteenth Amendment and the Bill of Rights* (Norman: University of Oklahoma Press, 1989); Earl M. Maltz, "Fourteenth Amendment Concepts in the Antebellum Era," *American Journal of Legal History* 32 (1988): 305–346, 337; Raoul Berger, *Government by Judiciary: The Transformation of the Fourteenth Amendment* (Indianapolis, IN: Liberty Fund, 1997); and Philip Hamburger, "Privileges or Immunities," *Northwestern University Law Review* 105 (2011): 61–147.

11. Amar, *The Bill of Rights*, 174–180.

12. Russell Hittinger, introduction to *Rights and Duties: Reflections on Our Conservative Constitution*, by Russell Kirk (Dallas, TX: Spence Publishing, 1997), xxiii–xxvi.

13. Steven D. Smith, *The Rise and Decline of American Religious Freedom* (Cambridge, MA: Harvard University Press, 2014).

14. Amar, *The Bill of Rights*, 236.

15. Amar, *The Bill of Rights*, 288.

16. Hamburger, "Privileges or Immunities," 61.

17. Hamburger, "Privileges or Immunities," 62. Kurt Lash's well-received book, *The Fourteenth Amendment and the Privileges and Immunities of the Fourteenth Amendment*, argues contrary to Hamburger that the language used in cession treaties like the Louisiana Purchase defined the enumerated rights of citizens and was the extent of the rights granted by the Privileges or Immunities Clause in the Fourteenth Amendment and that it is a misreading of the evidence to tie directly the rights of the Fourteenth Amendment to the Privilege and Immunities Clause of Article IV of the Constitution.

18. James Madison, *Writings* (New York: Literary Classics of the United States, 1999), James Madison to Thomas Jefferson, October 8, 1788, 419–420.

19. Virginia Constitution of 1776; New Jersey Constitution of 1776; Delaware Constitution of 1776; Maryland Constitution of 1776; North Carolina Constitution of 1776; Georgia Constitution of 1777; New York Constitution of 1777; South Carolina Constitution of 1778; Massachusetts Constitution of 1780; and New Hampshire Constitution of 1783.

20. Nathan S. Chapman and Michael W. McConnell, "Due Process as Separation of Powers," *Yale Law Journal* 121, no. 7 (2012): 1672.

21. Michael W. McConnell, "Ways to Think about Unenumerated Rights," *University of Illinois Law Review* 2013, no. 5 (2013): 1985.

22. McConnell, "Ways to Think about Unenumerated Rights," 1985.

23. McConnell, "Ways to Think about Unenumerated Rights," 1988.

24. McConnell, "Ways to Think about Unenumerated Rights," 1989.

25. McConnell, "Ways to Think about Unenumerated Rights," 1990.

26. McConnell, "Ways to Think about Unenumerated Rights," 1989; *Roe v. Wade*, 410 U.S. 113, 152–154 (1973).

27. Paul Benjamin Linton, "Enforcement of State Abortion Statutes after Roe: A State-by-State Analysis," *University of Detroit Mercy Law Review* 67, no. 2 (1990): 158–161, and McConnell, "Ways to Think about Unenumerated Rights," 1990.

28. *Lawrence v. Texas*, 539 U.S. 558 (2003).

29. *Planned Parenthood of Southeastern Pa. v. Casey*, 505 U. S. 833, 851 (1992).

Chapter 3. The Meaning of Obergefell

1. Transcript of Oral Argument, *Obergefell v. Hodges*, 135 S. Ct. 2584 (2015) (Nos. 14-556, 14-562, 14-571, 14-574), 2015 WL 1929996, at *38.

2. Ilya Somin, *Volokh Conspiracy*, "A Great Decision on Same-Sex-Marriage but Based on Dubious Reasoning," June 26, 2016, accessed October 29, 2018, https://www.wash ingtonpost.com/news/volokh-conspiracy/wp/2015/06/26/a-great-decision-on-same -sex-marriage-but-based-on-dubious-reasoning.

Chapter 4. The Republican Principle

1. Fred Barnes, "Trump's Intellectuals," *Weekly Standard* 21, no. 37 (June 6, 2016): 14.

2. Charles Murray, "Trump's America," *Wall Street Journal*, February 13–14, 2016.

3. Murray, "Trump's America."

4. Tyler Cowen, *Marginal Revolution*, "What the Hell Is Going On?" May 25, 2016, accessed 10/29/2018, http://marginalrevolution.com/marginalrevolution/2016/05/what -in-the-hell-is-going-on.html.

5. Tyler Cowen, "What the Hell Is Going On?," *Marginal Revolution*, May 25, 2016, accessed 10/28/2016, https://marginalrevolution.com/marginalrevolution/2016/0/what -in-the-hell-is-going-on.html.

6. Randy Barnett, *Restoring the Lost Constitution: The Presumption of Liberty*, rev. ed. (Princeton, NJ: Princeton University Press, 2013).

7. William F. Buckley Jr. and Charles Kesler, eds., introduction to *Keeping the Tablets: Modern Conservative Thought* (New York: Perennial Library, 1988), 33.

8. Leo Strauss, *Natural Right and History* (Chicago: University of Chicago Press, 1953): 1.

9. Charles Kelser, "What's Wrong with Conservatism," American Enterprise Institute Bradley Lecture series, June 8, 1998.

10. Harry Jaffa, *Crisis of the House Divided: An Interpretation of the Issues in the Lincoln-Douglas Debates* (Chicago: University of Chicago Press, 2008), 327–329.

11. Jaffa, *Crisis of the House Divided*, 329.

12. Alexis de Tocqueville, *Democracy in America* (1840; rprt., Indianapolis, IN: Liberty Fund, 2010), "Of the Point of Departure and Its Importance for the Future of the Anglo-Americans," 1:62–64.

13. Augustine, *City of God* (New York: Random House, 2000), book 19, ch. 17, 696.

14. G. K. Chesterton, *What I Saw in America* (London: Hodder & Stoughton, 1922).

15. Willmoore Kendall, "How to Read The Federalist," in *Contra Mundum* (Lanham, MD: University Press of America, 1994), 417.

16. John Courtney Murray, *We Hold These Truths: Catholic Reflections on the American Proposition* (New York: Sheed & Ward, 2005), 7.

17. Murray, *We Hold These Truths*, 7.

18. Murray, *We Hold These Truths*, 9.

19. Murray, *We Hold These Truths*, 10.

20. Kendall, "The True Sage of Woodstock," in *Contra Mundum*, 78–79.

21. Kendall, "The True Sage of Woodstock," 79.

22. Kendall, "The Intensity Problem and Democratic Theory," in *Contra Mundum*, 469–506.

23. Eric A. Posner and Adrian Vermeule, *Executive Unbound: After the Madisonian Republic* (New York: Oxford University Press, 2011).

24. Kendall cites in footnote 24 of "The Two Majorities," in *Contra Mundum*, authority from *Federalist* No. 58 for its proposition that preventing the majority from having its way reverses "the fundamental principle of free government. It would no longer be the majority that would rule." Similarly, Kendall highlights *Federalist* No. 22 for reference that the touchstone of republican government is that "the sense of the majority shall prevail."

25. George W. Carey, ed., *The Federalist*, Gideon ed. (Indianapolis, IN: Liberty Fund, 2001), "No. 9," 39.

26. Kendall, *Contra Mundum*, "The Intensity Problem and Democratic Theory," 469–506.

27. Alexander Hamilton, John Jay, and James Madison, *The Federalist*, ed. George W. Carey, James McClellan. Gideon ed. (Indianapolis: Liberty Fund, 2001), "No. 64," 336.

28. Kendall, "The Two Majorities," in *Contra Mundum*, 202–227.

29. Kendall, "The Two Majorities," 224.

30. Kendall, "The Two Majorities," 225.

Chapter 5. A Constitution in Full: Written and Providential

1. Robert Moffitt, "Constitutional Politics: The Political Theory of Orestes Brownson," *Political Science Reviewer* 8, no. 1 (1978): 135–172, 156.

2. Peter A. Lawler and Richard Reinsch II, "Orestes Brownson and the Unwritten Foundation of American Constitutionalism," *Modern Age* 58, no. 2 (Spring 2016): 31–41.

3. Lawler and Reinsch, "Orestes Brownson and the Unwritten Foundation of American Constitutionalism," 32.

4. A Congregationalist in his early life and then a committed Presbyterian in his teenage years, Brownson left the Calvinist fold out of his belief that it denigrated reason, and he became a universalist clergyman at the age of twenty. Brownson then tilted toward Unitarianism, which soon gave way to transcendentalism and his melding of social-progress theology and political action, or what might be described as a quest to redivinize humans and politics.

5. Orestes A. Brownson, *The American Republic: Its Constitution, Tendencies and Destiny* (1865; rprt., Wilmington, DE: ISI Books, 2003), 40.

6. Brownson, *The American Republic*, 45.

7. Brownson, *The American Republic*, 249.

8. Brownson, *The American Republic*, 21.

9. Brownson, *The American Republic*, 21.

10. Brownson, *The American Republic*, 21.

11. Brownson, *The American Republic*, 21.

12. Brownson, *The American Republic*, 25.

13. Brownson, *The American Republic*, 221.

14. Brownson, *The American Republic*, 189.

15. Brownson, *The American Republic*, 190.

16. Brownson, *The American Republic*, 257.

17. Thomas I. Cook and Arnaud B. Leavelle, "The American Republic," *Review of Politics* 4, no. 2 (January 1942): 173–193, 181–182.

18. Brownson, *The American Republic*, 191.

19. Brownson, *The American Republic*, 185.

20. Brownson, *The American Republic*, 185. "In the Declaration of Independence they declared themselves independent states indeed, but not severally independent. The declaration was not made by the states severally, but by the states jointly, as the United States. They unitedly declared their independence; they carried on the war for independence, won it, and were acknowledged by foreign powers and by the mother country as the United States, not as severally independent sovereign states." 135–136.

21. Brownson, *The American Republic*, 136. The Articles of Confederation would seem to create a problem for Brownson on this point. However, Brownson defends his thesis on two grounds: (1) The Articles never departed from an essential understanding of "nation" or of United States. The States may have voted separately, but this was a compromise position for smaller states and was shown as ineffective as early as 1782—five years after its formation—when New York called for a reconsideration of the Articles of Confederation because of its threat to the "nation." (2) The Articles were a provisional government, emerging during a united resistance, and in need of repair soon after its formation because of its insufficiencies. Its unworkability, for Brownson, was owing to the fact that it had broken with the essential unity that had held the colonies together as dependents and as an insurrectionary body. Moreover, both the Philadelphia Convention of 1787 and the state ratifying conventions had properly debated the Articles' weaknesses and the need for a revised charter document that accorded more nearly to the original form of America.

22. Brownson, *The American Republic*, 98–99.

23. Brownson, *The American Republic*, 91.

24. Brownson, *The American Republic*, 127.

25. Brownson, *The American Republic*, 112.

26. Brownson, *The American Republic*, 257.

27. Brownson, *The American Republic*, 255.

28. Brownson, *The American Republic*, 3.

29. Stanley Parry, "The Premises of Brownson's Political Theory," *Review of Politics* 16, no. 2 (April 1954): 194–211, 202.

30. Orestes Brownson, *Essays and Reviews Chiefly on Theology, Politics, and Religion* (New York: D. and J. Sadlier, 1852): 306–307.

31. Brownson, *The American Republic*, 120–121.

32. Parry, "The Premises of Brownson's Political Theory," 204.

33. Brownson, *The American Republic*, 99.

34. Brownson, *The American Republic*, 84.

35. Brownson, *The American Republic*, 86.

36. Brownson, *The American Republic*, 49.

37. Brownson, *The American Republic*, 222. "The tendency to this sort of democracy has been strong in large sections of the American people from the first, and has been greatly strengthened by the general acceptance of the theory that government originates in compact. The full realization of this tendency, which, happily, is impracticable save in theory, would be to render every man independent alike of every other man and of society, with full right and power to make his own will prevail." 222–223.

38. Brownson, *The American Republic*, 225.

39. Brownson, *The American Republic*, 229.

40. Woodrow Wilson, *The New Freedom* (New York: Doubleday, Page, 1913), 46–47.

41. Ronald J. Pestritto and William J. Atto, eds., *American Progressivism: A Reader* (Lanham, MD: Lexington Books, 2008): 2.

42. Pestritto and Atto, *American Progressivism*, 222.

43. Pestritto and Atto, *American Progressivism*, 155.

44. Pestritto and Atto, *American Progressivism*, 250.

45. Brownson, *The American Republic*, 225.

46. William Voegeli, *Never Enough: America's Limitless Welfare State* (New York: Encounter Books, 2010).

47. Allan Carlson, *The American Way: Family and Community in the Shaping of the American Identity* (Wilmington, DE: ISI Books, 2003), 56–60.

48. Carlson, *The American Way*, 64–79.

49. Allan Carlson, "The Social Conservative Case for the New Deal," Regional Meeting of the Philadelphia Society, October 8, 2005.

Chapter 6. A Question of Loyalty

1. Harold Koh, "Transnational Legal Process," *Nebraska Law Review* 75, no. 1 (1996): 181–208.

2. Jeremy Rabkin, Review of *Taming Globalization: International Law, the U.S. Constitution, and the New World Order* by Julian Ku and John Yoo, *Engage* 13, no. 2 (July 2012): 120–121.

3. Pierre Manent, "City, Empire, Church, Nation," *City Journal* 22, no. 3 (2012): 48–57.

4. Pierre Manent, *Democracy without Nations? The Fate of Self Government in Europe* (Wilmington, DE: ISI Books, 2007), 82.

5. Manent, *Democracy without Nations*, 82.

6. Manent, *Democracy without Nations*, 80.

7. Orestes Brownson, *The American Republic: Its Constitution, Tendencies and Destiny* (1865; rprt., Wilmington, DE: ISI Press, 2003), 33–34.

8. Brownson, *The American Republic*, 33.

9. Russell Hittinger, *The First Grace: Rediscovering the Natural Law in a Post-Christian World* (Wilmington, DE: ISI Press, 2003), 13. Hittinger also points us to Thomas Hobbes's rendering of man in *De Homine*: "Politics and ethics (that is, the sciences of just and unjust, of equity and inequity) can be demonstrated a priori; because we ourselves make the principles—that is, the causes of justice (namely, laws and covenants)—whereby it is known what justice and equity, and their opposites injustice and inequity, are," 13.

10. Hittinger, *The First Grace*, 14.

11. Brownson, *The American Republic*, 32–35.

12. Brownson, *The American Republic*, 36–37.

13. Brownson, *The American Republic*, 37.

14. John Locke, "Of Property," in *Second Treatise of Civil Government*, book II, ed. Thomas Hollis (London: A. Millar, 1764), §40.

15. Brownson, *The American Republic*, 39.

16. Harvey Mansfield, "On the Majesty of the Law," *Harvard Journal of Law & Public Policy* 36, no. 1 (Winter 2012): 117–129, 122.

17. Mansfield, "On the Majesty of the Law," 122–123.

18. Mansfield, "On the Majesty of the Law," 123.

19. Brownson, *The American Republic*, 108.

20. Brownson, *The American Republic*, Peter A. Lawler's "Introduction to the ISI Edition," xix.

21. Brownson, *The American Republic*, 32.

22. Brownson, *The American Republic*, 32.

23. Brownson, *The American Republic*, 31–32.

24. Brownson, *The American Republic*, 32.

25. Willmoore Kendall, *The Conservative Affirmation in America* (Chicago: Regnery Gateway, 1985), "The Social Contract: The Ultimate Issue between Liberalism and Conservatism," 85.

26. Kendall, *The Conservative Affirmation in America*, 85.

27. Brownson, *The American Republic*, 75.

28. Jacques Maritain, *Man and the State* (Washington DC: Catholic University of America Press, 1998) 49.

29. Maritain, *Man and the State*, 51.

30. Maritain, *Man and the State*, 40.

31. Maritain, *Man and the State*, 41.

32. Maritain, *Man and the State*, 43–44.

33. Brownson, *The American Republic*, 87.

34. Brownson, *The American Republic*, 88.

35. Brownson, *The American Republic*, 50.

36. Brownson, *The American Republic*, 49.

37. Brownson, *The American Republic*, 50.

38. Brownson, *The American Republic*, 54.

39. Brownson, *The American Republic*, 77.

40. Brownson, *The American Republic*, 54.

41. Brownson, *The American Republic*, 50–51.

42. Brownson, *The American Republic*, 53.

43. Brownson, *The American Republic*, 53.

44. Ralph Hancock, "Brownson's Political Providence, with Some Preliminary Comparisons with Tocqueville's Providential Statesmanship," *Perspectives on Political Science* 37, no. 1 (Winter 2008): 17–22.

45. Hancock, "Brownson's Political Providence," 18.

46. Brownson, *The American Republic*, 91.

47. Brownson, *The American Republic*, 15.

48. Hancock, "Brownson's Political Providence," 18.

49. Brownson, *The American Republic*, 83.

50. Brownson, *The American Republic*, 45.

51. Brownson, *The American Republic*, 83–84.

52. Brownson, *The American Republic*, 16.

53. Brownson, *The American Republic*, 83.

54. Brownson, *The American Republic*, 85.

55. Brownson, *The American Republic*, 84.

Chapter 7. Constitutional Thomism

1. Orestes A. Brownson, *The American Republic: Its Constitution, Tendencies and Destiny* (1865; rprt., Wilmington, DE: ISI Books, 2003), 91–108.

2. Orestes A. Brownson, "Liberalism and Progress," in *Seeking the Truth: An Orestes Brownson Anthology*, ed. Richard M. Reinsch II (Washington, DC: Catholic University of America Press, 2016), 402–403.

3. Michael P. Zuckert, *The Natural Rights Republic* (Notre Dame, IN: University of Notre Dame Press, 1996); Randy E. Barnett, *Restoring the Lost Constitution: The Presumption of Liberty*, rev. ed. (Princeton, NJ: Princeton University Press, 2013).

4. Zuckert, *The Natural Rights Republic*, 49, 54.

5. Zuckert, *The Natural Rights Republic*, 148–201.

6. Zuckert, *The Natural Rights Republic*, 200–201.

7. Michael P. Zuckert, *Launching Liberalism: On Lockean Political Philosophy* (Lawrence: University Press of Kansas, 2002): 162.

8. Zuckert, *Launching Liberalism*, 162.

9. Zuckert, *Launching Liberalism*, 166.

10. Alexis de Tocqueville, *Democracy in America* (1840; rprt., Indianapolis: Liberty Fund, 2010): 2:402–425.

11. Zuckert, *The Natural Rights Republic*, 171.

12. Zuckert, *The Natural Rights Republic*, 145.

13. Zuckert, *The Natural Rights Republic*, 120, quoting Thomas Pangle, *The Ennobling of Democracy: The Challenge of the Postmodern Era* (Baltimore: Johns Hopkins University Press, 1992).

14. Zuckert, *Launching Liberalism*, 142.

15. Lee Ward, *John Locke and Modern Life* (New York: Cambridge University Press, 2010); Michael P. Zuckert, *Natural Rights and the New Republicanism* (Princeton: Princeton University Press, 1994).

16. Zuckert, *Launching Liberalism*, 142.

17. Zuckert, *The Natural Rights Republic*, 255n57.

18. Ward, *John Locke and Modern Life*, 294.

19. Zuckert, *The Natural Rights Republic*, 128–129.

20. Zuckert, *The Natural Rights Republic*, 103.

21. Zuckert, *Launching Liberalism*, 165–166.

22. Tocqueville, *Democracy in America*, 4:1245–1261.

23. Tocqueville, *Democracy in America*, 3:881–886.

24. Sara Henary, "The Problem of Human Equality in Locke's Political Philosophy: Responses to Jeremy Waldron and Michael Zuckert," Paper presented at the conference Stuck with Virtue, Berry College, Mount Berry, GA, November 4, 2010.

25. Ward, *John Locke and Modern Life*, 229.

26. Ward, *John Locke and Modern Life*, 229.

27. Augustine, *City of God* (Edinburgh: T&T Clark, 1888), 228–304.

28. Remi Brague, *The Law of God: The Philosophical History of an Idea* (Chicago: University of Chicago Press, 2007).

29. Peter A. Lawler, "The Logos in Western Thought," *Modern Age* 51, no. 1 (Winter 2009): 42–46.

30. Ward, *John Locke and Modern Life*, 232.

31. Augustine, *City of God*, 223–224.

32. Ward, *John Locke and Modern Life*, 232.

33. Ward, *John Locke and Modern Life*, 245–247.

34. Ward, *John Locke and Modern Life*, 249.

35. Peter A. Lawler, *Modern and American Dignity: Who We Are as Persons and What That Means for Our Future* (Wilmington, DE: ISI Books, 2010), 157–184.

36. Ward, *John Locke and Modern Life*, 258.

37. Ward, *John Locke and Modern Life*, 258.

38. Tocqueville, *Democracy in America*, 3:726–736.

39. Chantal Delsol, *The Unlearned Lessons of the Twentieth Century* (Wilmington, DE: ISI Books, 2006), 194–195.

40. Tocqueville, *Democracy in America*, 1:45–73; B. Danoff and L. Herbert, eds., *Alexis de Tocqueville and the Art of Democratic Statesmanship* (Lanham, MD: Lexington Books, 2011); Peter A. Lawler, "Tocqueville on How to Praise the Puritans Today," in Danoff and Herbert, *Alexis de Tocqueville and the Art of Democratic Statesmanship*, 179–198.

41. Tocqueville, *Democracy in America*, 1:45–73.

42. Brownson, *The American Republic*, Introduction essay by Peter A. Lawler, 1–123.

43. Tocqueville, *Democracy in America*, 3:881–886.

44. Tocqueville, *Democracy in America*, 1:45–73.

45. Tocqueville, *Democracy in America*, 3:742–753.

46. Zuckert, *Launching Liberalism*, 215.

47. G. K. Chesterton, *What I Saw in America* (London: Hodder & Stoughton, 1922).

48. R. L. Bruckberger, *Images of America*, trans. C. G. Paulding and Virginia Peterson (New York: Viking Press, 1959), 193–194.

49. Bruckberger, *Images of America*, 99.

50. John Courtney Murray, "Law or Prepossessions?," *Law and Contemporary Problems* 14, no. 1 (Winter 1949): 23–43, 29.

51. John Courtney Murray, *We Hold These Truths: Catholic Reflections on the American Proposition* (Lanham, MD: Sheed & Ward, 2005), 45.

52. Murray, *We Hold These Truths*, 53.

53. George Will, "Progressives Are Wrong about the Essence of the Constitution," *Washington Post*, April 16, 2014.

54. Patrick J. Deneen and Susan J. McWilliams, eds., *The Democratic Soul: A Wilson Carey McWilliams Reader* (Lexington: University Press of Kentucky, 2011), 229–235.

55. Deneen and McWilliams, *The Democratic Soul*, 331.

56. Deneen and McWilliams, *The Democratic Soul*, 331.

57. Rev. Martin Luther King Jr., "Letter from a Birmingham Jail," April 16, 1963.

58. Brownson, *The American Republic*, 221–246.

59. Brownson, *The American Republic*, 229–230.

60. Brownson, *The American Republic*, 237.

61. Walker Percy, *The Last Gentleman* (New York: Farrar, Straus and Giroux, 1966).

62. Walker Percy, *Lost in the Cosmos: The Last Self-Help Book* (New York: Farrar, Straus and Giroux, 1983).

63. Walker Percy, introduction to *Lanterns on the Levee: Recollections of a Planter's Son*, by William Alexander Percy (Baton Rouge: Louisiana State University Press, 1989), vii–xviii.

64. Percy, introduction, xiii.

65. Percy, introduction, xiii.

66. Percy, introduction, xiii.

67. Tocqueville, *Democracy in America*, 3:881–884.

68. Walker Percy, *Signposts in a Strange Land* (New York: Farrar, Straus and Giroux, 1991), 326–339.

69. Tocqueville, *Democracy in America*, 4:987–993.

70. Tocqueville, *Democracy in America*, 3:881–884.

71. Bruckberger, *Images of America*, 89–93.

Bibliography

Amar, Akhil Reed. "The Bill of Rights and the Fourteenth Amendment." *Yale Law Journal* 101, no. 6 (April 1992): 1193–1284.

——. *The Bill of Rights: Creation and Reconstruction.* New Haven, CT: Yale University Press, 1998.

Augustine. City of God (Edinburgh: T&T Clark, 1888).

Barnes, Fred. "Trump's Intellectuals." *Weekly Standard* 21, no. 37 (June 6, 2016): 14.

Barnett, Randy. *Restoring the Lost Constitution: The Presumption of Liberty.* Rev. ed. Princeton, NJ: Princeton University Press, 2013.

Benedict XVI, Pope. *Deus Caritas Est.* Washington, DC: United States Conference of Catholic Bishops, 2006.

Berger, Raoul. *The Fourteenth Amendment and the Bill of Rights.* Norman: University of Oklahoma Press, 1989.

——. *Government by Judiciary: The Transformation of the Fourteenth Amendment.* Indianapolis, IN: Liberty Fund, 1997.

Brague, Remi. *The Law of God: The Philosophical History of an Idea.* Chicago: University of Chicago Press, 2007.

Brownson, Orestes A. *The American Republic: Its Constitution, Tendencies and Destiny.* 1865; rprt., Wilmington, DE: ISI Books, 2003.

——. *Essays and Reviews Chiefly on Theology, Politics, and Religion.* N.p.: D. and J. Sadlier, 1852.

——. *The Works of Orestes A. Brownson.* Vols. 3, 12–13. Detroit: H. F. Brownson, 1900.

——. *The Works of Orestes A. Brownson.* Vol. 17: *The Federal Constitution.* New York: AMS Press, 1966.

Bruckberger, R. L. *Images of America.* Translated by C. G. Paulding and Virginia Peterson. New York: Viking Press, 1959.

Buckley, William F., Jr., and Charles Kesler, eds. *Keeping the Tablets: Modern Conservative Thought.* New York: Perennial Library, 1988.

Carlson, Allan. *The American Way: Family and Community in the Shaping of the American Identity.* Wilmington, DE: ISI Books, 2003.

———. "The Social Conservative Case for the New Deal." Regional Meeting of the Philadelphia Society, October 8, 2005.

Chapman, Nathan S., and Michael W. McConnell. "Due Process as Separation of Powers." *Yale Law Journal* 121, no. 7 (2012): 1672–1807.

Chesterton, G. K. *What I Saw in America.* London: Hodder & Stoughton, 1922.

Cook, Thomas I., and Arnauld B. Leavelle. "The American Republic." *Review of Politics* 4, no. 2 (January 1942): 77–90.

Cowen, Tyler. "What the Hell Is Going On?" *Marginal Revolution.* May 25, 2016. Accessed October 28, 2018. http://marginalrevolution.com/marginalrevolution/2016/05/what-in-the-hell-is-going-on.html.

Curtis, Michael Kent. *No State Shall Abridge: The Fourteenth Amendment and the Bill of Rights.* Durham, NC: Duke University Press, 1986.

Danoff, B., and L. Herbert, eds. *Alexis de Tocqueville and the Art of Democratic Statesmanship.* Lanham, MD: Lexington Books, 2011.

Delsol, Chantal. *The Unlearned Lessons of the Twentieth Century.* Wilmington, DE: ISI Books, 2006.

Deneen, Patrick J., and Susan J. McWilliams, eds. *The Democratic Soul: A Wilson Carey McWilliams Reader.* Lexington: University Press of Kentucky, 2011.

Fairman, Charles. "Does the Fourteenth Amendment Incorporate the Bill of Rights? The Original Understanding." *Stanford Law Review* 2, no. 1 (1949): 5–139.

Hamburger, Philip. "Privileges or Immunities." *Northwestern University Law Review* 105, no. 1 (2011): 61–147.

Hamilton, Alexander, John Jay, and James Madison. *The Federalist.* Edited with introduction by George W. Carey, James McClellan. Gideon ed. Indianapolis: Liberty Fund, 2001.

Hancock, Ralph. "Brownson's Political Providence, with Some Preliminary Comparisons with Tocqueville's Providential Statesmanship." *Perspectives on Political Science* 37, no. 1 (Winter 2008): 17–22.

Henary, Sara. "The Problem of Human Equality in Locke's Political Philosophy: Responses to Jeremy Waldron and Michael Zuckert." Paper presented at the conference Stuck with Virtue, Berry College, Mount Berry, GA, November 4, 2010.

Hittinger, Russell. *The First Grace: Rediscovering the Natural Law in a Post-Christian World.* Wilmington, DE: ISI Books, 2003.

Jaffa, Harry. *Crisis of the House Divided: An Interpretation of the Issues in the Lincoln-Douglas Debates.* Chicago: University of Chicago Press, 2008.

Kelser, Charles. "What's Wrong with Conservatism." American Enterprise Institute Bradley Lecture series, June 8, 1998.

Kendall, Willmoore. *The Conservative Affirmation in America.* Chicago: Regnery Gateway, 1985.

———. *Contra Mundum*. Lanham, MD: University Press of America, 1994.

Kirk, Russell. *Rights and Duties: Reflections on Our Conservative Constitution*. Dallas, TX: Spence Publishing, 1997.

Koh, Harold. "Transnational Legal Process." *Nebraska Law Review* 75, no. 1 (1996): 181–208.

Lasch, Christopher. *The True and Only Heaven: Progress and Its Critics*. New York: Norton, 1991.

Lash, Kurt T. *The Fourteenth Amendment and the Privileges and Immunities of American Citizenship*. New York: Cambridge University Press, 2014.

Lawler, Peter A. "The Logos in Western Thought." *Modern Age* 5, no. 1 (Winter 2009): 42–46.

———. *Modern and American Dignity: Who We Are as Persons and What That Means for Our Future*. Wilmington, DE: ISI Books, 2010.

———. "Tocqueville on How to Praise the Puritans Today." In *Alexis de Tocqueville and the Art of Democratic Statesmanship*, ed. B. Danoff and L. Herbert, 179–198. Lanham, MD: Lexington Books, 2011.

Lawler, Peter, and Richard M. Reinsch, II. "Orestes Brownson and the Unwritten Foundation of American Constitutionalism." *Modern Age* 58, no. 2 (Spring 2016): 31–41.

Linton, Paul Benjamin. "Enforcement of State Abortion Statutes after Roe: A State-by-State Analysis." *University of Detroit Mercy Law Review* 67, no. 2 (1990): 157–259.

Lloyd, Gordon. *Law and Liberty*. "The Constitutional Liberty of the Anti-Federalists." March 2013. Accessed October 28, 2018. http://www.libertylawsite.org/liberty-forum/the-constitutional-liberty-of-the-antifederalists/.

Locke, John. *Second Treatise of Civil Government*. London: A. Millar, 1764.

Madison, James. *Writings*. New York: Literary Classics of the United States, 1999.

Maltz, Earl M. "Fourteenth Amendment Concepts in the Antebellum Era." *American Journal of Legal History* 32, no. 4 (1988): 305–346.

Manent, Pierre. "City, Empire, Church, Nation." *City Journal* 22, no. 3 (Summer 2012): 48–57.

———. *Democracy without Nations? The Fate of Self-Government in Europe*. Wilmington, DE: ISI Books, 2007.

Mansfield, Harvey. "On the Majesty of the Law." *Harvard Journal of Law & Public Policy* 36, no. 1 (Winter 2012): 117–129.

Maritain, Jacques. *Man and the State*. Washington, DC: Catholic University of America Press, 1998.

McConnell, Michael W. "Ways to Think about Unenumerated Rights." *University of Illinois Law Review* 2013, no. 5 (2013): 1985–1997.

Moffitt, Robert. "Constitutional Politics: The Political Theory of Orestes Brownson." *Political Science Reviewer* 8, no. 1 (1978): 135–172.

Murray, John Courtney. "Law or Prepossessions?" *Law and Contemporary Problems* 14, no. 1 (Winter 1949): 23–43.

——. *We Hold These Truths: Catholic Reflections on the American Proposition*. Lanham, MD: Sheed & Ward, 2005.

Parry, Stanley. "The Premises of Brownson's Political Theory." *Review of Politics* 16, no. 2 (April 1954): 194–211.

Percy, Walker. *The Last Gentleman*. New York: Farrar, Straus and Giroux, 1966.

——. *Lost in the Cosmos: The Last Self-Help Book*. New York: Farrar, Straus and Giroux, 1983.

——. *Signposts in a Strange Land*. New York: Farrar, Straus and Giroux, 1991.

Percy, William Alexander. *Lanterns on the Levee: Recollections of a Planter's Son*. Baton Rouge: Louisiana State University Press, 1989.

Pestritto, Ronald J., and William J. Atto, eds. *American Progressivism: A Reader*. Lanham, MD: Lexington Books, 2008.

Posner, Eric A., and Adrian Vermeule. *Executive Unbound: After the Madisonian Republic*. New York: Oxford University Press, 2011.

Rabkin, Jeremy. Review of *Taming Globalization: International Law, the U.S. Constitution, and the New World Order* by Julian Ku and John Yoo. *Engage* 13, no. 2 (July 2012): 120–121.

Reinsch, Richard M., II. "Orestes Brownson's Freedom of the Church." *Logos* 20, no. 4 (Fall 2017): 112–123.

——, ed. *Seeking the Truth: An Orestes Brownson Anthology*. Washington, DC: Catholic University of America Press, 2016.

Smith, Steven D. *The Rise and Decline of American Religious Freedom*. Cambridge, MA: Harvard University Press, 2014.

Somin, Ilya. *Volokh Conspiracy*. "A Great Decision on Same-Sex-Marriage but Based on Dubious Reasoning." June 26, 2015. Accessed October 28, 2018. https://www.washingtonpost.com/news/volokh-conspiracy/wp/2015/06/26/a-great-decision-on-same-sex-marriage-but-based-on-dubious-reasoning.

Strauss, Leo. *Natural Right and History*. Chicago: University of Chicago Press, 1953.

Tocqueville, Alexis de. *Democracy in America*. 4 vols. 1840; rprt., Indianapolis, IN: Liberty Fund, 2010.

——. *Democracy in America*. London: Penguin Books, 2003.

Voegeli, William. *Never Enough: America's Limitless Welfare State*. New York: Encounter Books, 2010.

Ward, Lee. *John Locke and Modern Life*. New York: Cambridge University Press, 2010.

Wilson, Woodrow. *The New Freedom*. New York: Doubleday, Page, 1913.

Zuckert, Michael P. *Launching Liberalism: On Lockean Political Philosophy*. Lawrence: University Press of Kansas, 2002.

——. *Natural Rights and the New Republicanism*. Princeton, NJ: Princeton University Press, 1994.

——. *The Natural Rights Republic*. Notre Dame, IN: University of Notre Dame Press, 1996.

Cases and Constitutions

Duncan v. Louisiana, 391 U.S. 145 (1968).

Lawrence v. Texas, 539 U.S. 558 (2003).

Obergefell v. Hodges, 135 S. Ct. 2584 (2015) (Nos. 14-556, 14-562, 14-571, 14-574), 2015 WL 1929996, Transcript of Oral Argument.

Planned Parenthood of Southeastern Pa. v. Casey, 505 U. S. 833 (1992).

Roe v. Wade, 410 U.S. 113 (1973).

West Virginia State Board of Education v. Barnette, 319 U.S. 624 (1943).

Index